New Perspectives on China's Relations with the World

National, Transnational and International

EDITED BY

DANIEL JOHANSON, JIE LI & TSUNGHAN WU

E-INTERNATIONAL RELATIONS PUBLISHING

E-International Relations
www.E-IR.info
Bristol, England
2019

ISBN 978-1-910814-47-5

This book is published under a Creative Commons CC BY-NC 4.0 license. You are free to:

- **Share** – copy and redistribute the material in any medium or format
- **Adapt** – remix, transform, and build upon the material

Under the following terms:

- **Attribution** – You must give appropriate credit, provide a link to the license and indicate if changes were made. You may do so in any reasonable manner, but not in any way that suggests the licensor endorses you or your use.
- **Non-Commercial** – You may not use the material for commercial purposes.

Any of the above conditions can be waived if you get permission. Please contact info@e-ir.info for any such enquiries, including for licensing and translation requests.

Other than the terms noted above, there are no restrictions placed on the use and dissemination of this book for student learning materials/ scholarly use.

Production: William Kakenmaster
Cover Image: VojtechVlk

A catalogue record for this book is available from the British Library.

E-IR Edited Collections

Series Editors: Stephen McGlinchey, Marianna Karakoulaki & Agnieszka Pikulicka-Wilczewska
Books Editor: Cameran Clayton
Editorial assistance: Daniele Carminati, Fernanda de Castro Brandão Martins, Hayden Paulsen & Yiming Yu.

E-IR's Edited Collections are open access scholarly books presented in a format that preferences brevity and accessibility while retaining academic conventions. Each book is available in print and digital versions, and is published under a Creative Commons license. As E-International Relations is committed to open access in the fullest sense, free electronic versions of all of our books, including this one, are available on our website.

Find out more at: http://www.e-ir.info/publications

About the E-International Relations website

E-International Relations (www.E-IR.info) is the world's leading open access website for students and scholars of international politics, reaching over 3.5 million readers each year. E-IR's daily publications feature expert articles, blogs, reviews and interviews – as well as student learning resources. The website is run by a registered non-profit organisation based in Bristol, UK and staffed with an all-volunteer team of students and scholars.

About the Editors

Daniel Johanson received his PhD from King's College, London. His research focuses on how Chinese foreign policy has evolved and adapted to address issues of international concern, specifically on China's interactions with Sudan, Iran, and North Korea.

Jie Li received his PhD in History at the University of Edinburgh. His doctoral project (Sovietology in Post-Mao China, 1980–1999) examined the Chinese official and intellectual evolving perceptions of Soviet socialism in the 1980s and 1990s. He has published a number of commentaries on contemporary Chinese affairs as well as book reviews and papers on a variety of historical scholarship. He is currently teaching Chinese language and culture in Hong Kong.

Tsunghan Wu is a PhD candidate at the Lau China Institute, King's College London. His research interests focus on international relations, nationalism, ethnic conflicts and the Tibetan issue. His PhD deals with the politics of China's nation-building in Tibet in the post-1949 era.

Abstract

As China's role and influence throughout the world continues to grow, understanding this evolution becomes ever more important. This book is dedicated to exploring new trends and themes in Chinese foreign policy, with the aim of adding new insights to the existing literature and opening up opportunities for further specialised research. The book is divided into to three sections: National, touching on issues within China and its periphery; Transnational, looking at how concepts and people influence power; and finally, International, examining China's interactions with the other regions and nations. The chapters work together to offer a sweeping overview of a multitude of new perspectives on China's interactions and activities throughout the world.

Contributors

Ilaria Carrozza is a PhD candidate in International Relations at the London School of Economics and Political Science, working on Sino-African security relations and foreign policy analysis. She was the editor of *Millennium: Journal of International Studies*, Vol. 45, and has previously worked as a consultant for the United Nations Economic and Social Commission for Asia and the Pacific (UNESCAP).

Benjamin Creutzfeldt is a Resident Fellow at the Woodrow Wilson International Center for Scholars. Prior to this he was the Resident Postdoctoral Fellow for Sino-Latin American-US Affairs at the SAIS Foreign Policy Institute at Johns Hopkins University in Washington, DC. He earned a degree in Chinese Studies from the University of Durham (UK) and earned his MA from SOAS, whereupon he joined Christie's as an auctioneer and expert for Chinese porcelain and works of art. He has studied and worked extensively in China and co-founded multiple start-up companies. He received his PhD in 2015 for research on China's foreign policy towards Latin America.

Nori Katagiri is Associate Professor of Political Science at Saint Louis University. He is also Visiting Research Fellow, Air Staff College, Japan Air Self-Defence Force and Fellow Cohort 4 of the Mansfield Foundation's US-Japan Network for the Future. Prior to Saint Louis University, he taught at Air War College, a graduate degree program for senior military officers and officials of the US government and foreign nations. He is the author of *Adapting to Win: How Insurgents Fight and Defeat Foreign States in War* (University of Pennsylvania Press, 2015). He received his PhD degree in Political Science from the University of Pennsylvania.

Neville Chi Hang Li is a Teaching Assistant at the University of Bath. His previous appointment was at City University of Hong Kong, serving as a Senior Research Associate. He received his PhD in Politics, Languages and International Studies from the University of Bath. His research interests focus on Politics and International Relations in Asia-Pacific, Critical Security Studies, Political Demography and New Media and Political Communication. His PhD dissertation entitled *Securitization of Population Dynamics in the People's Republic of China*, examines the ideational relationship between security and demography with both the Copenhagen School and the Paris School approaches.

Tony Tai-Ting Liu is a Visiting Research Fellow at the Institute for Advanced Studies on Asia, The University of Tokyo, and a Research Fellow at the Center for Contemporary China Studies, National Chung Hsing University. He held previous research positions at the Australian Catholic University and University of Tubingen. His research interests include International Relations Theory, International Political Economy, East Asia international relations, and Chinese foreign policy.

Gustav Sundqvist is a PhD student at Åbo Akademi University. He specialises in Chinese politics and his doctoral work focuses on the roles of civil society, diffusion and ideology in democratisation processes.

Casper Wits is a Postdoctoral Research Associate at the Faculty of Asian and Middle Eastern Studies at the University of Cambridge. He is a historian of modern East Asia and his research focuses on diplomatic and international history during the Cold War, especially Sino-Japanese relations in this period. At Cambridge he is associated with the ERC research project "The Dissolution of the Japanese Empire and the Struggle for Legitimacy in Postwar East Asia, 1945–1965" – http://warcrimesandempire.com.

Shu Liang (Karl) Yan is a PhD candidate in Political Science at the University of Toronto. Karl's research focuses on the effects of China's grand strategy on its economic statecraft. Karl is currently investigating the reform and 'going out' of the Chinese railway sector along Belt and Road countries.

Claudia Zanardi is a PhD candidate in the War Studies Department of King's College, London where she researches French, British and German foreign and security policies towards China and China's military modernisation. Previously, she worked at the European Institute for Security Studies (EUISS) and the Assembly of the West European Union (WEU), and she produced research for the OECD-GOV Directorate and the International Secretariat of Amnesty International (Paris Office). She was part of the European China Resource Advise Network (ECRAN), a Taiwan Fellow researcher of the Ministry of Foreign Affairs of the Republic of China (ROC) in 2015, and since 2017 a Global Royster Fellow at the University of North Carolina at Chapel Hill.

Contents

INTRODUCTION

    CHINA'S RELATIONS WITH THE WORLD: CHANGING AGENDA, NEW ISSUES, AND ONGOING DEBATES
    Daniel Johanson, Jie Li & Tsunghan Wu   1

PART ONE - NATIONAL

1. SWITCHING BETWEEN ACCOMMODATION AND SUPPRESSION: CHINA'S NATION-BUILDING STRATEGIES AND UNITED FRONT WORK FOR TIBETAN LEADERSHIP
   Tsunghan Wu   8

2. THE CHANGING SECURITY DIMENSION OF CHINA'S RELATIONS WITH XINJIANG
   Claudia Zanardi   24

3. MECHANISMS BEHIND DIFFUSION OF DEMOCRACY IN THE PEARL RIVER DELTA REGION
   Gustav Sundqvist   43

4. "ONE COUNTRY, TWO SYSTEMS" UNDER SIEGE: RIVAL SECURITISING ATTEMPTS IN THE DEMOCRATISATION OF HONG KONG
   Neville Chi Hang Li   60

PART TWO - TRANSNATIONAL

5. PUBLIC DIPLOMACY: CHINA'S NEWEST CHARM OFFENSIVE
   Tony Tai-Ting Liu   77

6. CAN CHINA LINK THE BELT AND ROAD INITIATIVE BY RAIL?
   Shu Liang (Karl) Yan   87

7. THE TRANSNATIONAL IN CHINA'S FOREIGN POLICY: THE CASE OF SINO-JAPANESE RELATIONS
   Casper Wits   104

8. SOVIET FOREIGN POLICY IN THE EARLY 1980S: A VIEW FROM CHINESE SOVIETOLOGY
   Jie Li   115

PART THREE - INTERNATIONAL

9. OVERCOMING THE GREATEST DISTANCE: CHINA IN LATIN AMERICA
   Benjamin Creutzfeldt   134

10. CHINA'S MULTILATERAL DIPLOMACY IN AFRICA: CONSTRUCTING THE SECURITY-DEVELOPMENT NEXUS
    Ilaria Carrozza   142

11. BECOMING A 'RESPONSIBLE POWER'?: CHINA'S NEW ROLE DURING THE JCPOA NEGOTIATIONS
    Daniel Johanson   159

12. THE EVOLUTION OF SINO-JAPANESE RELATIONS: IMPLICATIONS FOR NORTHEAST ASIA AND BEYOND
    Nori Katagiri   174

NOTE ON INDEXING   184

China's Relations with the World: Changing Agenda, New Issues, and Ongoing Debates

DANIEL JOHANSON, JIE LI & TSUNGHAN WU

In the late fall of 2016, the editors of this volume met and discussed concepts for what would later become this book. At the time we agreed that a new collection of research dedicated to exploring new trends and themes in Chinese Foreign Policy would be an essential addition to the existing literature and would allow for further specialised exploration into new and exciting topics. As China's role and influence throughout the world continues to grow, understanding this evolution is ever more important. Having an idea of how China's policies and strategies have adapted – be it on concepts of power, China's internal politics, regional actors, bilateral relations, or international actors – will enable us to further comprehend Chinese actions and priorities.

Quickly we settled on a framework for the book based around three key areas: Firstly, national – touching on issues within China and its periphery. Secondly, transnational – looking more at how concepts and people influence power. And, finally, international – examining China's interactions with other regions and nations. The breadth of research in the book presents a multitude of new perspectives on China's interactions and activities throughout the world. From China's periphery to global issues and how policies are influenced, the chapters work together to further define Chinese foreign policy and inform us on how it has developed.

National

The National section of this book consists of four chapters. The authors of these chapters have focused on ethnic minorities (Tibetans and Uyghurs), democratic development in the Pearl River Delta region, and the issue of Hong Kong. In their discussions, these chapters engage with themes concerning China's security, and the means by which the Chinese Communist Party (CCP) utilises and manages domestic tensions. With the comprehensive social transformation brought about by modernisation and the politico-economic reforms of recent decades, China has not only enjoyed success on the global stage, but Beijing has also acknowledged, albeit cautiously, the emergence of potential challenges. Indeed, these chapters provide analysts with exploratory insight into the Chinese government's actions and reactions to these new challenges.

The first two chapters focus on China's periphery – looking at Beijing's approach to Tibet and Xinjiang, respectively. Both authors delineate a precise picture by examining a wide and varied range of documents concerning the CCP's practice in ethnic minority regions. First, Tsunghan Wu outlines China's commitment to constructing a unitary multi-ethnic state and a combined united front, aligned to the former, for the Tibetan ethnic minority. Crucially, he distinguishes two distinct strategies: accommodation and suppression, that the ruling Chinese Communist Party has employed towards the traditional Tibetan 'upper strata'. Given a social elite feature, this group of 'upper strata' enjoys significant influence throughout all levels of local society. As such, the CCP endeavours to bring their power and influence under their control. As argued by Wu, the CCP's flexible uses of accommodation and suppression have effectively integrated Tibet into the PRC state as a whole. Wu argues that while the strategy of accommodation was implemented during the 1950s and 1980s, Beijing now relies on the strategy of suppression. An 'apparent' social order could be achieved from governmental view – however, the dynamics of ethnic conflict have evolved, both publicly and locally, which has conversely eroded the socio-politico-economic inducement policies that Beijing offered the Tibetans. At present, Tibet still poses a threat to China's nation-building.

In the second chapter Claudia Zanardi depicts the evolution that the Chinese periphery has experienced since 1949. Through a multi-layer examination, Zanardi argues that the issue of Xinjiang is strongly related to Beijing's Uyghur policies and the Uyghur's embedment in both the pan-Turkic-Speaking nationalist and pan-Islamist networks in differing eras. In both networks, the Uyghurs are perceived as disloyal and a security threat to China's territorial integrity. As a consequence, the CCP adopted a repressive policy – though a certain degree of tolerance was evident in the 1980s. However, there is some similarity to the situation in Tibet whereby Beijing's policies fan Uyghur discontent and threaten a potential eruption of protest. Inequality, due to the uneven distribution of economic development along ethnic lines further exacerbates the conflict.

The next two chapters move on to assess the situation in other majority-Han regions in mainland China. Gustav Sundqvist first shifts our attention to the Pearl River Delta region, focusing on a vital topic when considering modern China – democratisation. In his chapter he investigates the impact of Hong Kong and Taiwan with regard to local democratisation development (a process termed as democratic diffusion). The author conducted this research mainly through interviews with twenty respondents from labour non-governmental organisations (LNGOs) based in Hong Kong and Guangdong province in southern China. His findings identify four mechanisms: consulting, financing, provision of free space and provision of international networks through which democracy diffuse in the region. Questions regarding the existence of a Chinese civil society and the suitability of democracy for Chinese society have long been important topics of debate. Sundqvist's work enhances this discussion and broadens our horizon concerning groups of labour organisation in mainland China. They not only have a strong desire for democratisation while living in a political system distinct from Hong Kong and Taiwan, but they also perceive both as sources of inspiration. A line of democratic diffusion is developing and expanding on a grassroots level through these identified mechanisms. In this sense, Sundqvist has set up a distinct landmark for follow-up studies.

The final chapter in this section by Neville Chi Hang Li shifts our attention to Hong Kong, where several anti-Beijing and pro-democracy demonstrations have occurred in recent years. The author analyses the political framework of 'one country, two systems', that Deng Xiaoping put in place to deal with any potentially problematic contradictions between the capitalist and socialist systems. Li refers to this as a 'political buffer' and suggests that its role is in danger. Referring to the concept of security developed by Barry Buzan and the Copenhagen School, Li contends that increasing conflict from both the pro-self-determination and the pro-establishment camps contribute to this. This chapter clarifies the basic viewpoints of these two groups and traces the origins of their distinct arguments. Specifically, the pro-self-determinists regard Hong Kong as the only referent object and thus seek full democracy and independence. On the other hand, the followers of the pro-establishment camp regard the entire state, i.e. the PRC, as the referent object. In this way, they avoid confrontation against the central government of Beijing. Clearly, these two stances are incompatible. Given the fact that both sides aim to securitise their referent objects, such an irreconcilable relationship of security competition can only lead to a growing sense of insecurity.

Transnational

The transnational section also consists of four chapters, each dealing with a unique aspect of Chinese foreign policy. Tony Tai-Ting Liu's investigation into China's public diplomacy looks at how 'telling a good story of China' and the concept of 'China Dream' have been utilised to cope with the widespread 'China threat theory' and improve China's status and image. The author also discusses the contributions of the Confucius Institutes and the China Cultural Centres with regard to China's public diplomacy endeavours. He concludes that by making such efforts, China seeks to move away from the popular image of 'China threat' to a more cordial image of China as a friendly and peace-loving nation.

Following on from this, Shu Liang Yan utilises a case study of China's High-Speed Railway project to illustrate that an infrastructural initiative such as this not only has a place on an economic agenda, but also aims to reshape the international political order in China's favour. In Yan's view, both the Belt and Road Initiative and the worldwide deployment of Chinese-made high-speed railways are concerted efforts launched by the Chinese government. The author argues that the common objective of both projects is building China's alliances through infrastructural construction. Both projects are served to connect continental Asia, change the regional power dynamic, forge a counter-hegemonic force against the Western liberal system and ultimately establish new international institutions that are in China's interest. However, Yan questions if the implementation of these public projects can adapt to different political institutions and business cultures as well as deal with countries with profoundly different domestic power dynamics.

Casper Wits argues that the achievement of Sino-Japanese diplomatic normalisation in 1972 and the Peace and Friendship Treaty in 1978, were the result of an intense process of bridge-building and (nominally) non-governmental contacts spanning decades. Central to these efforts was a transnational network involving people from both countries – to which the author refers as People's diplomacy (*renmin waijiao*) or People-to-People diplomacy (*minjian waijiao*). China and Japan both appear to look to the past to learn from the mechanisms that have contributed to the many achievements in post-war Sino-Japanese relations. This seems to be particularly true today as present bilateral relations are tense. People-to-People diplomacy offers a potential way to counteract the current downward spiral in bilateral relations. Such examples can provide us with a unique perspective for analysing modern China's relationship with Japan and the world in a broader twentieth century transnational history context. Wits's account shows that grass-roots transnational networks can be utilised to achieve political goals. History has shown us how civic action across borders changed seemingly rigid political realities throughout the Cold War.

The final chapter in this section by Jie Li focuses on how the changes in China's foreign policymaking combined with the shift in Sino-Soviet relations in the early 1980s affected the writing and thinking of Chinese scholars on the Soviet Union at that time. In the early 1980s, Chinese scholarly research into Soviet hegemony (*baquan zhuyi*), Soviet-Yugoslavian conflicts and Soviet-Third World relations all reflected Beijing's ambitions of challenging the orthodox Soviet model of economic development in the socialist world. This was in order to compete with the Kremlin for leadership amongst developing countries and to project a more benevolent image of Chinese socialism vis-à-vis Moscow. This chapter presents a picture of how Chinese scholars attempted to adjust their analyses to align with China's vision of itself and the world through their research on the formation and evolution of Soviet foreign policy. In the author's view, Chinese Soviet-watchers were not able to remain outside the confines of Chinese politics. The Party guideposts always transcended impartial academic research.

International

In the first chapter of this final section, Benjamin Creutzfeldt offers an overview of the history of the interaction between China and Latin America – tracing the historical roots from the Qing dynasty until the establishment of the People's Republic of China. The development of the relationship between China and Latin American countries has at times been slow, especially in comparison to other parts of the world. Since Jiang Zemin visited the region in 2001, however, relations and trade quickly grew. Creutzfeldt notes that what makes the relationship most interesting for observers of Chinese foreign policy is where the region fits into China's strategy. On the one hand, it provides necessary raw materials for China's growth. On the other, it offers potential support for 'a new global framework' where China's involvement could either end up supporting the existing elites, or enabling change.

The next chapter in this section by Ilaria Carrozza examines China's role in Africa, discussing China's socialisation to the international order and its work to utilise regional forum diplomacy and venues like the Forum on China-Africa Cooperation (FOCAC) as a means to socialise African leaders into a similar security narrative. Carrozza notes that many studies of socialisation fail to account for a bias in favour of the Western liberal order and its associated norms – and in the process neglect the give and take inherent in socialisation. She views China's use of FOCAC to have successfully created an accepted Sino-African narrative. In particular this appears to be China's reiteration that it too is a developing state and will continue to assist fellow developing countries in creating a shared future prosperity. Utilising this, China has been able to bring African leaders into the dialogue and in the process allow for

China to further help African development and play a more active role in African peace and security.

Following on from this, Daniel Johanson examines how China's role in the Joint Comprehensive Plan of Action (JCPOA) differs from its actions in earlier stages of the Iranian nuclear issue. As one of Iran's few remaining trading partners, China's role in the sanctions process that led to the agreement was essential – but also understudied and not well understood. What is telling is how China portrayed itself as 'active', 'constructive' and 'responsible'. This chapter shows that, at least in global issues that are not a core interest, China's actions will work within the system – for now at least.

The final chapter in this section, and of the book, is Nori Katagiri's examination of China's relationship with Japan and what it means for the region. Katagiri highlights two key factors that play a role in the relationship – the interpretation by each nation of the current state of their balance of power and the impact that the external environment plays. There is a mistrust between the two nations on security and military issues, stemming from a number of historical and modern issues. However, the increase in socioeconomic cooperation highlights a path for a better relationship. There are, of course, flashpoints that could cause things to change for better or worse: territorial disputes, North Korea, Taiwan, Southeast Asia and the uncertainty inherent in American foreign policy are mentioned in particular.

–

China undeniably plays a greater role in international affairs, and as this continues it is important to understand grand overarching questions like what its policies are, why they are, where change is occurring, and how they are changing. In the chapters that follow, we will see an excellent overview of the latest new perspectives in the study of Chinese foreign policy. The work in this volume not only updates our understanding of Chinese foreign policy, but also enables scholars to further this research and build upon it. The broad scope in themes and content should provide a wide overview of the study of Chinese foreign policy and the factors that influence it across the board. As you will see in the chapters that follow, these influences are many and each author brings their own unique perspective in analysing the issues at hand.

Part One

National

1

Switching between Accommodation and Suppression: China's Nation-Building Strategies and United Front Work for Tibetan Leadership

TSUNGHAN WU

This chapter investigates the People's Republic of China's (PRC) nation-building practice in Tibet over the past six decades and relates it to the evolving united front work employed by the Chinese Communist Party (CCP) towards Tibetan traditional elites. The chapter argues that the Chinese Party-state aims to construct a united multi-ethnic state which contains a superior Chinese national identity, whilst allowing the co-existence of plural ethnic identities. In line with this, the CCP strives to balance uniting the 'ethnic upper strata' with empowering autonomy for these ethnic elites. Specifically, in this way, the central regime had developed and switched its positions between deliberatively accommodating and collaborating with the Tibetan traditional elites, and suppressing them within this process. This chapter suggests that the former is applicable to the decades of the 1950s and 1980s, and the latter relates to the more recent era. The transiting dynamics have more to do with the state's perceptions to these traditional elites. The chapter observes that as the ruling authority regarded Tibetan behaviours and demands with dynamics threating to the construction of Chinese nationhood, the authority tightened its control, which, however, reversely undermined the effects of existing inducement policies on economic and cultural developments designed for Tibetans. Furthermore, such political control intensified international disputes over the CCP's statecraft.

In this chapter, I adopt a hybrid concept of nation-building. In other words, I do not further distinguish the concepts of state-building and nation-building, as some researchers may do in the previous literature. In most cases, the former refers to the degree of development of state institutions and relevant apparatus, whereas the latter focuses on the creation of national identity amid the population in a state (Call 2008, 5; Paris and Sisk 2009, 15). This chapter admits the usefulness of such a conceptual separation when analysing specific aspects, however, it favours a hybrid approach, for better understanding the operational process of nation-building. Moreover, a hybrid approach is in line with a fact that most policy makers and journalists do not further make distinctions in their daily practices (Call 2008, 5). Given these academic and practical merits, as a result, this hybrid position seems to be appropriate in examining Chinese nation-building in Tibet.

United front work is an important theme yet paid not enough attention in the existing researches. In this chapter it refers to a Chinese Communists' flexible strategy that is employed to build alliance containing as many collaborators (regardless targets' class, ethnicity, party backgrounds etc.) as possible, in order to achieve an ultimate goal (Van Ness 1970, 61; Qunpei 2008, 296). In its association to China's nation-building, as such, the united front work serves as a key political tool accessing to the targets and managing them.

The primary English and Chinese language sources utilised in this study include declassified archives and official documents over ethnic minority affairs and Tibetan policies. The author also reviewed historical records, selected works and speeches by PRC leaders on Tibetan affairs published by the China Tibetology Publishing House, CCP Party History Press and Central Party Literature Press. The quotes are translated by the author. By analysing these materials this chapter attempts to accurately gauge Chinese perceptions.

The chapter begins with an introduction to the PRC's nation-building regarding the national narrative. It then presents the Chinese government's means of operation in Tibet, in which the united front work for the ethnic upper strata occupies a key position. Two strategies: the united front of accommodation and the united front of suppression are summarised. Finally, the chapter presents an overview of China's operation over the past six decades. It concludes by suggesting that the CCP should reflect its strategies to overcome conflictual dynamics that have occurred in the process of nation-building.

Configuring China as a United Multiethnic State

Since the establishment of the PRC in 1949, the ruling Chinese Communist Party has upheld a nationalist narrative constructing China as a united multiethnic state (Fei 1989; Li 1980). The ethnic Han constitutes a clear majority with 92%, and the remaining 8% is composed of 55 ethnic minorities. Such a pluralistic and united configuration is claimed by the regime as a historical landmark. This narrative was derived from the Party's adaptions and compounds of the Stalinist theory of the 'nationality issue', which recognised the equal rights of all nationalities/ethnic groups in the world (Stalin 2012), and the Republican Chinese regime's linear narrative stating that all China's ethnic groups shared a common bloodline and history (Leibold 2007). The CCP sinicised the Soviet Model, and meanwhile, it aimed to balance ethnocultural diversity and national integration. As a result, for one thing, the Communist authority insisted on the indispensability of all ethnic groups within the state territory and their contributions to the modern Chinese nation. For another, the CCP denied ethnicities' separatism rights and the adoption of federation, but instead promoted a nationalist sentiment of multiethnic unity, to impose the socialist transformation on all areas of the state, and to design a regional ethnic autonomy system under the state's unitary administration (Wu 2012, 344–76; 2016).

As a nation envisaged to be socio-politically and spatially integrated into congruity (Gellner 1983), scholars have noticed the significance of a 'national narrative' behind the nation-builder's commitment. The narrative can be conceptualised as a blueprint, a value or a direction set by the nation-builders to be imposed onto the 'imagined community' (Anderson 2006). In its practices, the national narrative can reflect in constitution, laws, and official statements. Functioning as the core principle, the narrative instructs the establishments of most relevant policies and of institutions. In the case of China, 'a united multi-ethnic state', is a term that can be used interchangeably with the concept of 'national integrity and ethnic consolidation' (Guojia Tongyi Minzu Tuanjie国家统一民族团结), which constitutes a national narrative and is embedded in the CCP's nation-building operation at all levels.

'National integrity and ethnic consolidation' features a mutually reinforced concept. It is contended that if consolidation amidst all ethnic groups were to be achieved, national integrity would be complete; the Chinese nation, as a whole, would move towards common prosperity (Kim 2007, 462–465). In the PRC's official rhetoric, national integrity refers to three historical backgrounds. Firstly, the concept of 'big integrity' of the Chinese nation has been built since the Qin dynasty. Secondly, this integrity has been strengthened through inter-ethnic interactions over thousands of years. Finally, Chinese society has completed their national unification through the process of fighting against imperialists. In addition, ethnic consolidation signifies several aspects, including the opposition of discrimination among ethnic groups and the in-separatism of the Chinese nation (Tuanzhongyang Minzu Diqu Gongzuo Lingdao Xiaozu et al. 2013, 38–40).

Having played the role of a provisional constitution before the establishment of the Constitution in 1954, the Common Program of the Chinese People's Political Consultative Conference (Zhongguo Renmin Zhengzhi Xieshang Huiyi Gongtong Gangling中国人民政治协商会议共同纲领) of 1949, is regarded as one of the most important documents that feature this official PRC narrative. With regard to the state's stance on ethnicities, Chapter Six explores an implication that aims to construct a homogenised loyalty towards the party-state for all ethnicities, whilst allowing for the existence of ethnic distinction. It contends:

> Article 50: "All ethnicities within the boundaries of the People's Republic of China are equal. They shall unite and mutually help each other, and they shall oppose imperialism and their own public enemies, so that the People's Republic of China will become a big fraternal and co-operative family composed of all its ethnicities. Greater Nationalism [chauvinism] and Local Nationalism [ethno-nationalism] shall be opposed. Acts involving discrimination, oppression and splitting of the unity of the various ethnicities shall be prohibited" (Zhongyang Wenxian Yanjiushi 2005, 3).

> Article 51: "Regional autonomy shall be exercised in areas where ethnic minorities are concentrated and various kinds of autonomy organizations of the different ethnicities shall be established according to the size of the respective populations and regions…" (Zhongyang Wenxian Yanjiushi 2005, 3).

Moreover, an implication that the state should endeavour to impose inter-ethnic cohesion through politico-economic means is evident, as can be seen in Article 53:

> All ethnic minorities shall have freedom to develop their languages, to preserve or reform their traditions, customs and religious beliefs. The People's Government shall assist the masses of the people of all ethnic minorities to develop their political, economic, cultural and educational construction work (Zhongyang Wenxian Yanjiushi 2005, 3).

Upon the establishment of the Common Program, the CCP could initiate relevant projects, including the creation of the Ethnic Identification Project (Minzu Shibie民族识别), the fostering of ethnic Party cadres and the beginning of preparations for setting up the ethnic autonomous regions. The Program was also used as a guideline for the CCP to tackle ethnicity/nationality issues in China's peripheral areas in the early 1950s, as a scenario of the liberation of Tibet showed. The Party composed the principle of the Program to the '17-Point Agreement' to negotiate with the government of the Dalai Lama during the liberation process. Then, once the Constitution was founded, containing major aspects of the Program, corresponding laws and policies were designed in the following decades. With years of enforcement, amendment and supplementation, China had institutionalised a sophisticated system, framing inter-ethnic relationships and means of national integration. The PRC nation-building narrative had also shaped and reshaped its propaganda and agenda within a certain scope.[1]

Nation-building, The United Front Work of Upper Strata, and Tibet

From the outset, the CCP applied its national narrative nationwide. Flexibly, the Party implemented its nation-building practice along with socialist transformation, depending upon local conditions, drawing a distinction between the Han and the ethnic minority areas (Wang 2017, 153–57). Comparatively, it adopted a much more cautious attitude when imposing reforms on the latter regions. In the process, the CCP projected that the means of imposition should not violate the socialist doctrine that vindicated the principle of popular voluntarism. Rather, works should be conducted through the CCP's 'active persuasion' and collaboration with the traditional elites, termed as the 'patriotic ethnicity upper strata'. It does not matter in specific cases the authorities of these elites were based on the sacred or secular sources, even though the Communists advocated atheism. These actions were necessary, because as a new regime, the Communist's power had not yet penetrated down to a localised level. Therefore, the traditional figures, with their established connections, became important agents and must be united for the CCP.

While the Han makes up a majority in the CCP, the Party leadership endeavoured to avoid an impression that the nation-building manifested as a Han nationalist movement against the ethnic minorities. As such, the role of the 'patriotic' ethnicity upper strata was emphasised and they were, and still are, central to the CCP's united front work related to the ethnic minorities. Of all the ethnic minority areas, Tibet featured a typical and controversial case.

---

1   For example, in the Central Ethnic Work Conference, the notion of national integrity and ethnic consolidation was every time proclaimed. See Kim 2007, 445–7.

Until Chairman Mao launched the liberation of Tibet in 1950, this vast area had been under the rule of the Dalai Lama and his cabinet (Kashag) and had preserved their 'de facto independence' from the Chinese central authority since the collapse of the Qing Empire (Goldstein 1997, 30–36; Crowe 2013, 1104–1108). Although its sovereign status was never recognised by any foreign country, factors including demographic isolation/mono-ethnicity, limited external aid (mainly from the British Raj) and the Chinese government's long-term struggles with domestic warlords and Japanese invasion, contributed to Tibet's self-rule (Sperling 2004, 22–23).

The sending of a commercial delegation to the West (Sperling 2004, 23) and the exclusion of all officials of the Republican Chinese government on the eve of the establishment of the PRC demonstrated Tibet's attempt to achieve a greater degree of independence (Shakya 1999, 7–11). Perceiving this behaviour as a threat to China's sovereign and territorial integrity, the CCP employed a comprehensive policy combining united front appeal and military attack for the Tibetans. Considering their unique ethno-religious characteristics, Mao instructed at a largest degree befriending the Dalai Lama and the Panchen Lama as well as other Tibetan traditional elites, given their influence on local society (Mao 2001, 1; 16). During the process of signing the '17-Point Agreement', the Chinese also promised that 'current societal system would be maintained' as long as the Tibetans accepted that Tibet was part of China (Zhongyang Wenxian Yanjiushi 2005, 43–44). The CCP continued this stance until 1959 when the 'Lhasa uprising' took place. Prior to this, the Communists had paid special treatment to the Tibetan elites on many occasions. Not only were both the Dalai Lama and the Panchen Lama appointed to symbolic senior positions at the first meeting of the National People's Congress in 1954, but they were also deemed as leaders in the Preparatory Committee for the Autonomy Region of Tibet, established in 1956. According to the Chinese government, half of the 6,000 people of the upper strata were designated to various official institutes (Xizang Tongshi Bianweihui 2015, 123). Moreover, the Central government organised tours to visit Tibet, which explained the CCP's perspective to the local elites in an attempt to convince them of their intent. Alternatively, the authorities also invited these elites to visit the inland provinces (Xizang Tongshi Bianweihui 2015, 120–21; Jiefang Xizangshi Bianweihui 2008, 229–30).

While it is true that the flight of the Dalai Lama to India provoked the CCP's adaption of new policies and tougher control, broadly the implication of the united front work remained to a certain extent, which can be proven by the Party's collaboration with the left leadership. The following scenarios justified the CCP's lasting commitment, constructing China into a multi-ethnic state via uniting the upper strata. It is worth noting that the united front work related to Tibet is not only confined to the work by the United Front Work Department.

Beyond that, it also involved the State Ethnic Affairs Commission and State Administration for Religious Affairs. As can be seen, China's Tibetan policies have been mainly designed, instructed and practiced through these units. In short, through the examination of evolvement of Tibetan policies in the past six decades, this paper argues that the united front work of Tibetan elites constituted a key part of China's nation-building in Tibet. In addition, it has been identified that the CCP regime developed a duo strategy of accommodation and suppression towards Tibet.

Two Strategies of the United Front for the Tibetan Upper Strata

The strategies of accommodation and suppression were mainly identified based on the CCP's interactions with the Tibetan upper strata in the 1950s and the 1960s, respectively. With regard to accommodation, this paper argues that it refers to the commitment that the CCP aimed to conduct China's nation-building through increasingly inter-ethnic intimacy. During the 1950s, the CCP leadership offered a high degree of autonomy for the Tibetans. Also, many of the upper strata were appointed to senior positions within the government and public institutes, such as the Dalai Lama and Panchen Lama as mentioned in the last section. Most traditional Tibetan leadership accepted this way of arrangement because conversely they thought they could influence the policy-making process related to Tibet. On the other hand, the suppression strategy is referred to the CCP's tightening of control over the Tibetan elites while still claiming that efforts were made to maintain unity. The scope of autonomy granted to the upper strata turned conditional and aligned to what was fundamentally reliant to the edicts and interpretations of the Party-state. In specific cases the CCP's implementation of policies varies, but this paper contends that the types of these two strategies identified outlined the CCP's actions. In particular, the 1950s and 1980s represented periods of accommodation, while all other time periods experienced suppression.

Relevant questions may then be raised here: why and under what conditions would the CCP adjust its strategy? Inspired by the previous literature completed by Goldstein (1997), Han (2013), and Topgyal (2013; 2016), this paper attributes the influences of China's perception of ethno-nationalist sentiment to its Tibetan policies. As a primary argument, this paper forwards the idea that the transiting dynamics between two strategies were related to the CCP's perception of the commitments of these Tibetan traditional elites. This paper observes that when the ruling authority perceived the demands made by traditional elites to be detrimental to the Chinese national identity, while reinforcing Tibetan ethno-nationalist sentiment, the Party would adopt a strategy of suppression.

Switching between Accommodation and Suppression

The 1950s

Having liberated Tibet, the CCP leadership prioritised a notion of 'expansion and consolidation of the united front with the upper strata' above all missions with regard to the Tibetan affairs (Zhongyang Wenxian Yanjiushi 2005, 80–81). The purpose behind this commitment was to build and enhance friendship with the traditional Tibetan elites, through which the Party believed, it would be able to improve the inter-ethnic relationship and then persuade the elites themselves to act as facilitators for socialist transformation. Under the terms of the 17-Point Agreement, the CCP maintained the existing socio-politico-economic status of the upper class. Besides, Tibet was able to exempt itself from various socialist campaigns that had been launched in other regions of China in the 1950s. Finally, when knowing about the Dalai Lama's concerns over socialist reform, Mao immediately compromised to postpone the agenda until 'the Tibetans were ready' (Mao 2001, 154–55). These empirical cases reflected the CCP's allowance of a high degree of accommodation for social elites during that period. However, mutual coexistence between Beijing and Tibet would not push forward the expected positive integration in the passage of time. Rather, tensions continually escalated until the revolt in 1959. Afterwards, the Chinese authorities imposed a new strategy of suppression on the area, where it continued to collaborate with the remaining Panchen Lama.

The factors which have triggered the bilateral conflicts were multiple, but a key one was that Beijing perceived the Tibetan leadership's firm unwillingness to conduct socialist transformation as a plot to deny Central authority and even facilitate Tibet's independence movement (Zhongyang Wenxian Yanjiushi 2005, 217–220). Relatively, the Kashag's inactivity and tolerance of the Tibetan guerrillas stems from other ethnic Tibetan regions of China spreading to Tibet (and their receipt of US military aid) (Jiefang Xizangshi Bianweihui 2008, 339–52; Knaus 2003, 68–69), which furthermore raised Beijing's doubt (Han 2013, 135). As a consequence, the Chinese negated their previous strategy. Following the dissolution of the Kashag, Beijing purged a large number of the upper strata, who were suspected of engagement in the revolt.

The 1960s to the mid-1970s

The 1960s witnessed waves of far-leftist crusades represented by the Democratic Reform, the Socialist Reform, and then the Cultural Revolution, which continued until 1976 when Chairman Mao passed away. During this short period, Tibet experienced tremendous changes to its society's economic, cultural and value systems (Shakya, 1999, 287–88; Wang 2002, 94–96). The wealth and land redistribution to previously deprived serfs had improved their material conditions and reshaped the landscape of Tibet. However, under the Maoist notions of class-struggle and criticism of the Four Olds, (old customs, old culture, old habits and old thought) the Tibetan tradition - given its feudal and religious legacies - faced extreme distortion and destruction. Thousands of monasteries and temples were forced to close, ruined, or converted for alternative use (Woeser 2016). In this context, many of the remaining Tibetan upper strata, including the Panchen Lama, also experienced antagonism from the anti-religious and anti-traditional activists. Moreover, those who showed sympathy for the Tibetan traditional actors tended to be tagged as ethno-nationalists. The role of the Tibetan upper class was still nominally significant. In practice, however, their agency was very limited and illusory. In 1965, the Tibet Autonomous Region was established. While being described as 'autonomous', the implication was that Beijing had further institutionalised its incorporation of Tibet into the PRC state apparatus and centralised its power (China Report 1966, 28–32; Shakya 1999, 302–03).

The late-1970s to the 1980s

The rise of Deng Xiaoping in the post-Mao era was marked by the adoption of Reform and Opening Up announced at the Third Plenum of the 11th CCP Central Committee. Along with this came a revival of the strategy of accommodation towards the Tibetan upper strata by the CCP leadership. To portray a friendly and tolerant gesture, they released groups of Tibetan prisoners and removed labels from more than 6000 people who either took part in the 1959 rebellion or were considered to be related to 'reactionary' or 'counter-revolutionary' involvement before the end of the Cultural Revolution (Zhonggong Xizang Zizhiqu Weiyuanhui Dangshi Yanjiushi 2005, 312). A group of upper strata, including the Panchen Lama himself, had now been rehabilitated and reappointed to senior positions within the government.

In the 1980s, Hu Yaobang, then General Secretary of the Party, hosted the Tibet Work Forum twice, where the rehabilitated Tibetan upper strata attended. Having proclaimed the specialties of Tibet on these occasions, Hu highly valued the advice and perspectives from these traditional figures. The implication of strengthening inter-ethnic unity through these traditional elites was evident. In relation to this intent, the Chinese government proposed to increase the number of Tibetan cadres, provided funds to support the rejuvenation of Tibetan Buddhism and restoration of a number of monasteries and temples, as well as heralding religious practices in public. The Tibetan language was also claimed to be widely used in all official institutions in the

TAR (Wang 2011, 108–09). Moreover, the Party Central redefined the scope of the 'upper class people' to not only the former and incumbent political and religious leaders, but also the exiles and their families dwelling in China (Zhongyang Wenxian Chubanshe and Zhonggong Xizang Zizhiqu Weiyuanhui 2005, 365–66). The key reason for this enhancement of united work was that the CCP presumed that these upper-class people could help to promote the Party's policies to the masses more effectively than other Communists from different ethnic backgrounds. Adopting a liberalist stance, the central government emphasised that 'loving the country was the only measure', and sought to unite these leaders as much as possible (Sung 2011, 301; Wang 2011, 110–12).

The CCP presumed that its accommodating strategy could acquire greater support and loyalty from the Tibetans, but in reality, this did not occur. Firstly, more than 21 demonstrations and riots, led by monks, occurred between 1987 and 1989 (Karmel 1996, 491). It was also reported that 138 incidents took place during the period between 1987 and 1992 (Schwartz 1994, 186). Initially Beijing regarded the protests as the result of the government's insufficient appraisal of power. However, the increase in disturbances, as well as slogans calling for the return of the Dalai Lama and Tibetan independence, caused the central government to view the situation as a crisis. Beijing soon faced higher pressure from the successful inter-nationalisation of the Tibetan issues by the exiled Dalai Lama and the exiled Tibetan government that drew the attention of the world inside and outside of China. This resulted in the political conservatives in the CCP leadership dominating the Tibetan policy-making process once more. Hu's withdrawal from his position is believed to have been connected with the instability of Tibet.

The aftermath of the Panchen Lama's death witnessed a new wave of monk demonstrations in March 1989. In his response, Hu Jintao, the former Chinese president who served as the party secretary of the TAR at that time, imposed martial law. The law itself was lifted one year later, but the implication was that the government again switched its strategy towards the upper strata to a hard-line approach.

The post-1990 era

While the strategy Beijing adopted towards the Tibetan upper strata returned to suppression, its commitment has been far more sophisticated than the pre-Reform and Opening Up era. Since the 1990s, under a notion of 'grasping with both hands', the CCP government has dually embarked upon political authoritarianism and economic developmentalism, which have contained a great investment in infra-structure and modernisation projects in Tibet on an unprecedentedly large scale (Fisher 2009). In its association, the government provided generous funds to the development of Tibetan Buddhism. By doing this, however, the CCP has attempted to stifle the political freedom of the population, the clergy in particular, to ensure the stability and implementation of the Party-led nation-building agenda. Various inducement policies for economic interests and crusades for regulation were also put into practice at the same time (Mukherjee 2010, 476–78; Topgyal 2016, 51–66).

On the occasion of the National United Front Work Forum, launched in 1993, then-President Jiang Zemin, introduced a term known as the 'co-adaption of religion and socialism'. Having been called 'co-adaption', it essentially meant that religion in China must obey the guidance of the Party-state, and religion was not allowed to interfere with issues defined as political (Zhu 2014, 307). However, religion can be utilised for facilitating China's integrity and ethnic consolidation. In his speech at the Third Tibet Work Forum of 1994, Jiang stated clearly:

> Tibet is a place where the population believe Tibetan Buddhism...[we] must comprehensively and correctly implement the Party's religious policy, guarantee the appropriate religious activities, and strengthen monastic management according to law and the principle of separation of church and state. Religion is not allowed to intervene in political and social affairs...[we] should strengthen the education and management of the monks, uniting them for safeguarding national integrity and ethnic consolidation...With regard to ethnicity and religious work, the patriotic upper strata should play a positive role... (Zhongyang Wenxian Yanjiushi 2005, 461–462).

Moreover, deliberate regulations have been employed to the areas of monastery and temple management – interfering with affairs regarding worship and reincarnation. The patriotic education campaign was also launched in 1996 (Zhao 2004, 236), targeting monasteries and temples throughout Tibet. It has become a governmental tool to control monastic activities and their education curricula to subordinate the state's confinement of religion. The campaign calling for discrediting the Dalai Lama took place amongst the clergy. The dispute over the search for the 11th Panchen Lama in the mid-1990s and the flight of the 17th Karmapa to India in 2000 represent important cases that revealed the CCP's commitments towards Tibetan Buddhism. The publication of 'Measures on the Management of the Reincarnation of Living Buddhas' in 2007, a policy that requires all Tibetan lamas wishing to reincarnate to obtain prior approval by the government, is another recent case confirming that the state wants to guarantee its future control over the selection process of Tibetan lamas (Arpi 2013, 547; Dumbaugh 2008, 7).

Conclusion

This chapter contributes to the literature with several new aspects. Firstly, it reveals a relationship that the CCP regime's united front strategies for the Tibetan upper strata were framed by China's nation-building politics. In addition, these strategies showed dynamics of flexibility relying on the situations. This argument is against a horizon that many of the Tibetan studies claim the rigidness of China's policies. Thirdly, this chapter offers a vivid example of Beijing's dilemmas in its ethnic minority areas. On the one hand, the authority remained in doubt whether the provision of accommodation led to the growing of Tibetan ethno-national identity by the traditional elites. On the other, a strategy of suppression, adopted to stabilise Tibet, did not lead to a smoother route for nation-building. The occurrences of the 14 March Incident in 2008 and the occasional, yet endless wave of Tibetan self-immolations since 2009, in both of which religious groups constituted an important role, marked the fact that the government's current commitment resulted in widespread discontent. It is without doubt that such discontent undermined the authority's efforts to reconstruct Tibet with a considerable amount of resources over the years. Therefore, the Chinese government has always been covered by a sense of insecurity. Revisiting its strategies and exploring alternative and appropriate means will be necessary in order to successfully attain national integration and the unification of a multi-ethnic China.

References

Anderson, Benedict. 2006. *Imagined Communities: Reflections on the Origin and Spread of Nationalism*. Verso Books.

Arpi, Claude. 2013. "China's Leadership Change and Its Tibet Policy." *Strategic Analysis* 37 (5): 539-557.

Call, Charles. 2008. *Building States to Build Peace*. Lynne Rienner Publication.

China Report. 1966. "Tibet: Autonomy or Integration?: The 'Tibetan Revolution' Is at An Uncertain Stage. Peking Has Tightened Its Control but Its Position Is Not Invulnerable in Tibet." *China Report* 2: 28–32.

Crowe, David M. 2013. "The 'Tibet Question': Tibetan, Chinese and Western Perspectives." *Nationalities Papers* 41 (6): 1100–1135.

Dumbaugh, Kerry. 2008. *Tibet: Problems, Prospects, and US Policy*. CRS Report for Congress.

Fei Xiaotong. 1989. "Zhonghua Minzu De Duoyuan Yiti Geju [The Cultural Pluralistic Entity of the Chinese Nation]." *Journal of Peking University (Philosophy and Social Sciences)* 4: 1–19.

Fischer, Andrew M. 2009. "The Political Economy of Boomerang Aid in China's Tibet." *China Perspectives* (3): 38–53.

Gellner, Ernest. 1983. *Nations and Nationalism*. Oxford: Blackwell.

Goldstein, M. C. 1997. *The Snow Lion and the Dragon: China, Tibet, and the Dalai Lama*. University of California Press.

Han, Enze. 2013. *Contestation and Adaptation: The Politics of National Identity in China*. Oxford University Press.

Jiefang Xizangshi Bianweihui. 2008. *Jiefang Xizangshi* [History of Liberation of Tibet]. Beijing: CCP Party History Press.

Karmel, Solomon M. 1995. "Ethnic Tension and the Struggle for Order: China's Policies in Tibet." *Pacific Affairs* 68 (4): 485–508.

Knaus, Jenneth K. 2003. "Official Policies and Covert Programs: The US State Department, the CIA, and the Tibetan Resistance." *Journal of Cold War Studies* 5 (3): 54–79.

Kim, Binggao. 2007. *Minzu Lilun Tonglun* [Introduction of Minzu Theories]. Beijing: Press of the Central University for Nationalities.

Leibold, James. 2007. *Reconfiguring Chinese Nationalism: How the Qing Frontier and Its Indigenes Became Chinese*. Springer.

Li, Weihan. 1979. "Zhongguo Ge Shaoshu Minzu He Minzu Guanxi [China's Ethnic Minorities and Interethnic Relationship]." *Zhongguo Minzu* [China's Ethnic Groups] 3: 8–19.

Mao, Zedong. 2001. *Maozedong Xizang Gongzuo Wenxuan* [Selection of Mao Zedong on Tibetan Works]. Beijing: China Tibetology Press.

Mukherjee, Kunal. 2010. "China–Tibet Relations from 1950 Until 2008: the Interaction between Religion, Nationalism, and Reform." *The Korean Journal of Defense Analysis* 22 (4): 467–483.

Paris, Roland, and Sisk, Timothy D. 2009. "Introduction: Understanding the Contradictions of Postwar Statebuilding." In, *The Dilemmas of Statebuilding: Confronting the Contradictions of Postwar Peace Operations*, edited by Roland Paris and Timothy D. Sisk, 1–20. London: Routledge.

Qunpei, Gesang, ed. 2008. *Minzu, Zongjiao, Tongyi Zhanxian Lilun He Zhengce* [Ethnicity, Religion, United Front Work Theory and Policy]. Lhasa: Xizang Renmin Press.

Song, Yuehong. 2011. *Dangdai Zhongguo De Xizang Zhengce Yu Zhili* [Modern China's Tibet Policy and its Governance]. Beijing: Renmin Press.

Stalin, Joseph. 2012. *Marxism and the National Question*. London: CPGB-ML.

Topgyal, Tsering. 2013. "Identity Insecurity and the Tibetan Resistance against China." *Pacific Affairs* 86 (3): 515–538.

Topgyal, Tsering. 2016. *China and Tibet: The Perils of Insecurity*. London: Hurst & Company

Tuanzhongyang Minzu Diqu Gongzuo Lingdao Xiaozu, Zhongyang Minzu Daxue Zhongguo Minzu Lilun Yu Minzu Zhengce Yanjiuyuan, Zhongyang Tuanxiao Gongqingtuan Gongzuo Lilun Yanjiusuo. eds. 2013. *Minzu Diqu Tuanganbu Duben* [Textbooks for League Cadres in Ethnic Minority Areas]. Beijing: China Youth Publishing Group.

Schwartz, Ronald. D. 1994. *Circle of Protest: Political Ritual in the Tibetan Uprising*. Columbia University Press.

Sperling, Elliot. 2004. *The Tibet-China Conflict: History and Polemics*. Washington, DC: East-West Center.

Tsering, Shakya. 1999. *The Dragon in the Land of Snows*. London: Pimlico.

Van Ness, Peter. 1970. *Revolution and Chinese Foreign Policy: Peking's Support for Wars of National Liberation*. Berkeley: University of California Press.

Wang, Lixiong. 2002. "Reflections on Tibet." *New Left Review* 14: 79–111.

Wang, Maoxia. 2011. *Deng Xiaoping Yu Xizang Gongzuo: Cong Heping Jiefang Dao Gaige Kaifang* [Deng Xiaoping and the Works on Tibet: From Peaceful Liberation and Reform and Open]. Beijing: China Tibetology Press

Wang, Xiaobin. 2013. *Zhongguo Gongchandang Xizang Zhengce Yanjiu* [The CCP's Tibet Policies Research]. Beijing: Renmin Press.

Wang, Ke. 2017. *Xiaoshi De Guomin: Jindai Zhongguo De Minzu Huayu Yu Shaoshu Minzu De Guojia Rentong* [Disappearing Citizens: Modern China's Narrative on Nation/Ethnicity and National Identity of the Ethnic Minorities]. The Chinese University of Hong Kong.

Woeser, Tsering. 2016. *Shajie* [Forbidden Memory. Tibet during the Cultural Revolution]. Taipei: Dakuai Wenhua.

Wu, Zhe. 2012. "Renqun Fenlei Yu Guozu Zhenghe: Zhonggong Minzu Shibie Zhengce De Lishi Xiansuo Yu Zhengzhi Mianxiang [Human Grouping and National Integration: CCP's Ethnic Identification Policy and Its Historical Source and Political Implications]." In *Liangan Fenzhi: Xueshu Jianzhi, Tuxiang Xuanchuan Yu Zuqun Zhengzhi* [Divided Governance of Cross-Strait: Academics Setting, Image Propaganda and Ethnic Politics], edited by Yu, Miin-ling, 319–95. Taipei: Institute of Modern History, Academia Sinica.

Wu, Zhe. 2016. "Minzu Quyu Zizhi Zhidu De Lishi Yu Xianshi [History and Reality of Ethnic Regional Autonomy]." *Wenhua Zongheng* 45: 88–93.

Xizang Tongshi Bianweihui. 2015. *Xizang Tongshi Dangdai Juan* [History of Tibet Modern Era]. Beijing: China Tibetology Press.

Zhao, Suisheng. 2004. *A Nation-state by Construction: Dynamics of Modern Chinese Nationalism*. Stanford University Press.

Zhongyang Wenxian Yanjiushi and Zhonggong Xizang Weiyuanhui. 2005. *Xizang Gongzuo Wenxian Xuan Bian 1949–2005* [Selected Writing of Works on Tibet 1949–2005]. CCCPC Party Literature Press.

Zhonggong Xizang Zizhi Qu Weiyuanhui Dangshi Yanjiushi. 2005. *Zhongguo Gongchandang Xizang Lishi Dashiji* [Historical Records of Chinese Communist Party on Tibet]. Beijing: CCP Party History Press.

Zhu, Xiaomin. 2014. *Xizang Qian Yan Wenti Yanjiu* [The Leading Issue on Tibet]. Beijing: China Tibetology Press.

2

The Changing Security Dimension of China's Relations with Xinjiang

CLAUDIA ZANARDI

The main purpose of this paper is to show how the security dimension of the People's Republic of China's relations with Xinjiang, has been changing. With 22 million residents in 2010, the Xinjiang Uyghur Autonomous Region (XUAR) is China's largest and westernmost region rich in natural resources such as oil, gas and uranium. It is also a connectivity hub across Eurasia, and crucial to the renewal of the ancient Silk Road. The region encourages the development of China's new Silk Road Economic Belt, which is part of the Belt and Road Initiative put forward by President Xi Jinping.

Since the founding of the People's Republic of China (PRC), Beijing has attempted to incorporate Xinjiang into the Chinese state through land reform and the building of infrastructure. The overarching argument of this article is that Xinjiang's security increasingly shifted from a domestic to a regional issue that required securitising trade with the Central Asian Republics (Kazakhstan, Kyrgyzstan, Tajikistan, Turkmenistan, and Uzbekistan). The Chinese focus on economic development and repressive policies towards Turkic-speaking Muslims in Xinjiang became a radicalising factor causing the Uyghur's growing embeddedness in international terrorist networks.

The concept of security that China applies to Xinjiang mirrors a realist definition of national security as the preservation of China's national territory and institutions. The region constitutes a security concern for the Chinese Communist Party (CCP) because its independence would likely trigger the independence of other regions, such as Tibet. Hence, ethnic and religious dimensions become subordinate to national unity. The use of violence is required to repress any opposition to a unified China based on Han nationalism, and the economic dimension has become a major tool in the repressive measures.

The Communist Making of Xinjiang as a Chinese Territory

Although other Muslim minorities live in Xinjiang, the Uyghur issue dominates regional security concerns because Uyghurs are the largest minority. Despite being Muslim, Turkic-speaking people in Xinjiang have fragmented 'oasis identities' (Rudelson 1997): for instance, Uyghur and Hui have conflictual relations. More sinicised and better integrated, the Hui enjoy greater freedom. Since it is not possible in this short chapter to consider the differences among these minorities, the focus will be on the Uyghur who represent Xinjiang's main Muslim community.

The Communists' 'peaceful liberation' (heping jiefang) of Xinjiang prompted thousands of Uyghur to flee China. The PRC approved a plan for transferring Han from coastal regions to Xinjiang (Joniak-Lüthi 2013) and encouraged migration as a 'patriotic duty' (Dillon 2004, 25). The national land reform had an anti-pan-Islam/Turkish connotation in Xinjiang since it redistributed the land owned by mosques and religious organisations 'to break down the traditional social structure and religious authority' (Dillon 2004, 35).

China also set up the Xinjiang Production Construction Company (XPCC), a civilian-military organisation, to reclaim land through agriculture and construction, which included demobilised Communists, former KMT soldiers and Han settlers and became a part of 'a four-in-one system of joint-defence linking the PLA, the Armed Police, the XPCC and ordinary people, playing an irreplaceable special role' (Xinhua 2003). In the aftermath of the Sino-Soviet split (1960) it also served to counter the Soviet influence.

In 1954, a pan-Turkic revolt supported by exiled Uyghurs in Turkey tried to establish a Muslim state in Xinjiang. Its failure pushed other Uyghurs to flee China. One year later, and according to Mao Zedong's desire to show how minorities lived peacefully together within the PRC, Xinjiang became an autonomous region, XUAR. However, it remained tightly controlled by military commander of Xinjiang General Wang Zhen and the Party Chief in Xinjiang Lieutenant General Wang Enmao, both Han. During the Great Leap Forward (1958–62), which was paralleled by the Sino-Soviet Split, China's repression of Soviet sympathisers in Xinjiang brought the closure of Islamic organisations and caused the migration of further waves of Turkic-speaking Muslims to the USSR, especially in 1962. The Uyghuristan People's Party, which sought independence from the PRC and became the East Turkistan

People's Revolutionary Party (ETPRP) open to all Turkic-speaking Muslims in Xinjiang, asked for military and political help to organise a revolt against Beijing, but its plot was discovered in 1969.

The Cultural Revolution (1966–1976) brought havoc in the XUAR. For instance, the powerful Party Chief Wang Enmao resigned, and the PLA had to intervene in 1971 to restore order. The Cultural Revolution also saw the resettlement of thousands of Han from coastal provinces, particularly from Shanghai, to Xinjiang to work at the XPCC. After the break with Moscow, the US became a secondary threat as the USSR's proximity to China made it Beijing's major threat (Nathan 2012, 89). This is corroborated by the expansion of the Lanzhou military region, which in 1985 incorporated the Urumqi's military command to counter the Soviet threat (Shichor 2004, 130). Since during the Cultural Revolution many clerics were killed or fled Xinjiang, when Deng Xiaoping's reforms revived the Islamic culture and religion in the 1980s there were no longer Imams to teach Islam in Xinjiang. Subsequently, authorized and underground Koranic schools (madrassas) flourished with connections to Salafists (Castest 2017).

The 1980s tolerance towards Muslim culture and religion within China aimed at gaining the favour of Muslim countries such as Saudi Arabia and, thus, increase bilateral economic ties. The Secretary General of China's Communist Party (CCP) Hu Yaobang proposed more autonomy and reforms for Xinjiang because at that time Muslims were perceived as less dangerous than Tibetans: they lacked both a unified leader and international support (Dillon, 2004, 37). The backside of this favourable policy toward Islamic culture and traditions was an increasing influence of Saudi Salafism among Muslim Chinese, who traditionally followed another tradition of Islam: Sufism (Dillon 2004, 15). Madrassas often had connections with the Salafists (Castest 2017) and taught fundamentalist Islam to Uyghur such as Hasan Mahsum (Acharya Arabinda 2010, 54).

The revival of Islam and Uyghur's culture also triggered anti-Chinese sentiments. In 1981, the Eastern Turkistan Prairie Fire Party was promptly repressed for preaching the use of force to create a Turkistan Islamic Republic in Xinjiang. From 1985 to Tiananmen (1989), Uyghur students in Xinjiang demonstrated and Uyghur's discontent re-emerged as more nationalistic. When the Party's conservative faction side-lined Hu, protests were repressed, several madrassas closed and Pan-Turkish authors and religious leaders who hold divergent views from official historiography were censored or imprisoned. As a result, enhanced censorship, policing, and political and religious control sparked rebellions; Hasan Mahsum established the East Turkish Islamic Party (ETIP/ETIM) inspired by two short-lived historical precedents: the 1st Turkic-Islamic Republic of Eastern Turkestan (TIRET), from 1933 to 1934, and the 2nd East Turkistan Republic (ETR), from 1944 to 1949 (Forbes 1986, 169). The ETIP's goal was to establish an Islamic Republic under the sharia law, but Mahsum's planned insurrection was discovered (1990). Consequently, the central government's approach to the Uyghur issue changed radically in the 1990s: religious leaders had to be appointed by the government and respect the Party's line, official institutions were created to teach the authorised version of Islam, and the entire society was put under tight surveillance.

Securitising Trade with New Central Asian (CA) Republics

In the 1980s, China's western regions, and thus Xinjiang, started looking for trading opportunities with the Middle East. Delegations of Islamic and Middle Eastern organisations went to northwest China (Yu 1989) to discuss trade, investment and labour opportunities in the Middle East, and Turkey and Saudi Arabia financed religious projects (Dillon 2004, 44). In 1985, Xinjiang sent delegations to Turkey and Saudi Arabia. The outcome was their funding of religious and cultural programmes: for instance, the Islamic Development Bank founded projects for $4,060,000 in China's western regions, such as at the Ningxia Academy, the Ningxia Tongxin Arabic Language School, and the Xinjiang and Beijing Islamic Academies (Dillon 2004, 44).

In 1992, Central Document N.4 instructed opening the northwest to trade with CA through Turkic-speaking communities. New infrastructure and telecommunications facilitated its integration with CA and the rest of China and the exploitation of Xinjiang's natural resources, particularly oil. Although Beijing initially relied on the Uyghur diaspora, by the mid-1990s ties between Xinjiang's Uyghur and the diaspora were restricted as potentially dangerous: opportunities for small traders, mainly Uyghur shrunk since they no longer could find Han or CA partners (Laruelle 2012, 118,120). Consequently, cross-border trade became increasingly monopolised by State Owned Enterprises (SOEs).

China also feared the negative impact of the Chechnyan wars of 1994–5 and 1999–2009 (Oresman 2003). In 1995, a demonstration by 50,000 claiming the incorporation of Ghulja (Yining in Chinese) to Kazakhstan was neutralised by the PAP and the PLA (Dillon 2004, 69). Since China forecasted massive social and ethnic unrest in Xinjiang, in 1996 the Standing Committee of the Politburo issued Central Document N.7 (caccfreedomsherald.org s.d.), restricting religious activities, and strengthening military and security readiness.

At the same time, China's counter-insurgency relied less upon the PLA and increasingly on paramilitary forces, the local police, and the militia. Although surveillance shifted to society and the PLA increasingly operated in support of the PAP, demonstrations continued. The killings of local party members, bureaucrats and official imams, and the sabotage of communications infrastructure culminated in the Ghulja uprising (1997) known as 'beating, smashing and looting' (Xu 1999). Xinjiang's government created 'special guard units from the XPCC' to control infrastructures. Bomb attacks in Xinjiang and Beijing were traced back to Turkey and Chinese authorities spoke about building a 'steel wall' to securitise Xinjiang (Shichor 2004).

Since China equates separatism with criminals, the following 'Strike Hard' campaign (1996–7) targeted activists as criminals and relied heavily on XPCC's Public Security Department (Dillon 2004, 88). In 1997, the Uyghur demonstrated against the Strike Hard campaign, the growing religious and cultural restrictions, and the increasing migration of Han. They called for Beijing to respect their autonomy, but China's security forces crashed down the protests, triggering three days of rioting: thousands of Uyghur were arrested, some were shot, and several mosques and schools were closed (Freund Larus 2012, 242). Consequently, new policies were adopted that focused on religion as a source of opposition.

Furthermore, religious leaders were replaced by loyal Han, and Uyghur leaders had to back official positions. Heavy surveillance was completed by grass roots control through residential street committees, Party members, neighbours, working groups, and local associations. The authorities clamped down on unofficial religious activities, madrassas and mosques (Dillon 2004, 105–6) and in 1996 any Islamic-related material required official authorisation (Dillon 2004, 85). The XPCC's Discipline Inspection Commission and Supervisory Committee increased its informants, and police pressured Uyghur and their neighbours to report suspicious activities (Wayne 2008, 22). In 2001, residents received new ID cards, reporters needed new press cards, and restrictive regulations were issued (e.g. foreign or unauthorised Uyghur Imams were banned) (Dillon 2004, 72–3). The following year, China pushed forward its 'development of the West' (Lai 2002).

Importing Security Challenge from Central Asia

The Soviet collapse saw the establishment of independent republics through coloured revolutions that China feared as a potential source of instability. The CA republics resumed their relations with China and its Uyghur population. When CA Uyghur lost Soviet support, many Uyghur migrated to Europe and North America (Kamalov 2009, 130) where they established the World Uyghur Congress (WUC) in 2004. Current president Rebiya Kadeer is a former

Uyghur businesswoman who traded with CA (Kazakhstan) and was a symbol of China's successful minority policy. A member of the National Committee of the People's Political Consultative Committee, she lost her seat when she refused to denounce her husband for plotting against China (Kadeer 2009). Imprisoned for 'passing on classified information to foreigners' (Dillon 2004, 82), her sentence brought for the first time worldwide attention to the Uyghur issue, whilst China wanted to prevent any internationalisation of its domestic problem (Clarke 2010).

Under Soviet rule, Moscow often mobilised its Uyghur communities against China. For instance, it allowed the publication of the anti-Chinese 'Voice of East Turkestan' calling for the UN to address the Uyghur's issue (Kamalov 2009, 125). In the 1990s, renewed ties between CA Uyghur and their Chinese cousins strengthened the support to Xinjiang's Uyghur. For instance, a CIS-International Uyghur Union was set up in 1992 in Kazakhstan to support Uyghur' self-determination and Human Rights in Xinjiang.

China considers pan-Islamist and pan-Turkic movements as destabilising forces and wants to avoid a sanctuary for independentist Uyghur in CA. Despite this, CA governments do not support Xinjiang's independence – their condescending policy towards their Uyghur communities worried Beijing. A 1999 census put the number of Uyghur in Kazakhstan at 210,300, the largest diaspora in CA (Kamalov 2009, 121), which has an estimated 300,000 Uyghur (Laruelle 2012, 20-21). At the beginning of the 1990s, Kazakhstan saw a mushrooming of Uyghur pro-independence organisations such as the United Revolutionary Front of East Turkistan (URFET), the Uyghur Liberation Organisation (ULO), the International Uyghur Union (IUU) promoting democracy, Human Rights, and self-determination for Uyghur in Xinjiang (Smith 1996, 20). Consequently, the Friendship Declaration between Kazakhstan and China (1995) included the common goal of fighting separatism.

China's trade policy towards the new CA republics required first the settlement of the borders. Beijing's self-restraint in negotiating a bilateral settlement and long-term economic prospects gave it more leverage over CA governments. China also boosted its stance against the 'three evils' (separatism, extremism, and fundamentalism) by initiating the Group of Five (1996), later institutionalised in the Shanghai Cooperation Organisation (SCO, 2001), which includes a Regional Anti-Terrorist Structure (RATS, 2004) (Debata 2007, 206-7). Beijing cultivates bilateral relations with Muslim countries to obtain their public support for its policy in Xinjiang and to deter them from supporting the Uyghur's cause (Brynjar 2013, 247) (Kondapalli 2010, 245-6). It also combined political pressure on CA countries to dissolve anti-Chinese groups with indirect practices to buy political elites. Since

Xinjiang's stability is crucial to CA governments, due to proximity reasons and their Uyghur communities, they continuously balance complacency towards Beijing with the need to prevent discontent among their majoritarian Muslim populations.

Uyghur's Growing Embedment in International Terrorist Networks

The current insurgency in Xinjiang is linked to the Afghan resistance to the Soviet occupation. In the 1980s, anti-Soviet forces in Pakistan already referred to Central Asia and Xinjiang as 'Temporary occupied Muslim Territory' (Scheuer 2002, 21). Some Uyghur were also trained as jihadi soldiers and Moscow's defeat by Islamist guerrilla renewed the Uyghur's hope for independence (Wayne 2008, 23).

When China started restricting Uyghur's cultural freedom and Islamic education, many Uyghur fled to Afghanistan which had no extradition treaty with the PRC. In 2002, China identified 400 Uyghur fighting in Afghanistan (Fuller 2004, 342) and later asserted that 1,000 Uyghur had been trained there and posed a threat to China (Wayne 2008, 10). For instance, the Baren revolt (1990) was organised through a network of mosques, foreign fighters reportedly came from Afghanistan (Wayne 2008, 7), and China traced insurgents' weapons to Mujahidin in Afghanistan. In Kazakhstan and Kyrgyzstan Pakistani consulates gave visas for Uyghur to study in fundamentalist madrassas, and some fought in Pakistan's Kashmir (R. Gunaratna 2002, 51). Indian intelligence also reported that Pakistan trained Uyghur, and Pakistani pan-Islamic jihad groups instructed Uyghur in Baluchistan: fundamentalist groups such as Jamaat-e-Islami, Jamaat-e-Tablighi, and Lashkar-e-Toiba helped Uyghur insurgents (R. Gunaratna 2002, 145).

With connections to Bin Laden, Hasan Mahsum established ETIP in 1990 (Schmidt 2013, 269). It became operational in 1997 when he brought its headquarters to the Taliban's stronghold in Afghanistan (R. a. Gunaratna 2015, 244). It trained Uyghur recruited at mosques to launch an unsuccessful jihad to create an East Turkistan Republic in Xinjiang (Dillon 2004, 63). The ISAF's bombing killed Mahsum (2003) and weakened the organisation that moved to Waziristan under Abdul Haq where he strengthened ties with Al Qaeda and the Islamic Movement of Uzbekistan (IMU). However, Uyghur fighters were not numerous (Brynjar 2013, 247) and disagreement between nationalists and conservative Islamists within the ETIP undermined the organisation. Finally, its allegiance to the leader of the Taliban Mullah Omar limited its action: the Taliban courted Beijing to counterbalance the US and forbade the ETIP from targeting China (Brynjar 2013, 248).

During the Soviet occupation of Afghanistan, Beijing cooperated with Washington. It subsidised mules and $200–400 million worth of weapons to the Mujahidin (Crile 2003, 268–9) and the PLA had facilities in Peshawar and near the Pakistani border with Afghanistan where it employed 300 military advisers. In 1985, the PLA opened military camps in Xinjiang to train the Mujahidin with 'Chinese weapons, explosives, combat tactics', etc. (Shichor 2004). Later, China also had diplomatic ties with the Taliban in Afghanistan, where Chinese telecoms built infrastructure in exchange for cooperation on the Uyghur's diaspora. Consequently, the Taliban handed two Uyghur fighters to China (Palmer 2004, 4).

In the aftermath of 9/11, Jiang Zemin launched another strike hard campaign (2001–2002) domestically while rushing to declare China's support for the US after Washington initiated the Global War on Terror (GWOT). Jiang Zemin offered to tackle terrorism in Xinjiang. Subsequently, Washington opened an FBI office in Beijing, helped China build signals intelligence (SIGINT) in Xinjiang, and Beijing obtained more room to manoeuvre with covert operations against Uyghur militants abroad (Wayne 2008, 87). Since China's priority was to keep Xinjiang a domestic issue, its contribution to GWOT remained limited. Furthermore, Beijing perceived the presence of American military bases in CA in the framework of the GWOT as a destabilising development in its periphery since they provided the US with a potential platform for hostile actions against China. In fact, Washington has regularly been accused of implementing direct and indirect actions to undermine the Chinese government through supporting Human Rights and democratic development in Xinjiang, and also Tibet. Beijing believes that the colour revolutions in the former USSR were fomented by the US, and aimed for regime change in China too (Nathan 2012, 92).

Beijing used the threat of terrorism to justify repressive policies at home because it considered everybody 'fighting for an independent state in the north-western province of Xinjiang' to be a terrorist (Chung 2002). This is the reason why, although the US included the East Turkestan Islamic Party (ETIP) in the Department of State's Terrorist Exclusion List (State 2004), it refused to include the WUC, the East Turkestan Liberation Organization, and the East Turkestan Information Centre. Actually, Washington supports the WUC through the National Endowment for Democracy (NED) funded by the Congress. Traditionally, the NED provides funding to the Uyghur American Association that promotes religious freedom and Human Rights in Xinjiang (Mackerras 2011, 26-7). Despite the Chinese pressure, Washington also refused to repatriate 22 Uyghurs in Guantanamo, two of whom were supposedly members of the ETIP (Jankoviak 2004, 318).

Economic Development and Repressive Policy towards Turkic-Speaking Muslims as Radicalising Factors

Although China's constitution states that ethnic groups are equal, China maintains quite a paternalistic attitude towards its minorities. The Constitution also guarantees their freedom of religion; however, religions must accommodate (Saunders 2017) socialism because Beijing fears their interference and requires religious organisations to register with the Religious Affairs Bureau. Since religion equals ignorance, Uyghur are also considered to be primitive, thieves and increasingly as terrorists (Kantian 2007, 64, 73), while those Uyghur who receive Chinese education are criticised by other Uyghur for sacrificing their culture (Kantian 2007, 17) in exchange for better economic opportunities.

As in Tibet, China's policy towards Xinjiang is increasingly based on both repression and 'forced' economic development. It is not by accident that in 2016 China nominated Chen Quanguo, former governor of Tibet, as the Party Secretary of Xinjiang. Furthermore, that same year the ongoing major military reform reduced the military regions from seven to five theatres (Saunders 2017): the incorporation of the Chengdu and Lanzhou MR in a broader Western Area Command including Tibet and Xinjiang highlights the CPC's increasingly unified vision of security in these two autonomous regions and their connections to neighbouring areas.

Beijing equates prosperity with long-term stability and identifies Chinese nationalism with Han nationalism on which the Chinese dream is based (Meyer 2016). Oasis towns near the southern border of the Taklimakan desert are the bastions of Uyghur culture, as well as China's poorest areas. Although separatist and Islamist movements have been flourishing in those areas (Dillon 2004, 5–6), deprivation is not the only root of terrorism; rich Muslims also embrace terrorism and there is evidence that Hui are slowly radicalising (Acharya Arabinda 2010). Over the last decade, Xinjiang has been developing fast, but such economic development has disproportionally benefited the Han settlers whilst subjecting the Uyghur on their own land (Bovingdon 2010). As a result, Uyghur's socio-economic marginalisation/discrimination undermines societal stability and China's policies towards the Uyghur may facilitate the interpretation of 'Islam as an ideology of national liberation' (Laruelle 2012, 180) and increase inter-ethnic conflict.

In fact, the riots in 2009 were the deadliest ethnic clashes in decades (around 200 casualties) and demonstrated the failure of China's approach to Xinjiang. In 2010, when the first Xinjiang Work Forum was held, Xinjiang's security budget doubled (Cui 2010), and Wang Lequan was replaced by a member of the Politburo, Zhang Chunxian (Simpson 2010), as Xinjiang's Party Secretary. Whilst Muslim countries kept a low profile (Mackerras 2011, 37) terrorist organisations called for reprisal. For instance, Al Qaeda in the Maghreb threatened Chinese expatriates and investment; Al Qaeda's top leader Abu Yahya al-Libi, called for the Uyghur to fight China, and the TIP's leader, Abdul Haq al-Turkistani, incited Muslims to target Chinese interests abroad (Mackerras 2011, 38; Stratfor 2009).

Thanks to connections with Al Qaeda, the ETIP reappeared in the mid-2000s as TIP, and currently operates in Syria with around 200 fighters, and during the Arab Spring (2010-12) encouraged Uyghur to fight for Sunni Muslims. Turkey facilitated Uyghur's travelling to fight in Syria through an association for cultural education founded in Turkey in 2016. China discovered that people working in the Turkish Embassy in China were illegally distributing passports to Uyghur to help them reach Syria (BBC 2015). In addition to CA, South East Asia (SEA) also became a route for reaching Turkey and Syria: in 2016, Thailand repatriated 109 Uyghur out of 400 who were smuggled into camps. Therefore, there is growing concern about terrorism in SEA (Pantucci 2017). Furthermore, since those Uyghur illegally leaving Xinjiang have to rely on locals for protection, they often become easy targets for criminal groups.

Within the PRC, the car bombing in Tiananmen Square (2013) and the knife attack at Kunming rail station (2014) signalled the dangerous spreading of the Uyghur issue outside Xinjiang. Hence, in 2014 XUAR's security budget doubled again and the second Central Work Forum on Xinjiang recognised that 'Xinjiang's most sustained problem is the problem of ethnic unity' (Leibold 2014, 4). Nevertheless, this indirect admission that economic development is all that is needed is inadequate, and more efforts should focus on reducing ethnic differences through better ethnic integration (e.g. improving labour opportunities, bilingual education, and economic conditions especially in the south) remains a rebranding of hanification.

China's counterterrorist actions remain limited by its view of separatism as criminal activity. This blurs the distinction between criminal and political offences (Dillon 2004, 112) and responds to China's attempt to criminalise terrorism per se, notwithstanding the political motives of the perpetrators (Clarke 2010) For instance, in 2002 for the first time an official document addressed the terrorist threat in Xinjiang claiming that ETIP had a dozen bases in the region (Wayne 2008, 44), and in 2003 a pilot-anti-terror squad was set up in Beijing (Lam 2003) and later replicated it in 36 cities, even if they were anti-riot squads (Wayne 2008, 78). Although China has become more prominent on UN global counter-terrorism, passed its first anti-terror act (2015), and now holds regular counterterrorism exercises, it still lacks counter-terrorism experience and capability. Beijing's increasing disillusion with the SCO in dealing with terrorism, explains the creation of the 'Quadrilateral Cooperation and Coordination Mechanism' (RadioFreeEurope/RadioLiberty 2016) between China, Pakistan, Tajikistan, and Afghanistan where China runs military camps to help train Afghan police (Snow 2017). In fact, the deteriorating security situation in neighbouring Afghanistan is a growing source of worry for Beijing. For instance, in 2017 the State Commissioner for counterterrorism and security, Cheng Guoping, questioned whether Afghanistan would become another haven for terrorists (Reuters 2017).

Overall, the Uyghur issue is gaining increased importance within Al Qaeda and domestic and international dimensions are increasingly entangled. For instance, in 2016 Al Qaeda Ayman al-Zawahiri acknowledged Hasan Mahsum as a jihadi leader and praised the jihad against the Han 'atheist colonisers' (Joschelyn 2016). In 2017, a video of Isis showed some Uyghur fighting in Iraq and threatened China to cause 'rivers of blood' (Hincks 2017). This highlights China's increasing need to protect its citizens and economic interests abroad due to the fact that terrorist attacks on Chinese expatriates are increasing. For example, in 2015 a terrorist attack in Mali killed Chinese executives of China Railway Construction Corporation, ISIS executed a Chinese citizen, in 2016 the Chinese embassy in Bishkek was targeted by a Uyghur network operating in CA (Dzyunbenko 2016), and in 2017 ISIS killed two Chinese citizens in Pakistan (Rasmussen 2017). This increase in security threats to Chinese businesses and citizens in CA underlines the security challenge of China's Belt and Road Initiative, which is a pillar of China's economic expansion through internationalisation.

Conclusion

China acknowledges separatism as the main threat to Xinjiang's stability and blames hostile foreign forces, mainly the US, for backing Human Rights, minority rights, the spreading of democratic values, and the insurgency in Xinjiang (e.g. through the Uyghur World Congress). However, rioters are traditionally indigenous, though increasingly embedded in global jihad networks. Beijing fears an independent Xinjiang because it would likely threaten the territorial integrity of the PRC by triggering other autonomous regions, such as Tibet, to push for independence. Therefore, China implements a pervasive surveillance system, the increasing militarisation of the region, repressive policies towards Uyghur, and 'forced Hanicisation' (Laruelle 2012, 179) of Xinjiang, which made the ratio of Turkic-speaking Muslims drop from around 90% at the end of the 1940s (Forbes 1986, 6), to roughly half of the population in the 2010s (Han and Paik 2017, 39).

China uses a carrot and stick approach including intense security crackdowns and forced economic development. On the one hand, Strike Hard campaigns address political unrest, criminal activities and religious movements under the same banner. In 2017, the provincial government expanded a 2015 regulation forbidding Muslim names as 'overly religious' (Feng 2017). Passports have been seized (Hornby 2016), Muslim dress codes forbidden, and long beards banned (Reuters 2017). In 2017, the Hotan/Hetian prefecture issued a directive outlawing the teaching of Uyghur language at school, including in secondary school (Sulaiman 2017), and the XUAR Working Guidelines on the Accurate Registration and Verification of Population introduced biometric collection scheme for Xinjiang's residents, from 'DNA samples, fingerprints, iris scans and blood types' (Haas 2017).

On the other hand, despite Xinjiang's economy improving, economic opportunities benefit Han residents disproportionally, and favourable policies to attract Han enhance competition for land and water. Xinjiang per capita income remains behind the national average and the growing wealth gap between Han settlers concentrated in towns and Uyghur concentrated in underdeveloped rural areas, exacerbate social tensions. The WUC argues that development policies such as the opening of the Northwest to trade with CA, the development of the Western regions, the adoption of Fora in Xinjiang, and more recently the Belt and Road Initiative all result in the marginalisation of the Uyghurs (WUC 2016, 2).

China's repression of Uyghur culture and religion breeds resentment. The prohibition of formal religious education under the age of 18 and of informal religious education even if given privately by parents (Wayne 2008, 105), did not eradicate fundamentalism. Rather, these measures increased Uyghur's rancour. Cultural and religious constraint triggers violent protests (Purbrick 2017, 241), and Uyghur reach the Middle East or Turkey to study and/or fight for Islam. Though China's strategic partnership with Egypt, Saudi Arabia, Turkey, and Iran does not stop trade with Muslim countries, it does complicate China's relations with these countries. Therefore, by fearing the support of Muslim countries for Uyghur separatists, Beijing plays down 'proliferation concerns and supplies arms and problematic technology to them at generous prices' (Horner 2002, 44).

While China pushes for economic development in Xinjiang, tight media control and cyber-surveillance constrain the region's economic growth: access to the Internet is pervasive and control exceptionally extensive. Although security measures and censorship made it difficult to have reports on Xinjiang unrest, officers admit there are incidents (Pantucci 2017). This explains why Xi Jinping called again for setting up a 'Great Wall of Steel' in

Xinjiang (Reuters 2017). The militarisation of Xinjiang is increased by the use of new technology such as the use of drones. In 2013, the regional government ordered China Aerospace Science and Technology Corporation drones for targeting terrorists. It requested drone pilots after 100 people were killed in violence that erupted in Xinjiang in 2014 when Muslims reacted against the security measures during the Ramadan (Tatlow 2014).

Uyghurs perceive these measures as undermining their identity. Furthermore, counter-terrorist efforts include the use of drones and tracking devices on vehicles based on China's Beidou navigation satellite system (Phillips 2017). Hence, China's security policy towards Xinjiang will push regional development further as well as push further repressive policies, and there is no real alternative for Uyghurs to the dilemma of either resisting or sinicising.

References

Arabinda, A., Gunaratna, R. & Wang, P. 2010. *Ethnic Identity and National Conflict in China*. New York: Palgrave Macmillan.

Bovingdon, G. 2010. *The Uyghur: Strangers in their Own Land*. New York: Columbia University Press.

Brynjar, L. 2013. *Architect of Global Jihad. The Life of Al-Qaida Strategist Abu Mus'ab al-Suri*. New York: Columbia University Press.

Caccfreedomsherald.org, n.d. "China Communist Party Document #7." *caccfreedomsherald.org*, http://caccfreedomsherald.org/conf/doc7.html.

Charles, H. 2002. 'The Other Orientalism. China's Islamist Problem." *National Interest* 67: 37–45.

Chen, Y. 2014. *The Uyghur Lobby: Global Networks, Coalitions, and Strategies of the World Uyghur Congress*. London: Routledge.

Chung, C. 2002. "China's War on Terrorism: September 11 and Uighur Separatism." *Foreign Affairs* 81(4): 8–12.

Clarke, M. 2010. "China, Xinjiang and the Internationalisation of the Uyghur Issue." *Global Change, Peace & Security* 22(2): 213–29.

Clarke, M. 2008. "China's Integration of Xinjiang with Central Asia: Securing a 'Silk Road' to Great Power Status?" *China & Eurasia Forum Quarterly* 6(2): 89–111.

Clarke, M. 2010. "Widening the Net: China's Anti-Terror Laws and Human Rights in the Xinjiang Uyghur Autonomous Region." *The International Journal of Human Rights* 14(4): 542–58.

Congressional Research Service, Library of Congress. 2006. "US-China Counterterrorism Cooperation: Issues for US Policy, (Kan, S. A.)." CNR Report for Congress RL33001. June 27, 2006.

Crile, G. 2003. *Charlie Wilson's War: The Extraordinary Story of the Largest Covert Operation in History*. New York: Atlantic Monthly Press.

Cui, J. 2010. "Xinjiang Security Funding Increased by 90 Percent." *China Daily*. January 13, 2010.

Debata, M. R. 2007. *China's Minorities: Ethnic-religious Separatism in Xinjiang*. New Delhi: Pentagon Press.

Dillon, M. 2004. *Xinjiang - China's Muslim Far Northwest*. London: Routledge.

Dzyunbenko, O. 2016. "Kirghizstan Says Uighur Militant Groups behind Attack on China's Embassy." *Reuters*. September 7.

Ekholm, E. 2002. "Braiding of China Muslim Group as Terrorist is Disputed." *International Herald Tribune*. September 14–15.

Feng, E. 2017. "China Bans Name 'Mohamed' for Xinjiang Newborns." *Financial Times*. April 25, 2017.

Forbes, A. 1986. *Warlords and Muslims in Chinese Central Asia. A Political History of Republican Xinjiang 1911-1949*. Cambridge University Press, Cambridge MA.

Freund Larus, E. 2012. *Politics and Society in Contemporary China*. Boulder: Lynne Rienner Publishers.

Friedrich, J. 2017. "Sino-Muslim Relations: The Han, The Hui and The Uighurs." *Journal of Muslim Minority Affairs* 37(1): 55–79.

Fuller, G. E. and Lipman, J. N. 2004. "Islam in Xinjiang." In *Xinjiang: China's Muslim Borderland*, edited by F. S. Star, 320–52. New York: M.E. Sharpe.

Gunaratna, R. 2002. *Inside Al Qaeda: Global Network of Terror*. New York: Columbia University Press.

Gunaratna, R. and Oreg, A. 2015, *The Global Jihad Movement*. New York: Rodman & Littlefield.

Haas, B. 2017. "Chinese Authorities Collecting DNA from all Residents of Xinjiang." *The Guardian*. December 12.

Han, E. and Paik, C. 2017. "Ethnic Integration and Development in China." *World Development* 93: 31–42.

Hincks, J. 2017. "Uighur Militants Reportedly Threaten China in Isis Video." *The Times*. March 1.

Hornby, L. 2016. "China Orders Xinjiang Residents to Hand in Passports." *Financial Times*. November 24, 2016.

Horner, C. 2002. "The Other Orientalism: China's Islamist Problem." *The National Interest*. 67: 37–45.

Joniak-Lüthi, A. 2013. "Han Migration to Xinjiang Uyghur Autonomous Region: Between State Schemes and Migrants." *Zeitschrift für Ethnologie* 138(2): 155–74.

Joscelyn, T. 2016. "Zawahiri Praises Uighur Jihadists in Ninth Episode of 'Islamic Spring' Series." *longwarjournal.org*, July 7. http://longwarjournal.org/archives/2016/07/zawahiri-praises-uighur-jihadists-in-ninth-episode-of-islamic-spring-series.php.

Kadeer, R. with Cavelius, A. 2009. *Dragon Fighter: One Woman's Epic Struggle for Peace with China*. Carlsbad: Kales Press.

Kamalov, A. 2009. "Uyghur in the Central Asian Republics. Past and Present." In *China, Xinjiang and Central Asia. History, Transition and Crossborder Interaction into the 21st Century*, edited by C. Mackerras and M. Clarke, 115-50. New York: Routledge.

Kantian, B. 2007, *Under The Heel of The Dragon. Islam, Racism, Crime, and the Uighur in China*. Athens: Ohio University Press.

Kondapalli, S. and Mifune, E. 2010. *China and its Neighbours*. New Delhi: Pentagon Press.

Lai, H., H., 2002. "China's Western Development Program. Its Rationale, Impulsion and Prospects." *Modern China* 28(4): 432–66.

Lam, W. 2003. "Beijing Sets up Anti-Terror Squads." *CNN.com*. January 15, 2003. Accessed January 3, 2018. http://edition.cnn.com/2003/WORLD/asiapcf/east/01/14/China.terror/.

Laruelle, M. and Peyrouse, S. 2012. *The Chinese Question in Central Asia*. New York: Columbia University Press.

Leibold, J. 2014. "Xinjiang Work Forum Marks New Policy of Ethnic Mingling." *ChinaBrief* 14(12): 3–6.

Mackerras, C. 2011. 'The Disturbances in The Tibetan Areas and Urumqi 2008-2009: Implications for China's International Relations." In *China's Policies on its Borderlands and The International Implications*, edited by Y. Hao and B. K. Chou, 19–45. Singapore: World Scientific Press.

Mackerras, C. 2001. "Xinjiang at the Turn of the Century: The Causes of Separatism." *Central Asian Survey* 20 (3): 289–303.

McMillan, A., 2009. "Xinjiang and Central Asia. Interdependency-not Integration." In *China, Xinjiang and Central Asia. History, Transition and Crossborder Interaction into the 21st Century*, edited by C. Mackerras and M. Clarke, 94–114. New York: Routledge.

McMillen, D. H.1984."Xinjiang and Wang Enmao: New Directions in Power, Policy and Integration." *The China Quarterly* 99: 569–93.

Meyer, P., 2016. "Could Han Chauvinism Turn the 'Chinese Dream' into a 'Chinese Nightmare'?" *The Diplomat*. June 14.

Nathan, A. J. and Scobell, A. 2012. *China's Search for Security*. New York: Columbia University Press.

Oresman, M. and Steingart, D. 2003. "Radical Islamisation in Xinjiang – Lessons from Chechnya?" *The Central-Caucasus Analyst*. July 30.

Palmer, Amb. M. 2004. *Breaking the Real Axis of Evil: How to Oust the World's Remaining Dictators by 2025*. Lanham: Rodman and Littlefield.

Purbrick, M. 2017. '"Maintaining A Unitary State: Counter-terrorism, Separatism and Extremism in Xinjiang." *Asian Affairs* 18(2): 236–56.

Phillips, T. 2017. "China Orders GPS Tracking of Every Car in Troubled Region." *The Guardian*. February 21.

RadioFreeEurope/RadioLiberty. 2016. "China Forms Antiterror Alliance with Pakistan, Tajikistan, Afghanistan." *RadioFreeEurope/RadioLiberty*. August 5.

Rasmussen, S. E. and Baloch, K. 2017. "Isis Claims to Kill Chinese Couple Studying and Teaching in Pakistan." *The Guardian*. June 8.

Reuters. 2017. "China Sets Rules on Beard, Veils to Combat Extremism in Xinjiang." *Reuters*. March 30.

Reuters. 2017. "China's Xi Calls for 'Great Wall of Iron' to Safeguard Restive Xinjiang." *Reuters*. March 10.

Rudelson, J. and Jankoviak, W. 2004. "Acculturation and Resistance: Xinjiang Identities in Flux." In *Xinjiang: China's Muslim Borderland*, edited by F. S. Starr, 299–319. New York: M.E. Sharpe.

Saunders Phillip C. and Joel Wuthnow (2017) *Chinese Military Reform in the Age of Xi Jinping: Drivers, Challenges and Implications*. Washington D.C.: Center for the Study of Chinese Military Affairs (National Defense University).

Schmidt, A., ed. 2013. *The Routledge Handbook of Terrorism Research*. London: Routledge.

Scheuer, M. 2002. *Through Our Enemies' Eyes: Osama Bin Laden, Radical Islam, and the Future of America*, Brassey's, Washington D.C.

Shichor, Y. 2004. "The Great Wall of Steel: Military and Strategy in Xinjiang." In *Xinjiang: China's Muslim Borderland*, edited by F. S. Starr, 120–60. New York: M.E. Sharpe.

Simpson, K. 2010. "King of Xinjiang Wang Lequan Replaced by Man with A Spirit of Creative Thought." *Shanghaiist.com*. April 26. http://shanghaiist.com/2010/04/26/xinjiang-wang-lequan-replaced.php.

Smith, D. L. 1996. "Central Asia: a New Great Game?" *Strategic Studies Institute*. June 17.

Snow, S. 2017. "Chinese Troops Appear to Be Operating in Afghanistan, and The Pentagon Is OK with It." *MilitaryTimes.com*. March 5, 2017.

Sulaiman, E. 2017. "China Bans Uyghur Language in Schools in Key Xinjiang Prefecture." *Radio Free Asia*. July 28. http://www.rfa.org/english/news/uyghur/language-07282017143037.html.

Tatlow, D. K. 2014. "China Said to Deploy Drones after Unrest in Xinjiang." *New York Times*. August 19.

Tiezzi, S. 2015. "Deadly Terrorist Attack in Somalia Hits Chinese Embassy." *The Diplomat*. July 28.

Toops, S. 2016. "Spatial Results of the 2010 Census in Xinjiang." *Uighur Human Rights Project*. March 7. http://uhrp.org/featured-articles/spatial-results-2010-census-xinjiang.

US Department of State. 2004. *Pattern of Global Terrorism 2003*. US Department of State, Washington D.C., April. https://www.state.gov/j/ct/rls/crt/2003/31611.htm.

Wayne, M. I. 2008. *China's War on Terrorism. Counter- insurgency, Politics, and Internal Security*, London: Routledge.

Xinhua. 2003. "Role of Xinjiang Production, Construction Corps Important: White Paper on Xinjiang." *Xinhua*. May 26. http://www.cctv.com/lm/1040/31/5.html.

Xu, Y. 1999. *Xinjiang fandui minzu fenlienzhuyi douzheng shihua* [The Story of the Struggle Against Ethnic Separatism in Xinjiang]. Urumqi: Xinjiang People's Press.

Yu, Z. and Zhang, Y. 1989. *Da Xibei duiwai knifing de xin silu* [Thinking of Opening Up the Great Northwest to the World]. Yinchuan.

Zhuang, P. 2016. "Chinese Court Cuts Jail Terms for 11 Xinjiang Prisoners Convicted of Terror, Separatist Offences." *SCMP*. February 3. http://www.scmp.com/news/china/policies-politics/article/1908838/chinese-court-cuts-jail-terms-11-xinjiang-prisoners.

BBC. 2015. "China Breaks Turkish-Uighur Passport Plot." *BBC*. January 14.

Stratfor. 2009. "China: An Al Qaeda Call to Arms." *Stratfor*. October 7.

Interviews

Castest, Rémi, Paris, 8 June 2017

Pantucci, Raffaello, Paris, 8 June 2017

3

Mechanisms behind Diffusion of Democracy in the Pearl River Delta Region

GUSTAV SUNDQVIST

Since the early 2000s, scholars of democratisation have been increasingly interested in how democracy spreads from one political unit to the next in a process often called diffusion of democracy (Brinks and Coppedge 2006, 464; Gleditsch and Ward 2006, 917; Wejnert 2005, 55). Many have noted that the PRC government threatens democracy in Greater China by weakening Hong Kong's democratic institutions (Pepper 2008, 300; Sing 2004, 221; Wu 2015, 290) and threatening to annex Taiwan (Jacques 2009, 304; Schubert 2012, 66). Less attention has been paid to how Hong Kong and Taiwan contribute to democratic development in the mainland. Despite their limited resources, promoters of democracy in Hong Kong and Taiwan may still have a democratising impact on some sections of Mainland China's society. This chapter addresses this issue by studying the relationship between labour non-governmental organisations (LNGOs) in the Pearl River Delta (PRD) region of Southern China. The research question is 'How do LNGOs in Hong Kong contribute to democratic diffusion in the PRD?'

Democracy, Civil Society, and Diffusion

More maximalist definitions of democracy include not only free elections but also the rule of law (Weale 2007, 203), the protection of political and civil freedoms (Dahl 1998, 86), and the presence of intermediaries through whom citizens can influence politics between elections (Schmitter and Karl 1991, 78). These components of democracy are often channelled through the social sphere not belonging to the state or the market, termed civil society (Diamond 1999, 222). The main object of this study, labour-oriented civil society, is viewed here as a potentially democratising force. The study is restricted to LNGOs, because labour groups have historically played a prominent role in democratisation, especially in communist states.[1] Labour movements in authoritarian societies tend to focus on democracy-related issues such as institutions for class representation, freedom of association, and fair application of labour legislation (O'Donnell and Schmitter 1986, 53). Labour groups can have a strong influence on national politics since they can often mobilise protesters and disrupt the economy through strikes (Valenzuela 1989, 447). Because of their officially pro-worker ideology, the legitimacy of communist regimes is particularly sensitive to criticism from organised labour (Beetham 1991, 183; Shambaugh 2009, 50). Labour movements thus played a decisive role in the transition from communist dictatorships in Eastern Europe, particularly in Poland, where the trade union Solidarity was especially important (Grugel 2002, 105). LNGOs were also prominent actors in Asian democracy movements, such as the anti-Guomindang movement in Taiwan during the 1980s (Chan and Chiu 2015, 168). Based on historical experiences, there is reason to believe that organised labour may play a major role in any potential liberalisation of politics in China.

Although civil society and labour movements have historically been prominent actors in transitions from authoritarianism, it must be noted that not all civil society groups have a democratising impact. Although the number of non-governmental organisations (NGOs) in the PRC has increased dramatically, from 5,000 in 1990 to 500,000 in 2014 (Teets 2014, 11), most of these groups have a relatively non-political agenda and they generally do not aim to challenge the government (Foster 2001, 102; He and Huang 2015, 12; Hsu and Hasmath 2014, 533). Diamond (1999, 228) provides a proper analytical tool, based on five features, for measuring the democratising potential of civil society groups.[2] In this study, I developed an analytical tool inspired by Diamond's, adjusted to more efficiently assess the democratising capacity of the small and pressured civil society groups in the PRC. The features

---

1   Note that LNGOs should be distinguished from member-based trade unions. In state-corporatist systems such as the PRC or pre-democracy Taiwan, representation of important social groups is monopolised by the state. In Mainland China, there is thus no legal trade union except the party-controlled All-China Federation of Trade Unions (ACFTU). Any new workplace trade unions must be permitted by the higher levels of ACFTU. LNGOs often engage in activities traditionally performed by trade unions such as providing legal consultation. However, unlike ACFTU, most LNGOs' activities take place outside of the workplace and these groups are usually not allowed to visit factories. For a discussion on the difference between the official trade union and LNGOs see Chan and Chiu 2015, 157–165.

2   Diamond uses five features to assess the democratising capacity of civil societies: (1) self-government, (2) goals and methods, (3) organisational institutionalisation, (4) pluralism, and (5) density.

employed are *self-government*, *goals*, *methods*, *institutionalisation*, and *density*. The first feature addresses the extent to which civil society groups practice internal democracy; the second and third, the goals and methods of civil society groups in relation to democracy; the fourth, whether the internal management of civil society groups is efficient and institutionalised; and the fifth, whether civil society groups are able to survive and grow.

Diffusion can be defined as 'the spread of a practice within a social system, where the spread denotes flow or movement from a source to an adopter typically via communication, role modelling, and/or coercion' (Wejnert 2014, 35). Diffusion generally involves at least two actors, a source and a potential adopter, a communication channel linking them together, and an innovation (Rogers 1995, 18). In the case of China studied here, the innovation is democracy.

Although previous studies quite convincingly show that some kind of democratic diffusion effect exists, most of this work is based on large-N analyses of cross-state data (Brinks and Coppedge 2006, 464; Doorenspleet 2004, 322; Gleditsch and Ward 2006, 921; Kopstein and Reilly 2000, 17; Starr and Lindborg 2003, 495). Some theories on the diffusion mechanisms have been elaborated, but the understanding of how democratic diffusion actually works is still relatively underdeveloped (Yilmaz 2009, 95). According to existing theories, democracy can be diffused through two different mechanisms: imposition or emulation (Teorell 2010, 86). Imposition is described as an attempt to influence others towards democracy through either coercive or cooperative means (Levitsky and Way 2005, 21). Powerful and high-status actors are generally more able to influence weak and low-status actors than vice-versa (Fordham and Asal 2007, 32). Emulation occurs when one actor, due to changing external conditions or new information, decides to adopt a more democratic stance (Brinks and Coppedge 2006, 466; Elkins and Simmons, 2005, 39). In the latter case, an adopter of democracy such as a democratic polity or a democracy-promoting organisation provides information (intentionally or not) on conditions associated with moving towards democracy (Elkins and Simmons 2005, 42). Democracies on the borders and movements towards democracy elsewhere can remind people in authoritarian societies that democracy is achievable (Ambrosio 2007, 235; Huntington 1991, 100).

A problem of previous theories on the mechanisms of democratic diffusion is reliance on overly broad concepts. More detailed theories are thus needed to better understand how democracy is diffused at the grassroots level in different social and geographical contexts. This chapter aims to contribute to filling this gap in the research.

Method and Material

From a democratic diffusion perspective, the PRD can be seen as a critical case. The region includes two important political units: the semi-democratic former British colony of Hong Kong and the southern parts of the much more authoritarian Guangdong province, both under the supreme authority of the central PRC government and the Chinese Communist Party (CCP). Because of more freedom of speech and assembly in Hong Kong, civil society in sensitive fields such as labour and democracy promotion has much more political space there than in Guangdong (Collins and Cottey 2012, 59; Lo 2013, 943). In this study Hong Kong LNGOs (H-LNGOs) are treated as the main sources of diffusing democracy and Guangdong LNGOs (G-LNGOs) as the main potential adopters. Although some studies have discussed how H-LNGOs influence G-LNGOs (Chan 2013, 9; He and Huang 2015, 15; Xu 2013, 246) the democratising aspect of this relationship has so far received little attention.

The primary material in this study is 18 interviews with 20 respondents and some fieldwork notes. All interviews were conducted during three fieldwork trips in the PRD in 2015, 2016, and 2017. All but one of the interviews with respondents from H-LNGOs was conducted in English and all interviews with G-LNGO respondents were conducted in Mandarin. I transcribed the English material myself and had the Chinese material transcribed by a trusted Chinese research assistant. Responses have been further edited for clarity, but the original transcripts are available by request. The interviews were semi-structured, and respondents were asked relatively broad questions about their organisations' activities and cooperation networks. Eight H-LNGOs and five G-LNGOs were covered. According to respondents from four of the Hong Kong groups, 12 H-LNGOs focused on mainland issues in 2017. The material thus involves a large sample of the H-LNGOs and may be generalisable to the whole community of these groups. Due to the state's suppression of mainland labour groups, there is no certain knowledge of the exact number of G-LNGOs, but estimates vary between 30 and 50 (Franceschini 2014, 480; Fu 2017, 448; Xu 2013, 246). The sample of these groups is thus hardly generalisable. Still, the information provided by G-LNGOs can be compared with that from H-LNGOs to deepen our understanding of how strategies to influence actors in the mainland are received. Following Xu (2013, 246), the organisations are identified by codes to protect their confidentiality (H1, H2, H3, G1, G2, G3, etc.). Information on the coding of the LNGOs are provided on my webpage under the 'research' tab.[3] A confidential version of the transcribed interviews can be provided on demand to readers qualified not to misuse the information.

---

[3] http://www.gustavsundqvist.com

Analysis

In this section, I argue that H-LNGOs mainly use four different strategies: (1) consulting, (2) financing, (3) providing free space, and (4) providing international networks to diffuse democracy in the PRD. The four categories were developed inductively during the analysis of the material. In the final discussion, I elaborate on the extent to which these strategies can also be perceived as mechanisms through which democracy can be spread. The appendix summarises how respondents from H-LNGOs described their groups' most salient strategies and how respondents from G-LNGOs described their groups' responses to these strategies.

Consultation

Consultation seems to be an important strategy of H-LNGOs to promote democratic diffusion in the PRD. Respondents from seven of the H-LNGOs told me that their groups participated in training sessions and workshops in Guangdong, and all the Hong Kong groups provided online, telephone, or face-to-face consultation to their mainland partners. Regarding the content of this consultancy, respondents from all but one of the H-LNGOs stated that they aimed to influence their cooperation partners to involve themselves in methods and activities more related to democracy such as elections, collective action and advocacy. One respondent from H2 told me the organisation used workshops to encourage G-LNGOs to become involved in trade union activities, which is sensitive in Mainland China, where all unions are supposed to be controlled by the state:

> one content was to let them decide a goal and see what they could do between the time span of one year in order to improve working conditions. They decided that their goal was to elect a trade union. When I returned in May, perhaps May 20, in the middle of May 2014, they started to take action, and declared they would elect a trade union.

Representatives from seven of the H-LNGOs also said that they consulted with their Guangdong partners to encourage their *institutionalisation*. As one respondent from H8 said, one aim was to raise the level of organisation among often scattered activists:

> we do believe in organisations, we do believe in organising, so we stress that organising is possibly the most important aspect for the sustainability of a labour movement, so we try to bring up this kind of messages, but, you know, whether others buy

this kind of messages or not, it is up to them.

Except respondents from G3, the Guangdong activists generally played down the impact H-LNGOs had on the *methods* and *institutionalisation* of Guangdong groups. However, most Guangdong respondents were in frequent contact with H-LNGOs and some noted that their Hong Kong partners provided some good advice in these fields. Respondents from five of the H-LNGOs also told me that they used consultation to influence the goals of Guangdong partners in a more democratic direction. As one representative of H5 reported, their organisation promoted concepts related to democracy such as freedom of speech and freedom of association:

> of course we would like to see democratic development in China, yes. So, at the moment of course we would not say that we are going to pull down the CCP openly, it would be political suicide, yes. And, and, also we understand it is kind of hard to call for just democracy with workers because they don't necessarily understand, firstly and secondly they won't be able to relate their own lives to that, their own well-being with that, so we actually frame it in another way... We actually started to talk about that from the three basic labour rights, the right to strike, the right to organise and the right to collective bargaining, so it is more connected to workers' consciousness, at the same time promoting some values of free society, like for example freedom of association, freedom of speech and the important value of deciding on your own life.

Respondents from three of the five G-LNGOs told me that interaction with actors overseas, especially organisations from Hong Kong and Taiwan, changed the Guangdong activists' views on politics in a democratic direction. However, the Guangdong activists usually emphasised that although they received ideological inspiration from abroad, they still had to develop indigenous strategies to achieve democracy, as demonstrated in the following conversation with one respondent from G2:

> *Interviewer*: 'You still think that communication with people in Taiwan and Hong Kong was meaningful?'
> *Respondent*: 'Yes... it opened our horizons... now, the whole background is clear for us.'
> *Interviewer*: 'Did they also talk about like human rights and democracy?... Do you think this is meaningful?'
> *Respondent*: 'Yes, certainly... the work we do will eventually end there.'

> *Interviewer:* '... so foreign actors influence you a bit but not very much and this influence is mostly in the ideological field?'
> *Respondent:* 'Yes, because usually I still believe that we must rely on ourselves and explore our own road. Only then will we know how to realise democracy here.'

There seems to have been great variety in how much Hong Kong groups have influenced the ideology of particular mainland activists. One respondent from G3 noted that some mainland activists were especially influenced by ideas from Hong Kong:

> *Interviewer:* 'Your colleague told me that you talk about how to practice democracy.'
> *Respondent:* 'Yes, we have studied this topic recently, but we still do not have any strong political ideas... but if you compare, there are some colleagues who go abroad and think that everything there is good... their political consciousness has been enlightened.'

Representatives from four H-LNGOs also said that their groups used consultation to promote democratic *self-government* among G-LNGOs, as demonstrated by this respondent from H2:

> during our trainings we may mention that they should elect their workers' representatives. During the bargaining process, they should elect workers' representatives or workers' representatives should take in all the demands from the workers and see what they need. Then they should present their demands to the management. This is perhaps a performance of democracy.

One respondent from G3 also noted that interactions with H-LNGOs influenced their organisation's internal governance in a democratic direction:

> we think that several Hong Kong groups have a relatively thick cultural atmosphere. They always say that things should be done together, discussed together, and they talk relatively democratically. I think that their atmosphere is a bit better than it is here in the mainland. It is worth studying this, and referring to this... so, now when we do things, when we do things together, then all of us first talk about it, we walk into the final results together. If it is a huge decision, you cannot decide about it by yourself.

Financing

Financing also seems to be a prime strategy of H-LNGOs to diffuse democracy in the PRD. Many respondents said that financing and consultation were especially important in the past, as many G-LNGOs were originally established by Hong Kong activists. According to one respondent, who is also a prominent scholar on Chinese labour groups, at least ten of the 30 to 50 G-LNGOs were established by Hong Kong groups, most of them around the turn of the millennium. Respondents from three of the Hong Kong groups told me their organisations had founded labour groups in Guangdong, and one respondent from G3 stated that her organisation was originally established by H4: 'one of their methods was to establish libraries. They established libraries in industrial areas and used this method to give workers service and to organise work, so at that time our colleagues from H4 went to the mainland to search, for instance, for workers to train, and they also contacted some social worker students and social worker professionals. So, they found perhaps four people, workers and social worker students, and they established G3, just like that.'

All five G-LNGOs seem to have received funding from Hong Kong partners, either recently or further in the past. The Guangdong activists said that they had no other choice but to rely upon funding from Hong Kong or foreign countries to finance projects more related to democracy, since mainland foundations usually only support charity projects. Respondents from two of the H-LNGOs said they conditioned financing to steer their mainland partners towards activities such as advocacy, collective action, and collective bargaining. As one employee from H2 said: 'it sounds strange but the foundation of our organisation is that we believe that collective bargaining is the way. So then if they want to work with migrant kids, they are free but not with our funding.' By providing funding, H-LNGOs seem to aim at influencing the methods of Guangdong partners working towards democracy and increasing the density of G-LNGOs.

Due to tightening political control of foreign funding of NGOs, Guangdong groups involved in sensitive activities face increasing hardship. The Foreign NGO Management Law, which came into effect in 2017, requires the Public Security Bureau to exert stricter control over the flow of financing between Hong Kong and mainland NGOs. As a result, respondents from G2, G3, and G5 told me it was increasingly hard to receive legal founding for sensitive activities. The director of G5 stated that he was prepared to lay off all his employees and continue his activism on his own: 'at least I can use my pencil to carry out my work… and who would employ me anyway? Who would employ a man who would just start a strike?' One Hong Kong activist told me that the director of G1 also planned large staff cuts as a consequence of the deteriorating political climate.

Provision of Free Space

The literature on social movements in authoritarian societies uses 'free space' to refer to spatial or organisational loopholes that allow some administrative freedom (Bedford 2009, 30; Johnston 2005, 111). Having more civil freedoms than Mainland China, Hong Kong can be perceived as a relatively free space in the PRC. It should, however, be noted that civil freedoms in Hong Kong have deteriorated in recent years. According to the Freedom House Index (2017), civil liberties in Hong Kong have slowly decreased every year since 2014. The Hong Kong activists I interviewed admitted that they were worried about the city's political trajectory. Nevertheless, as one activist from H1 said, they usually still perceive the political climate in Hong Kong to be much freer than that in the mainland: 'even though the so-called freedom of expression is deteriorating in Hong Kong, compared to the environment in the mainland, we still have a relatively safe and open space to talk about things like this.'

One strategy used by H-LNGOs to facilitate democratic diffusion in the PRD seems to be sharing Hong Kong's free space with Guangdong partners by inviting mainland activists to participate in workshops on sensitive issues organised in the city. Respondents from seven of the H-LNGOs told me they regularly invited mainland partners to participate in activities held in Hong Kong and five Guangdong respondents from three of the G-LNGOs said they had participated in such events. Permanent residents in Guangdong usually only must meet some minor formalities and pay a small fee to be permitted to go to Hong Kong. Five of the respondents raised the advantages of arranging activities in the city. As the director of H7 told me: they are coming up more [laughs] because we cannot organise meetings in [mainland] China anymore... although some harassment also happens in Hong Kong, it is still good. For them it is easier to come to Hong Kong, but if we organise some meetings outside China [PRC], there would be more difficult, then they have to get a visa.'[4]

As stated by a respondent from G3, workshops in Hong Kong were also appreciated by G-LNGOs: 'we often participate in their trainings and activities. In addition, we often use their groups to contact Hong Kong workers and understand more about Hong Kong workers. We communicate with Hong Kong workers and learn from them. We get some inspiration from them, we

---

4   Note that the respondent, who spoke English during the interview, sometimes uses the term China when she only refers to Mainland China, but sometimes also includes Hong Kong in the concept.

learn and then we use it in the mainland.' The director of H7 told me that their group had even invited mainland workers involved in a legal conflict with a large multinational company to come to Hong Kong and protest in front of the company's office building. I also sometimes experienced Hong Kong as a free space for mainland activists participating in protest activities. During the rally in Hong Kong on 1 May 2017, I met the director of G5, who I had interviewed a year earlier in the Guangdong city of Dongguan.

It should be mentioned that two respondents from Hong Kong and two from Guangdong also mentioned disadvantages to organising activities for mainland partners in Hong Kong. As reported by one employee at H8, mainland activists entering Hong Kong face political risks: 'after leaving the country they are always interrogated by the police, before and afterwards. Instead of bringing them trouble, we prefer to go inside and meet them.'

International Networks

Finally, H-LNGOs seem to use their international networks to promote democratic diffusion in the PRD. Because of the relatively free political space in Hong Kong and the good English language skills of Hong Kong activists, H-LNGOs have many cooperative ties with international actors. This probably explains why H-LNGOs are better funded than G-LNGOs. Respondents from six of the H-LNGOs told me that their groups receive foreign funding, mostly from labour unions, churches, and democracy-promoting agencies in Europe and the USA. The funding H-LNGOs provide for groups in the mainland thus generally has its origin in the West.

Respondents from seven of the H-LNGOs also used their international networks to help their mainland partners put pressure on multinational companies involved in labour conflicts and legal disputes. One respondent from H3 stated that they often used their contacts with Taiwan LNGOs to pressure Taiwanese companies: 'we have connections with the Taiwan groups, and then sometimes if there are any cases or some workers' struggles related to Taiwanese-owned factories, then we contact them, to see if they can give any support to the workers.' This respondent also told me that the Taiwanese groups usually respond by organising protests and by spreading information about these cases through social media. The director of G1 also said it was helpful to contact foreign media to put pressure on companies: 'we advise workers to first find media, of course, not domestic media but foreign media. Because after foreign media enters, some local governments will put pressure on companies.'

Finally, international networks are also used to pressure authorities in

Mainland China to respect civil rights. The most prominent cases have been when Chinese authorities have detained labour activists such as Wu Guijun (detained in May 2013, then released in May 2014), Zeng Feiyang (detained in December 2015, then given a four-year suspended sentence), and Meng Han (detained in December 2015, then sentenced to 21 months in prison). Respondents from two of the H-LNGOs told me they were actively involved in these campaigns, and seven of the eight Hong Kong groups also signed online petitions protesting these cases. One respondent from H8 was particularly involved in the campaigns to free Zeng Feiyang and Meng Han: 'we have written to international unions as well as NGOs, international NGO platforms such as the Clean Clothes Campaign, etcetera, etcetera, in you know, different campaigns that we all work on together in a coordinating kind of fashion in bringing this campaign possible.' The respondent from H8 argued that foreign labour unions had some leverage on the Chinese government because the ACFTU depends upon the goodwill of foreign unions to strengthen its role in international labour organisations.

Discussion

From the analysis, it seems clear that H-LNGOs have at least some potent strategies for spreading aspects of democracy to their Guangdong partners. Since the total population of H-LNGOs are limited and respondents from the groups often mention the same strategies, it is plausible to see these methods as corner stones in the community's attempts to contribute to democratic diffusion in the PRD. In general, H-LNGOs seem to use consultation, financing, sharing of free space, and international networks as main strategies to influence their partners in a democratic direction. Whether these strategies may be described as mechanisms through which democracy spreads is more difficult to determine, not least because the study involved a relatively limited number of G-LNGOs. There seems to be plenty of evidence suggesting that financing from Hong Kong groups has been necessary for increasing and sustaining the density of G-LNGOs involved in democracy related activities. There are also interesting cases suggesting that consultation from Hong Kong activists has inspired G-LNGOs to orient themselves in a democratic direction, not least in the fields of goals and self-government. The free space of Hong Kong also appears to increase some G-LNGOs' opportunities to receive information, and to provide them inspiration on how to develop their activities and ideas in a more democratic direction. The international networks provided by H-LNGOs also seem to provide G-LNGOs with some leverage against their adversaries. Thus, these four strategies at least seem to work as mechanisms in some cases. However, more research is needed to gain a deeper understanding on the breadth and impact of these mechanisms.

In interview studies, interest should be directed not only to what is said, but also to what is left unsaid. One aspect of this study that deserves further attention is that none of the G-LNGOs' respondents expressed any ambition to influence H-LNGOs in any direction. There was also no evidence suggesting that Hong Kong activists perceived their organisations as under the influence of mainland groups. It thus seems that the H-LNGOs exert unilateral influence on G-LNGOs. One plausible explanation for the hierarchical structure of the LNGO network may be the disparity in resources, knowledge, and freedom between H-LNGOs and G-LNGOs.

In the bigger picture, this study may be a first step in developing a better understanding of how democratic diffusion works on a grassroots level. Financing, consultation, and international networks may be perceived as different dimensions of the imposition mechanism. Actors in a more democratic community can use these tools to strengthen civil society actors in authoritarian societies, to influence them to orient themselves in a more democratic direction, and to increase the costs for regimes that aim to supress them. Consultation and free space can be perceived as dimensions of the emulation mechanism. By visiting democratic societies and receiving advice from democratic actors, members of civil society groups from authoritarian societies can gather information on the benefits and drawbacks of democracy and may also develop a better understanding of how democracy should and could be achieved.

Abbreviations

PRC	People's Republic of China
CCP	Chinese Communist Party
LNGO	Labour non-governmental organisation
H-LNGO	Hong Kong based labour non-governmental organisation
G-LNGO	Guangdong based labour non-governmental organisation
PRD	Pearl River Delta region

References

Ambrosio, T. 2007. "Insulating Russia from a Colour Revolution: How the Kremlin Resists Regional Democratic Trends." *Democratization* 14 (2): 232–52.

Beetham, D. 1991. *The Legitimation of Power*. Atlantic Heights, NJ: Humanities Press International.

Bedford, S. 2009. *Islamic Activism in Azerbaijan: Repression and Mobilization in a Post-Soviet Context*. PhD. Stockholm University.

Brinks, D. and Coppedge, M. 2006. "Diffusion Is No Illusion: Neighbor Emulation in the Third Wave of Democracy." *Comparative Political Studies* 39 (4): 463–89.

Chan, C. 2013. "Community-Based Organizations for Migrant Workers' Rights: The Emergence of Labour NGOs in China." *Community Development Journal* 48 (1): 6–22.

Chan, C. and Chiu, Y. 2015. "Labor NGOs under State Corporatism." In *Chinese Workers in Comparative Perspective*, edited by A. Chan, 157–173. Ithaca: Cornell University Press.

Collins, N. and Cottey, A. 2012. *Understanding Chinese Politics: An Introduction to Government in the People's Republic of China*. Manchester: Manchester University Press.

Dahl, R. 1998. *On Democracy*. New Haven: Yale University Press.

Diamond, L. 1999. *Developing Democracy: Toward Consolidation*. Baltimore, MD: Johns Hopkins University Press.

Doorenspleet, R. 2004. "The Structural Context of Recent Transitions to Democracy." *European Journal of Political Research* 43 (3): 309–35.

Elkins, Z. and Simmons, B. 2005. "On Waves, Clusters, and Diffusion: A Conceptual Framework." *The Annals of the American Academy of Political and Social Science* 598 (1): 33–51.

Fordham, B. and Asal, V. 2007. "Billiard Balls or Snowflakes? Major Power Prestige and the International Diffusion of Institutions and Practices." *International Studies Quarterly* 51 (1): 31–52.

Foster, K. 2001. "Associations in the Embrace of an Authoritarian State: State Domination of Society." *Studies in Comparative International Development* 35(4): 84–109.

Franceschini, I. 2014. "Labour NGOs in China: A Real Force for Political Change?" *The China Quarterly* 218(1): 474–92.

Freedom House, 2017." Hong Kong." Accessed July 31, 2017. https://freedomhouse.org/report/freedom-world/2015/hong-kong.

Fu, D. 2017. "Fragmented Control: Governing Contentious Labor Organizations in China." *Governance* 30 (3): 445–62.

Gleditsch, K. and Ward, M. 2006. "Diffusion and the International Context of Democratization." *International Organization* 60 (4): 911–33.

Grugel, J. 2002. *Democratization: A Critical Introduction*. Basingstoke: Palgrave.

He, A. and Huang, G. 2015. "Fighting for Migrant Labor Rights in the World's Factory: Legitimacy, Resource Constraints and Strategies of Grassroots Migrant Labor NGOs in South China." *Journal of Contemporary China* 24 (93): 471–92.

Hsu, J. and Hasmath, R. 2014. "The Local Corporatist State and NGO Relations in China." *Journal of Contemporary China* 23 (87): 516–34.

Huntington, S. 1991. *The Third Wave: Democratization in the Late Twentieth Century*. Norman: University of Oklahoma Press.

Jacques, M. 2009. *When China Rules the World: The Rise of the Middle Kingdom and the End of the Western World*. London: Allen Lane.

Johnston, H. 2005. "Talking the Walk: Speech Acts and Resistance." In *Repression and Mobilization*, edited by C. Davenport, H. Johnston and C. Mueller, 108–137. Minneapolis: University of Minnesota Press.

Kopstein, J. and Reilly, D. 2000. "Geographic Diffusion and the Transformation of the Postcommunist World." *World Politics* 53 (1): 1–37.

Levitsky, S. and Way, L. 2005. "International Linkage and Democratization." *Journal of Democracy* 16 (3): 20–34.

Lo, S. 2013. "The Role of a Political Interest Group in Democratization of China and Hong Kong: The Hong Kong Alliance in Support of Patriotic Democratic Movements of China." *Journal of Contemporary China* 22 (84): 923–43.

O'Donnell, G. and Schmitter, P. 1986. *Transitions from Authoritarian Rule: Tentative Conclusions about Uncertain Democracies*. Baltimore, MD: Johns Hopkins University Press.

Pepper, S. 2008. *Keeping Democracy at Bay: Hong Kong and the Challenge of Chinese Political Reform*. Lanham, MD: Rowman & Littlefield.

Rogers, E. 1995. *Diffusion of Innovations*. 4th ed. New York, NY: Free Press.

Schmitter, P. and Karl, T. 1991. "What Democracy Is... and Is Not." *Journal of Democracy* 2(3): 75–88.

Schubert, G. 2012. "Taiwan's Political Evolution from Authoritarianism to Democracy and the Development of Cross-Strait Relations." In *European Perspectives on Taiwan*, edited by J. Damm and P. Lim, 66–83. Wiesbaden: Verlag für Sozialwissenschaften.

Shambaugh, D. 2009. *China's Communist Party: Atrophy and Adaptation*. Berkeley, CA: University of California Press.

Sing, M. 2004. *Hong Kong's Tortuous Democratization: A Comparative Analysis*. London: Routledge Curzon.

Starr, H. and Lindborg, C. 2003. "Democratic Dominoes Revisited: The Hazards of Governmental Transitions, 1974-1996." *The Journal of Conflict Resolution* 47 (4): 490–519.

Teets, J. 2014. *Civil Society under Authoritarianism: The China Model*. New York, NY: Cambridge University Press.

Teorell, J. 2010. *Determinants of Democratization: Explaining Regime Change in the World, 1972–2006*. Cambridge: Cambridge University Press.

Valenzuela, S. 1989. "Labor Movements in Transitions to Democracy: A Framework for Analysis." *Comparative Politics* 21 (4): 445–72.

Weale, A. 2007. *Democracy*. 2nd ed. Basingstoke: Palgrave Macmillan.

Wejnert, B. 2005. "Diffusion, Development, and Democracy, 1800-1999." *American Sociological Review* 70 (1): 53–81.

Wejnert, B. 2014. *Diffusion of Democracy: The Past and Future of Global Democracy*. New York: Cambridge University Press.

Wu, C. 2015. "Dance with the Dragon: Closer Economic Integration with China and Deteriorating Democracy and Rule of Law in Taiwan and Hong Kong?" *Hong Kong Law Journal* 45 (1): 275–94.

Xu, Y. 2013. "Labor Non-Governmental Organizations in China: Mobilizing Rural Migrant Workers." *Journal of Industrial Relations* 55(2): 243–59.

Yilmaz, H. 2009. "The International Context." In *Democratization*, edited by C. Haerpfer, P. Bernhagen, R. Inglehart and C. Welzel: 92–106. New York: Oxford University Press.

Appendix

Tables 1 and 2 show how respondents from H-LNGOs described their groups' most salient strategies and how respondents from G-LNGOs described their groups' responses to these strategies.

Table 1. Strategies of H-LNGOs	
	H-LNGOs (N=8)
Consultation	
Providing consultancy to G-LNGOs	H1,H2,H3,H4,H5,H6,H7,H8
Using consultancy to improve G-LNGOs' institutionalisation	H2,H3,H4,H5,H6,H7,H8
Using consultancy to improve G-LNGOs' democratic methods	H2,H3,H4,H5,H6,H7,H8
Using consultancy to improve G-LNGOs' democratic goals	H2,H4,H5,H7,H8
Using consultancy to improve G-LNGOs' democratic self-government	H2,H4,H5,H7
Financing	
Establishing a new G-LNGO	H1,H3,H4
Providing financial resources for G-LNGOs	H2,H3,H4,H5,H6
Provision of free space	
Inviting Guangdong activists to LNGO activities in Hong Kong	H1,H2,H3,H5,H6,H7,H8
Inviting Guangdong activists to protest activities in Hong Kong	H7
International networks	
Using international networks to put pressure on actors in the mainland	H2,H3,H4,H5,H6,H7,H8
Using international networks to improve civil rights in the mainland	H3,H8

Table 2. G-LNGOs' responses to H-LNGOs' strategies	
	G-LNGOs (N=5)
Consultation	
Receiving consultancy from H-LNGOs	G2,G3,G4
Perceiving consultancy to have improved institutionalisation	G3
Perceiving consultancy to have improved democratic methods	G3
Perceiving consultancy to have improved democratic goals	G2,G3,G5
Perceiving consultancy to have improved democratic self-government	G3
Financing	
Having the organisation established by Hong Kong actors	G3,G4
Receiving financial resources from H-LNGOs	G1,G2,G3,G4,G5
Provision of free space	
Participating in LNGO activities in Hong Kong	G2,G3,G5
Participating in protest activities in Hong Kong	G5
International networks	
Using international networks to put pressure on actors in the mainland	G1
Using international networks to improve civil rights in the mainland	

4

"One Country, Two Systems" Under Siege: Rival Securitising Attempts in the Democratisation of Hong Kong

NEVILLE CHI HANG LI

The principle of "one country, two systems" is in grave political danger. According to the Joint Declaration on the Question of Hong Kong signed in 1984, and as later specified in Article 5 of the Basic Law, i.e. the mini-constitution of Hong Kong, the capitalist system and way of life in Hong Kong should remain unchanged for 50 years. This promise not only settled the doubts of the Hong Kong people in the 1980s, but also resolved the confidence crisis of the international community due to the differences in the political and economic systems between Hong Kong and the People's Republic of China (PRC). As stated in the record of a meeting between Thatcher and Deng in 1982, the Prime Minister regarded the question of Hong Kong as an 'immediate issue' as 'money and skill would immediately begin to leave' if such political differences were not addressed (Margaret Thatcher Foundation 1982).

Although "one country, two systems" was designed as a political buffer to avoid a direct clash between two political units, this chapter argues that the principle is politically threatened by two emerging securitising attempts throughout the democratisation of Hong Kong. The pro-self-determination camp (自決派) regards Hong Kong as the only referent object and suggests referenda on political reform (from a liberal perspective) or on independence (from a nationalist perspective) as emergency measures to securitise the democratisation of the city-state. Their securitising moves hit the nerves of the pro-establishment camp (建制派). The Hong Kong government and pro-

Beijing lawmakers condemn the pro-self-determination camp as "separatists" – they seek to set up laws in Hong Kong to prohibit treason against the PRC. Their counter-securitising moves have shifted the referent object from Hong Kong to the PRC, blurring the political separation that has existed up until now and endangering the organisational stability of both Hong Kong and the PRC.

Background

The "one country, two systems" principle serves as the solution to prevent a clash between two political units that have significant differences. Hong Kong owes its prosperity to a capitalist system, which it inherited during 156 years of British rule, while, since 1949, the PRC has been built upon socialism with Chinese characteristics. In addition to political and ideological differences, both political units do not share the same language, currency, degree of freedom and legal system. As a result, it would be politically irresponsible to forcefully put two political units together – this could bring catastrophic political instability to both Hong Kong and the PRC.

The mini-constitution of Hong Kong has various articles that reflect the principle of "one country, two systems." For example, Article 2 grants Hong Kong the right to 'exercise a high degree of autonomy and enjoy executive, legislative and independent judicial power.' Further, Article 9 certifies English as one of the official languages. A win-win situation was established; Hong Kong operates on its own terms and Beijing also has Hong Kong back under the umbrella of "one country, two systems" without causing a direct political and organisational collision – in addition to gaining economic prosperity from the Pearl of the Orient.

However, this political balance is being undermined due to the ambiguity of the Basic Law. Article 15 promises the democratisation of Hong Kong stating that 'the ultimate aim is the selection of the Chief Executive (CE) by universal suffrage upon nomination by a broadly representative nominating committee in accordance with democratic procedures.' Nevertheless, on 31 August 2014 the Standing Committee of the National People's Congress (NPCSC) issued a white paper that interpreted the meaning of the "broadly representative nominating committee" as a 1,200 member strong committee with a heavily pro-Beijing bias (Flowerdew and Jones 2016, 520–521). It was such an interpretation from Beijing that blurred the distinctions between Hong Kong and the PRC, hitting the nerves of Hongkongers and leading to the massive Occupy Movement in 2014. The NPCSC decision is one of the greatest political threats against various referent objects – such as Hongkongers' identity, political autonomy and democratisation. Hongkongers occupied three major urban areas for 79 days, hoping to overturn the NPCSC's decision. The internal and external legitimacy of both Hong Kong and the PRC has been eroded, not only because of the NPCSC's decision but also due to numerous incidents of police misconduct in the suppression of peaceful protesters – such as the firing of 87 rounds of teargas and the clandestine beating of a handcuffed protester (Bhatia 2016; Jones and Li 2016).

Undermining the "one country, two systems" disrupts the organisational stability of all involved political units and their citizens' well-being. In the rhetorical construction of Hongkongers, not only is their autonomy being existentially threatened, their way of life that has been guaranteed by the "one country, two systems" principle is also under siege. One of the central notions of the Occupy Movement – "I want true universal suffrage" – was aimed at reclaiming the democratisation promised by the Joint Declaration and the Basic Law (Li 2014). The array of incidents involving police misconduct also demonstrates how Hong Kong's law-enforcement system has been corrupted due to political reasons. All these discourses are centred on the rhetoric that Hong Kong's autonomy is politically threatened by influences from another political unit that undermines the principle of "one country, two systems".

During these securitising attempts, the discussion has moved towards autonomy, self-determination and even independence. Pro-establishment politicians and the Hong Kong government have attempted to counter-securitise the pro-democracy rhetoric by discursively framing the localism as "separatism" that threatens the PRC's national security. They have raised various emergency measures such as the legislation of Article 23 to prohibit treason against the PRC. This chapter engages with both securitising discourses and concludes that it does not matter which side successfully securitises the political security of Hong Kong in the future – it will be a lose-lose situation for both political units. This is because the political equilibrium established by the "one country, two systems" will inevitably be undermined.

Political Security and the Securitisation Framework

According to Buzan, political security refers to the organisational stability of a political unit, including its ideology, identity and institutions (Buzan 1991, 118). It clearly advocates a state-centrist perspective; indeed, the referent object of political security is the political unit itself – not the individuals. States are defined as organisations that 'exercise clear priority in some aspects over all other organisations with substantial territories. The term therefore includes city-states... and other forms of government....' (Tilly 1990, 1–2). Buzan et al. expand upon Tilly's definition by arguing that organisations, such as churches, also take on a political capacity; therefore it would be more appropriate to use the term 'political unit' to represent 'a collectivity that has gained a separate existence distinct from its subjects' (Buzan et al. 1998, 143).

In human security, the referent object of political security is regarded as the individual – the goal is to protect human rights from political repression (United Nations Development Project 1994, 32–33). Regarding the difference between the two approaches, Thomas and Tow pointed out that state-centric and people-centric securities are intertwined, and that political units can be a critical determining factor to either human security or human insecurity (Thomas and Tow 2002, 380). At the heart of security studies the following questions are continually asked: security for whom – for the general population? For state power itself? For dominant domestic constituencies? (Chomsky 2015).

The Copenhagen School has forged its own approach to provide an answer to these questions, namely the securitisation framework. The school argues that, in order for an issue to be considered as a threat, it is necessary to undergo a process of threat construction – i.e. to frame a non-politicised issue into a politicised one, and eventually a securitised one. To put it simply, securitisation refers to the process whereby a public issue is constructed into a threat (Buzan et al. 1998, 23–25). Non-politicised issues refer to matters that are not included in public discussion; therefore a state does not utilise its capacity to deal with it. An issue is politicised when it is included as a part of public policy. To successfully securitise an issue and construct it as a security threat requires: 1) the declaration of an existential threat towards a particular referent object; 2) the acceptance of relevant audiences; and 3) rights to be granted by the public to the securitising actors stating that they are able to break normal political procedures and carry out emergency measures in order to deal with the threat.

The Copenhagen School's framework studies how various securitising actors rhetorically present something as an existential threat towards a particular referent object; this chapter examines two rival discursive securitising attempts related to the democratisation of Hong Kong. On the one hand, the pro-self-determination camp has attempted to securitise Hong Kong as the only referent object; on the other hand, the pro-establishment camp has attempted to securitise PRC as the only referent object. Both securitising attempts are endangering the "one country, two systems"; currently, Hong Kong and the PRC are politically threatened, which will inevitably lead to a lose-lose situation.

Prior to the discursive analysis of these rival securitising attempts in Hong Kong, it is important to note that the securitisation framework is criticised by various scholars for its state-centric perspective (Eriksson 1999; Huysmans 1998; McSweeney 1996). In fact, Buzan et al. have specified political threats as threats against: 1) the internal legitimacy of a political unit, and 2) external legitimacy from other political units (Buzan et al. 1998, 144) – both are undeniably state-centric. Waever addresses these criticisms by emphasising how the analytical framework itself is open to various securitising actors to rhetorically present something as an existential threat (Waever 1999, 335). He further states that it is up to the relevant audiences to decide whether they are convinced by the state-centric rhetoric or not. Therefore, the securitisation framework is not inherently state-centric or people-centric; it is up to the relevant audiences to decide which security rhetoric they find most convincing. Indeed, it just so happens that, most of the time, states are the most influential securitising actors, which leads to a perception that the securitisation framework is a state-centric one.

The same situation occurs in the case of Hong Kong – the rival securitising actors do not start securitisation on a level playing field; for example, the pro-establishment camp is in a more advantageous position as they are the majority in the legislative council (LegCo) in Hong Kong. They take a pro-Beijing stance along with the Hong Kong government. They have more resources and propaganda channels to promote the securitising attempt to make the PRC as the referent object in Hong Kong. In contrast, pan-democrats are the minority in the LegCo; compared to the pro-establishment, they are in a less advantageous position to declare and convince the majority of Hongkongers about an existential threat to Hong Kong's autonomy and that the "one country, two systems" is being eroded. Although both camps are concerned with political security, and each securitising rhetoric is mainly about the organisational stability of a political unit, the major difference between them is that the pro-establishment camp and the Hong Kong government regard the PRC as the only referent object. In comparison, the pro-self-determination camp postulate that Hong Kong is the only referent object. The struggle and the rivalry between these securitising actors will now be examined.

From PRC Liberal to Hongkongers: Transformation of Securitising Attempts in the Pro-democracy Camp

Political security is about dealing with 'threats to the legitimacy or recognition either of political units or of the essential patterns (structures, processes or institution) among them' (Buzan et al. 1998, 144). In the securitisation framework, political units are regarded as the major referent object of the political sector, yet there are two main questions in the case of Hong Kong: what is the referent object and who are the securitising actors?

The government will usually be the securitising actor that presents their security argument when their organisational stability is being threatened. Nonetheless, this is not the case in Hong Kong. From the perspective of Hongkongers, the political insecurity that exists is due to the erosion of Hong Kong's autonomy. Conventionally, the Hong Kong government should declare themselves politically threatened, as there will be organisational instability if the issue is left unsettled. Yet, the Hong Kong government did not carry out any securitising move in relation to its autonomy with regard to the intervention from the Chinese Communist Party (CCP), such as the NPCSC's decision. This could be mainly due to the fact that the "one country, two systems" policy expires in 2047; there is the high possibility that the Hong Kong government will lose its autonomy and will eventually be controlled by Beijing. The responsibility then falls to pan-democrats and ordinary Hongkongers; this is why 1.2 million people rallied and occupied the streets in 2014. Indeed, their rhetoric in the occupy movement has been further developed as the localist rhetoric that regards Hong Kong as the referent object.

The development of security arguments among pro-democratic Hongkongers has been through a transformation. It has changed from leveraging Hong Kong's democratisation as an emergency measure to securitise the PRC's political reform (or democratisation), to regarding Hong Kong as a referent object and upholding the systemic referent object, i.e. "one country, two systems", in order to avoid political clashes. Despite progress, pro-self-determination politicians are not satisfied with the political equilibrium and "one country, two systems" theoretically means that Hong Kong is controlled by the CCP. They radicalise the localist rhetoric by pushing it towards the direction of self-determination and independence, constructing Hong Kong as the only referent object and eroding the political equilibrium that has been established by the "one country, two systems" policy.

Old Democrats: Leveraging the Democratisation of Hong Kong for China

While reviewing Hong Kong's socio-political transformation, Flowerdew lists Chris Patten's promotional discourse on the British legacy to Hong Kong as: 1) a capitalist economic system; 2) freedom of individuals; 3) independent judicial system; and 4) democratic political institutions (Flowerdew 1998; Flowerdew 2012). These elements serve as the ideological pillars that set Hong Kong apart from the PRC; therefore, "one country, two systems" is necessary to prevent clashes with regard to political ideology, political structure, the economic system and the judicial system. Regretfully, there are multiple incidents indicating that this political buffer is being eroded – the NPCSC's decision mentioned earlier serves as an example of this. Facing the erosion of the "one country, two systems" principle, Hongkongers keep protesting; various scholars have argued that such political participation contributes to building political awareness and localism within Hong Kong (Kaeding 2011; Lee 2015). The securitising attempts, putting Hong Kong as the referent object, are rooted within the development of localism in the city-state.

In fact, the securitising discourse that maintains Hong Kong as the referent object, which is regarded as localism, could be traced back earlier in 2012, when Hung noticed a British Hong Kong flag was raised during a protest for the first time to signify the British legacy to Hong Kong (Hung 2014). He further reviews the development of different rhetoric of local consciousness in Hong Kong; under his categorisation, the pro-democracy rhetoric is divided into 'seeing Hong Kong as a PRC liberal' and 'seeing Hong Kong as a Hongkonger.' Old democrats (民主派) in Hong Kong consider themselves as PRC liberals (not Hong Kong liberals) that regard China as the referent object and attempt to use the democratisation of Hong Kong as an emergency measure to leverage the democratisation of the PRC (Chan 2012). They believe that Hong Kong has both a role and responsibility to promote the PRC's political reform; they argue that Hong Kong is the only place in the PRC that could possibly have democracy due to the assurance of "one country, two systems".

Interestingly, from the CCP regime's perspective, leveraging Hong Kong's democratisation for PRC political reform is actually a political threat – not an attempt for political security. Old democrats failed to recognise the distinction between state and government. Although their securitising moves declared the Chinese nation as under threat and the government as requiring democratisation, this is still considered a threat to the sovereignty of the PRC. Indeed, Buzan argues that sovereignty grants the right for the political unit to decide the form of government – even if it adopts an authoritarian one (Buzan et al. 1998, 152). These old democrats failed to realise that the PRC regards their securitising moves a threat, rather than an attempt to achieve security within the Chinese regime; this perspective will be discussed in the section about the securitising attempt by the pro-Beijing camp. In relation to Hong Kong, these old democrats view the PRC as the referent object of political threat, whereas the democratisation of Hong Kong is simply an emergency measure to leverage political reforms in China.

Localising Democratisation: Hong Kong and "One Country, Two Systems" as the Referent Object

In contrast to 'seeing Hong Kong as a PRC liberal,' Chin has written a book called *On Hong Kong as a City-State*. It is regarded as the inspiration that has ignited the rising localism in Hong Kong, in other words 'seeing Hong Kong as Hongkongers' (Hung 2014). To put it simply, Chin argues that the rapid integration of Hong Kong and the PRC poses a prominent threat as it erodes the sociopolitical, economic and judicial system established during British rule in the city-state. Therefore, it is logical to declare Hong Kong as the major referent object and, for the purposes of political stability, to uphold the fading "one country, two systems" principle. Chin declares Hong Kong's ideology, identity and institutions as under an existential threat due to increasing Chinese interventions in the form of demographical, political, economic and cultural assimilation (Chin 2011). The emergency measure he suggests is to defend "one country, two systems" in order to draw a clear separation between the two political units and to maintain the political equilibrium. The major justification raised by Chin is that the PRC needs Hong Kong more than Hong Kong needs the PRC. His logic could be applied in various aspects – for example, Hong Kong as an international political unit can support the PRC in international organisations like the Asian Infrastructure Investment Bank in terms of funding and internationalising the Chinese currency. Therefore, it would be both in Hong Kong's and the PRC's interest to maintain "one country, two systems".

However, in order to sustain the interests of both political units, Hong Kong needs to maintain its autonomy. This is so it can preserve the confidence of the international community in the same manner the Joint Declaration helped it do in the 1980s. Thus, for the sake of both Hongkongers and the Chinese, "one country, two systems" must be securitised. This new perspective, which refers to Hong Kong as the referent object, ignited the flame of localism in Hong Kong. Simply put, the localisation of Hong Kong emerged by moving away from treating the PRC as the referent object.

As stated above, securitising actors are not placed on a level playing field. The rise of localism has motivated a new pro-democracy generation in the city-state; the occupy movement in 2014 is certainly one of the blossoms. Yet, the movement was suppressed by the Hong Kong government and the hope of upholding "one country, two systems" (and the democratisation of Hong Kong) was put into a deep freeze. In order to seize a more advantageous position and to persuade the relevant audiences, Chin joined the 2016 election of the LegCo in Hong Kong with local activist organisations, i.e. the Civic Passion and Proletariat Political Institute. As the leader of this election campaign, Wong Yeung-Tat raises the notion of a *de facto* referendum on constitutional reform of the Basic Law. He and Chin share the same view in maintaining Hong Kong as the major referent object and they argue that in order to survive the surging political clashes between the two political units, the only emergency measure is to launch a constitutional reform on the Basic

Law to sustain "one country, two systems" (Li 2016).

The manifesto for the localist election pact suggests reviewing various articles in the Basic Law as the emergency measure to securitise Hong Kong political security and the "one country, two systems". One of the main focuses is a review of Article 5 as to whether the capitalist system and way of life in Hong Kong should remain unchanged *beyond* 50 years. In line with Chin's argument, Wong suggests that, in order to maintain the political stability of Hong Kong, it is crucial to sustain the political buffer (Leung 2016). As this securitising move is not initiated by the Hong Kong government, the localist securitising actors attempted to get a mandate (support from the relevant audiences) in order to successfully securitise the political security of Hong Kong. They have planned two steps to reflect the legitimisation from the relevant audiences to put Hong Kong as the referent object. The first reflection is on all five of their candidates elected in all five electorates and, having cleared the first one, they can leverage their resignations in the LegCo to initiate a by-election *cum de facto* referendum. The question is then whether the result will reveal whether the Hong Kong people will legitimise the need for a constitutional reform as an emergency measure.

Disruption of 'One country, Two systems'

Radicalising a Securitising Move: Hong Kong as the Only Referent Object

Regretfully, the localist election campaign only got about 154,000 votes and one seat in five electorates. This was mainly due to a new rising political force that advocates the right to self-determination in Hong Kong and extinguished the localist rhetoric. Their notion of self-determination is widely shared among various new political parties including Youngspiration, Demosistō and the Hong Kong Lineup. In contrast to Chin and Wong's view, these political parties regard Hong Kong as the *only* referent object. They criticise that "one country, two systems" gives room for the PRC to intervene in Hong Kong's internal affairs. They seek a referendum on political reform (from a liberal perspective) or on independence (from a nationalist perspective). Yet, Hong Kong does not have a referendum law; the CCP condemns this proposal and calls it a violation of the Basic Law. The pro-self-determination camp regards their securitising move to self-determination as more effective than the localist rhetoric that attempts to sustain "one country, two systems". It turns out their radical rhetoric received more support from the people in Hong Kong than the pro-self-determination force that won six seats, roughly 240,000 votes, in the LegCo electoral college 2016.

Later, two legislators-elect of Youngspiration, Baggio Leung and Yau Waiching, raised a banner "Hong Kong is not China" during the oath-taking process in the LegCo. They took the oath to safeguard the interests of "the Hong Kong Nation" which explicitly put Hong Kong as the only referent object. This is their securitising attempt that was legitimised by their voters. Their securitising move not only offended both the pro-establishment and old pro-democracy Chinese (who see Hong Kong as a PRC liberal) but also led to the disqualification of their seats in LegCo, as the court ruled their oath as dishonest (Haas 2017a). The incident also opened a hole in the dam; the PRC reinterpreted the Basic Law and further disqualified four more pro-democracy legislators, claiming that their oaths were not "sincere and solemn" (Lau and Chung 2017). The only localist lawmaker Cheng is also being charged and facing the risk of disqualification. Regarding the serious external intervention of the PRC, Chin and localist legislator Cheng suggested all pan-democracy legislators resign and boycott the LegCo. However, both traditional pan-democracy and pro-self-determination camps heavily criticised the suggestion and claimed that they wanted to be re-elected in the LegCo – even though the PRC can disqualify legislators according to this new interpretation of Hong Kong's mini-constitution.

Localism in Hong Kong was initiated with the good will to maintain the political security equilibrium and the enduring "one country, two systems" principle. Yet, the rhetoric was radicalised by pro-self-determination politicians, which led to even more direct interventions and disruptions. There will be by-elections taking place in 2018. It could be an interesting future research piece to analyse whether the rhetoric shifts after the disqualification. Further, it will be intriguing to find out whether all the pan-democracy legislators will resign and boycott the LegCo and their re-election in order to fight and uphold "one country, two systems".

Pro-Beijing Camp: The PRC's National Security as the Only Referent Object

In response to the rise of the pro-self-determination securitising attempt, both Hong Kong and the CCP government attempted to counter-securitise the localist and pro-self-determination rhetoric by declaring the PRC's national security as being threatened. The Chief of the Chinese Liaison Office in Hong Kong, Wang, remarked that "one country, two systems" could be removed if it is leveraged to threaten the national security of the PRC (Radio Television Hong Kong 2017). This reveals that, whether traditional pan-democrats regard the democratisation of Hong Kong as a means to securitise China's political security, or pro-self-determination politicians attempt to detach themselves from "one country, two systems", both rhetorics are considered to be political threats to the PRC. The middle path is the constitutional reform proposed by Chin and Wong to sustain the "one country, two systems" principle in order to avoid clashes between the two political units. Yet, this securitising attempt did not receive sufficient endorsement from the Hong Kong people, and the PRC continues to intrude upon Hong Kong's internal business. This is because the masses in Hong Kong did not show their will to defend the political buffer.

In just a few months after the Occupy Movement, a new National Security Law of the PRC was passed in the NPCSC on 1 July 2015. There are multiple articles that counter-securitise the rhetoric of putting Hong Kong as the referent object. For example: Article 11 emphasises the preservation of sovereignty and territorial integrity of the PRC as a 'shared obligation of all Chinese people, including compatriots from Hong Kong, Macao and Taiwan'; and Article 40 further specifies Hong Kong and Macao as having a responsibility in preserving the national security of the PRC. It is clear that the communist regime regards the rhetoric of securitising Hong Kong's political security as a national security threat to its sovereignty, especially when there are rising pro-independence politicians after the occupy movement (Loh 2015).

Nevertheless, this national security threat would not erupt if the "one country, two systems" principle was not violated multiple times by the communist government. The Hong Kong government is also responsible as pro-Beijing politicians utilise the city-state's resources to speed up the integration of the two political units. This is due to the current "one country, two systems" only lasting for 50 years; indeed, there is no guarantee it will continue after 2047 (Li 2016). Combined with the fact that Hong Kong has not yet been democratised and the CE was elected in a pro-Beijing biased committee, localists have attempted to seek constitutional reform to extend the "one country, two systems" in order to maintain the organisational stability of the city-state. Indeed, as Article 15 of the National Security Law of the PRC clearly states, the political unit must 'persist in the leadership of CCP, maintaining the socialist system with Chinese characteristics, developing socialist democratic politics and completing socialist rule of law…', all these notions collide with the political, economic and legal system in Hong Kong, reminding us of the need to maintain "one country, two systems".

In line with the PRC's position, the pro-establishment politicians in Hong Kong also follow the rhetoric and have attempted to securitise the PRC's national security by the legislation of Article 23 in Hong Kong that prohibits treason against the communist government. The latest CE election in Hong Kong in 2017 is the only election since 1997 where only pro-establishment candidates have entered (mainly due to the pre-screening of the pro-Beijing nomination committee that the Occupy Movement protested against). Two strong potential candidates, Carrie Lam and John Tsang, both supported the legislation of Article 23 'to enact laws on its own to prohibit any act of treason, secession, sedition, subversion against the Central People's Government'. The proposed bill had led to half a million people protesting in 2003 due to serious concerns regarding freedom of speech. Perhaps unsurprisingly, the traditional pan-democratic politicians backed this securitising attempt, as they remained detached from the localisation of Hong Kong and continued to view the democratisation of Hong Kong as an emergency measure to securitise the democratisation of the Chinese nation.

In the manifesto of Tsang, it states that Hong Kong has a constitutional responsibility to enact local legislation to protect national security of the PRC according to Article 23 of the Basic Law. He proposed to use a 'white bill' to kick off the legislation and start with less controversial issues; by having this law they can 'ensure that the rights and freedoms of the people of Hong Kong are fully protected while safeguarding [the] national security [of the PRC].' Tsang puts heavy emphasis on securitising the PRC's national security; this securitising attempt shifts the referent object from Hong Kong to the PRC. Another strong CE candidate, Carrie Lam, also expresses similar views on the legislation of Article 23, putting the PRC as the only referent object. She adopts the same rhetoric to convince the election committee of the constitutional responsibility of this legislation, yet she also claimed that she noticed this is a highly controversial issue and will act cautiously. When Carrie Lam was elected by the 1,200 members of the election committee, Jasper Tsang, former LegCo president, also urged her to restart the legislation as soon as possible. The legislation of Article 23 has been a prominent issue and has been examined from legal and constitutional perspectives (Fu *et al.* 2005). It sparks questions such as whether it is reasonable for Hong Kong to be fully democratised prior to the legislation, or how the legislation would affect freedom and democratisation in Hong Kong. Yet, with the advantage of mobilising the government and public resources, the securitising attempt of the pro-Beijing camp to maintain the PRC as the referent object is clearly occupying an advantageous position. There is limited time for the people in Hong Kong to reflect their will before "one country, two systems" is completely undermined.

Conclusion

This chapter has engaged with the rival securitising attempts in Hong Kong. While the localism of Hong Kong has been radicalised by pro-self-determination politicians who support a full departure from the one country, two systems, pro-Beijing politicians are counter-securitising it by placing the PRC as the only referent object and are attempting to legislate Article 23 to suppress 'separatism' in Hong Kong. The rival securitising attempts have already shaken international confidence in Hong Kong; this will eventually hurt both Hong Kong and the PRC's national interests. The chairman of the Congressional-Executive Commission on China of America warns the new CE, Carrie Lam, that if Hong Kong is to become just another Chinese city under her leadership, America will reassess whether Hong Kong warrants special status under American law (Congressional-Executive Commission on China 2017). In line with concerns over the rapidly eroding autonomy, Moody's Investors Service has downgraded Hong Kong's local and foreign currency issuer rating from Aa1 to Aa2. This is specifically due to concerns over the legal and institutional arrangements that will be in place when one country, two systems expires (Moody's Investors Service 2017).

The Hong Kong government has also recently announced a plan to lease part of its new high-speed railway station to the PRC and to allow the Chinese Public Security to enforce Chinese laws, including national security laws and other laws that restrict freedom of speech (Haas 2017b). This would be a serious violation of the one country, two systems principle and brings political instability to Hong Kong and the PRC. It appears that the political equilibrium will inevitably be undermined; this will be a lose-lose situation for both political units. Although localists like Cheng, Chin and Wong are continuously deepening the securitising rhetoric of upholding one country, two systems to counter-balance the pro-Beijing and pro-self-determination camps (Cheng 2016; Cheng and Kan 2017; Chin 2011), there is not much time left for Hongkongers to make up their minds and decide which securitising rhetoric is most convincing for them. The by-elections will take place soon and it is critical for the public to urge all pan-democracy legislators to resign and boycott the LegCo and the re-election. This is the only way to take a firm stance against the violation of the one country, two systems principle by the PRC.

References

Bhatia, A. 2016. "Discursive Construction of the 'key' Moment in the Umbrella Movement." *Journal of Language and Politics* 15 (5): 551–568.

Buzan, B. 1991. *People, States & Fear: An Agenda for International Security Studies in the Post-Cold War Era*. Hemel Hempstead: Harvester.

Buzan, B., O. Waever, and J. de Wilde, 1998. *Security: A New Framework for Analysis*. Boulder: Lynne Rienner.

Chan, K. 2012. *China's Heavenly Doctrine and Hong Kong*. Hong Kong: Oxford University Press.

Cheng, C. T. 2016. *Civic Nationalism and State Formation*. Hong Kong: Passion Times.

Cheng, C. T. and J. Kan. 2017. *Ji ben fa gai liang zou yi* [Proposed Amendments to the Basic Law]. Hong Kong: Passion Times.

Chin, W. 2011. *On Hong Kong as a City State*. Hong Kong: Enrich Publishing.

Chomsky, N. 2015. *Because We Say So*. London: Hamish Hamilton.

Congressional-Executive Commission on China, 2017. "Statement on Hong Kong's Chief Executive Election." http://www.cecc.gov/media-center/press-releases/statement-on-hong-kongs-chief-executive-election.

Eriksson, J. 1993. "Observers or Advocates? On the Political Role of Security Analysts." *Cooperation and Conflict* 34 (3): 311–330.

Flowerdew, J. 1998. *The Final Years of British Hong Kong: The Discourse of Colonial Withdrawal*. London, New York: Macmillan and St. Martin's Press.

Flowerdew, J. 2012. *Critical Discourse Analysis in Historiography: The Case of Hong Kong's Evolving Political Identity*. Basingstoke: Palgrave Macmillan.

Flowerdew, J. and R. Jones. 2016. "'Occupy Hong Kong'." *Journal of Language and Politics* 15 (5): 521–528.

Fu, H., C. J. Petersen, and S. N. M. Young, eds. 2005. *National Security and Fundamental Freedoms: Hong Kong's Article 23 Under Scrutiny*. Hong Kong: Hong Kong University Press.

Haas, B. 2017a. "Hong Kong Charges pro-Independence Activists over China Protest." *The Guardian*, April 26, 2017. http://www.theguardian.com/world/2017/apr/26/hong-kong-police-detain-pro-independence-lawmakers-after-china-protest.

Haas, B. 2017b. "Anger at Plan to Let Chinese Police Patrol in Hong Kong." *The Guardian*, July 26, 2017. http://www.theguardian.com/world/2017/jul/26/anger-at-plan-to-let-chinese-police-patrol-in-hong-kong.

Hung, H. 2014. "Three Views of Local Consciousness in Hong Kong." *Asia-Pacific Journal* 12 (1): 1-10.

Huysmans, J. 1998. "Revisiting Copenhagen: Or, On the Creative Development of a Security Studies Agenda in Europe." *European Journal of International Relations* 4 (4): 479–505.

Jones, R. H. and N. C. H. Li. 2016. "Evidentiary Video and 'Professional Vision' in the Hong Kong Umbrella Movement." *Journal of Language and Politics* 15 (5): 569–591.

Kaeding, M. P. 2011. "Identity Formation in Taiwan and Hong Kong – How Much Difference, How Many Similarities?" in *Taiwanese Identity in the 21st Century: Domestic, Regional and Global Perspectives*, edited by G. Schubert and J. Damm, 258-79. London: Routledge.

Lau, C. and K. Chung. 2017. "Court Ruling Disqualifying Lawmakers 'a Declaration of War'." *South China Morning Post*, July 14, 2017. http://www.scmp.com/news/hong-kong/politics/article/2102609/four-more-hong-kong-lawmakers-disqualified-over-oath-taking.

Lee, F. L. F. 2015. "Social Movement as Civic Education: Communication Activities and Understanding of Civil Disobedience in the Umbrella Movement." *Chinese Journal of Communication* 8 (4): 393–411.

Leung, S. K. 2016. "Wong Yeung-Tat: Constitutional Referendum Is the Most Realistic Election Promise." *Passion Times*, March 24, 2016. http://www.passiontimes.hk/article/03-24-2016/29566.

Li, N. C. H. 2014. "The Growing Significance of New Media in Hong Kong's Social Movements." Paper presented at Global Insecurities International Conference. Bristol.

Li, N. C. H. 2016. "Demands for Constitutional Reform: One Year after Occupy Hong Kong." In *Changing World, Changing Lives Conference*. Bath.

Loh, D. 2015. *Hong Kong's Political Future After the 'Umbrella Revolution'*. Singapore: S. Rajaratnam School of International Studies.

Margaret Thatcher Foundation. 1982[Released 2013]. "China: Record of Conversation (MT-Vice Chairman Deng Xioaping of China) [Future of Hong

Kong] [MT's Annotated Copy]." http://www.margaretthatcher.org/document/122696.

McSweeney, B. 1996. "Identity and Security: Buzan and the Copenhagen School." *Review of International Studies* 22 (1): 81–93.

Moody's Investors Service. 2017. "Moody's Downgrades Hong Kong's Rating to Aa2 from Aa1 and Changes Outlook to Stable from Negative." https://www.moodys.com/research/Moodys-downgrades-Hong-Kongs-rating-to-Aa2-from-Aa1-and--PR_366144.

Radio Television Hong Kong. 2017. "'One Country, Two Systems' could Go: Wang Zhenmin." *Radio Television Hong Kong*, April 29, 2017. *http://news.rthk.hk/rthk/en/component/k2/1327827-20170429.htm*.

Thomas, N. and W. T. Tow. 2002. "Gaining Security by Trashing the State? A Reply to Bellamy and Mcdonald." *Security Dialogue* 33 (3): 379–382.

Tilly, C. 1990. *Coercion, Capital and European States, A.D. 990-1990*. Oxford: Basil Blackwell.

United Nations Development Project. 1994. *Human Development Report*. Oxford: Oxford University Press.

Waever, O. 1999. "Securitizing Sectors? Reply to Eriksson." *Cooperation and Conflict* 34 (3): 334–340.

Part Two

Transnational

5

Public Diplomacy: China's Newest Charm Offensive

TONY TAI-TING LIU

Since Joshua Kurlantzick (2007, 6) coined the term 'charm offensive' in 2007, the term has stuck in the study of International Relations to refer to China's use of soft power to improve its global status and image. While the idea of China charming the world with its economic and cultural prowess has not changed too much over the past decade, the ways Beijing has adopted to charm other states have diversified since. In conjunction with such developments, in recent years, the term 'public diplomacy' has come to replace charm offensive as China's latest efforts to improve its status and image through soft means.

As China's first official public diplomacy report points out, in simple terms, public diplomacy refers to various ways of conducting diplomacy or fostering bilateral exchange with other countries beyond the state level (Zhao and Lei 2015, 4). In other words, besides traditional state to state diplomacy carried out between governments, non-governmental organisations and individuals occupy a central role in China's latest foreign policy endeavour. Hinged on the concept of people-to-people relations, China seeks to move away from the popular image of 'China threat' to a more cordial image of China as a friendly and peace-loving nation.

Noting China's recent turn towards public diplomacy, this chapter seeks to address the topic in three sections. Part one examines the idea of public diplomacy and corresponding developments that took place in China since former President Hu Jintao's emphasis on the concept in 2009. Part two looks into the idea of 'telling a good story of China' – an important guiding principle of China's public diplomacy – and corresponding efforts Beijing has made towards it. Part three discusses the Confucius Institute and China Cultural Centres and their contributions towards the goals of 'telling a good story' and fostering people-to-people relations. This chapter concludes with some considerations on the challenges China may face in its public diplomacy endeavour.

From Peaceful Rise to Public Diplomacy

Despite abundant discussions on 'public diplomacy' in the West, the concept remains quite refreshing in the context of China. In 2009, speaking on the occasion of the 11th Conference of Chinese Diplomatic Envoys Stationed Abroad, Chinese President Hu Jintao expounded on the importance of public diplomacy in Chinese foreign policy. In Hu's words, '[China] should strengthen public diplomacy and humanities diplomacy and commence various kinds of cultural exchange activities in order to disseminate China's great culture' (*The 11th Conference of Chinese Diplomatic Envoys Stationed Abroad was held in Beijing*, 2009). Hu's address was significant, as the statement marked the first time China has considered the concept of public diplomacy on the level of national policy.

Since then, public diplomacy gradually developed into a notable priority in the succeeding Xi Jinping administration. In the party report of the 18th National Congress of the CCP that was released in 2012 alongside the confirmation of Xi Jinping as China's next president, Beijing clearly expressed the guideline of 'making good efforts to advance public diplomacy' (Xinhua 2012). In 2013, Xi Jinping followed up preceding calls for realising public diplomacy by introducing the corresponding concept of 'telling a good story of China and disseminating the voice of China.' 'Telling a good story of China' quickly became the central tenet of China's public diplomacy.

Under the state emphasis on public diplomacy, various public, private and academic institutions and organisations were established to carry out the function of reshaping China's global image. In terms of government, the Public Diplomacy Office was established in 2009 as the main official body for managing and coordinating tasks related to public diplomacy on the state and departmental levels. In the private sector, echoing Beijing's call for public diplomacy, a number of public diplomacy associations were subsequently established. In December 2012, the China Public Diplomacy Association was established in Beijing. The association serves as an informal channel for China to communicate with the world; the participation of academics and retired officials gives functions hosted by the association a track two or semi-official nature. On the regional level, 15 regional public diplomacy associations have been established across the nation in metropolitan centres such as Shanghai, Tianjin, Nanjing and Guangzhou (Han 2014). Academically, at least eight higher education and research institutes that focus on the study of public diplomacy were established across the country, including the Centre for Public Diplomacy at Tsinghua University (2011) and the School of International and Public Affairs at Jilin University (2013) among others.

Institutional establishment aside, it is important to recognise that public diplomacy did not grow out of a vacuum in China but came about following a series of adjustments in Chinese foreign policy to cope with the so called 'China threat theory'. In an essay in a 2005 issue of the influential *Foreign Affairs* magazine, Vice President of China's Central Party School Zheng Bijian articulated in simple terms that China seeks a 'peaceful rise' and not otherwise (Zheng 2005, 20). Nonetheless, despite China's peaceful intentions, as the term 'rise' also suggests the possibility of a powerful China becoming more assertive in international affairs, the term was eventually replaced with 'development' to suggest a less negative connotation. In the context of peaceful development, the Hu Jintao administration subsequently introduced the concept of 'harmonious worldview' and re-emphasised China's good neighbour policy (Tsai et al. 2011, 27–30). China's peaceful development, in other words, is realised through its emphasis on harmony.

Public diplomacy as China's new foreign policy emphasis came about in a similar vein. Following leadership turnover in 2013, Xi Jinping proposed the 'China Dream' as the new guiding concept for China in the near future. In Xi's words, 'China Dream is the great rejuvenation of the Chinese nation' (Central Committee of the Communist Party of China Party Literature Research Office 2013). Unfortunately, Xi's ideological calling provided little hints as to how China seeks to realise its rejuvenation or re-occupation of the centre stage of the world again. Such a void is perhaps covered by public diplomacy. In other words, in terms of the China Dream, part of how the Chinese nation will be rejuvenated rests with how well China conducts its public diplomacy, or an effort to improve China's global image. In such a case, similar to related concepts introduced in the Hu Jintao era, the China Dream and public diplomacy are proposed as interconnected and mutually reinforcing concepts. Under Xi Jinping, the China Dream is the grand ideological principle that will guide China's continued development in the near future while public diplomacy – similar to the 'good neighbour policy' – is one of the ways that Xi's vision will be realised.

Telling a Good Story of China

The guiding principle for China's public diplomacy drive is 'telling a good story of China' (讲好中国故事 *jianghao zhongguo gushi*), a guideline that has been repeated publicly by current Chinese President Xi Jinping since the 18th National Congress of the Chinese Communist Party (CCP). Noting the tendency of Chinese leaders since Jiang Zemin to pronounce their policy ambitions in short captivating phrases, 'telling a good story of China' is one of the latest notable phrases to follow in the string of announcements from the Three Represents to 'scientific outlook on development'. While 'telling a good story of China' has attracted global attention in recent years; interestingly, the concept is not entirely new. In 2010, John Naisbitt – a renowned futurist who was well known for his earlier writings on Asia's newly developed economies – together with Doris Naisbitt, published *China's Megatrends: The 8 Pillars of a New Society*, a volume that detailed China's rapid political, economic and social changes over the past two decades. The alleged idea for the volume, according to Naisbitt, came about through a conversation with ex-Chinese president Jiang Zemin in the 1990s, when Jiang invited him to tell a story of China (Ma 2009).

Regardless of the reception of Naisbitt's work, the idea of telling a good story became a foreign policy priority under Xi Jinping that is to be realised through various forms of public diplomacy. On 13 August 2013, in a speech given at the National Propaganda and Ideology Work Conference, Xi stressed the importance of establishing new forms of propaganda aimed at 'telling a good story of China and disseminating the voice of China' (*Xi Jinping: Propaganda Work is an Extremely Important Task of the CCP*, 2013). The 8/13 speech opened up the watershed for discussions on storytelling in China. While the political nature of Xi's call is easy to notice, the statement nonetheless paved the way for various efforts towards defining and realising its content. Among the discussions, Wang Yiwei's interpretation of telling a good story of China is worth noting:

> As Party Secretary Xi Jinping pointed out, the quest of the era is to tell the story of China and the mission of the era is telling a good story of China... first is to tell the development story of China and the ideals that support China's development... telling a good story of China means telling a good story of oneself and projecting the attraction of China through personal appeal... the story of China is multifaceted; there is success and there is also failure. The key is to tell the Chinese way or approach behind the story (Wang 2016).

Wang's description highlights three components to China's guideline that warrant attention. First, the story of China is about development, with economic development serving as the mainstay of the story. Second, the story of China is about the individual; individual success stories help to shape and project China's global image. Third, the story of China is a mixed success story; the Chinese experience or how China succeeded should be part of the story. Realised through public diplomacy, China's storytelling aspiration – an effort to improve the Chinese image abroad – has notably taken several forms since 2013.

In terms of development, not long after the 8/13 speech, Xi Jinping proposed the Belt and Road (B&R) initiative, an ambitious geopolitical project that seeks to integrate Asia, Europe and Africa into an intercontinental market and transport network. Alongside the B&R, the Silk Road Fund (SRF) and the Asia Infrastructure Investment Bank (AIIB) were subsequently established to finance the project. Jointly, the B&R, SRF and AIIB aim to improve trade and transport routes – channels that are facilitated by infrastructural development – around the world. Based on the integration and investment initiatives, Xi Jinping has expounded on the theme of development, most notably at the 2016 G20 Summit in Hangzhou, where he delivered a speech titled 'A New Starting Point for China's Development: A New Blueprint for Global Growth' (*Keynote Speech by H.E. Xi Jinping, President of the People's Republic of China, at the Opening Ceremony of the G20 Summit*, 2016) and at the 2017 Belt and Road Summit in Beijing, where Xi referred to China's historical connection with the Silk Road and elaborated on themes including economic, infrastructure, innovation and green development (*Full text of President Xi's speech at opening of Belt and Road Forum*, 2017). In addition, the Chinese government has invested great efforts in promoting the B&R through various methods, which includes the publication of the B&R Public Diplomacy Report (2016), the production of a major documentary series on the B&R (2016), and the release of a project theme song just ahead of the B&R Summit (2017).

On the other hand, regarding individuals, examples may be gleaned from the variety of ways through which China and the Chinese are presented. Concerning the B&R, such presentation can be observed from the frequent reference by the state to Zhang Qian and Zheng He, historical figures in China's ancient past who are regarded as the trailblazers for what came to be known as the Silk Road and China's maritime trade route respectively. Emphasis on the individual can also be observed from the B&R documentary series produced by China Central Television (CCTV), China's official broadcasting service. Besides interviews with influential figures and experts, the documentary is interwoven with the personal stories of some 60 common individuals who dwell along the B&R (CCTV 2016). Finally, China is represented by its political and business elites, or individuals who receive media attention internationally. Such an approach is exemplified by the so-called 'head of state diplomacy' that sees Chinese leaders promoting China's national image abroad. Since assuming the role of China's top leader in 2013, Xi Jinping has made official visits to more than a dozen states annually, consolidating China's foreign relations while gathering international spotlight on China through wide media coverage and reporting.

Tools of Public Diplomacy: Confucius Institute and China Cultural Centre

Although public diplomacy did not begin to take the form of official policy until 2013, the Chinese leadership had similar ideas in mind nearly a decade earlier. Under the Hu Jintao administration, the Confucius Institute, a state sponsored institution with the objective of teaching and promoting the learning of the Chinese language abroad, was established under Confucius Institute Headquarters, also known as the Hanban, in 2004. The Hanban is responsible for overseeing the operation of the global network of Confucius Institutes across the world. Amidst incessant discussions on China rising onto the world stage as a revisionist threat, the Confucius Institute was envisioned by Beijing as a way to reduce the anxieties surrounding China while promoting China's image as a benevolent and peaceful power abroad. Soft power, a term coined by political scientist Joseph Nye (2005), was the keyword associated with the Confucius Institute and China's adoption of soft means to improve its global image then.

Since the establishment of the first Confucius Institute in Korea in 2004, the number of China's language teaching institution grew rapidly. By the end of 2016, China had established 512 Confucian Institutes and 1073 Confucian Classrooms (programs established in high schools and primary schools) in more than 140 countries around the world (Hanban 2017). While the Confucius Institute is primarily a language teaching institution, it is inevitable that its curriculum and textbooks used in classrooms are infused with lessons and stories on Chinese history and culture. In such a sense, the Confucius Institute fits well with the guideline of 'telling a good story of China' and the objectives of China's public diplomacy. Meanwhile, through the organisation of cultural celebration events and language competitions, the Confucius Institute also enhances people-to-people relations through the direct interaction between foreign and Chinese participants and organisers. The annual 'Chinese Bridge' Chinese Proficiency Competition is a good example of the Confucius Institute's public diplomacy achievement. Through the organisation of language competitions across the world, China has not only provided a motivation for foreign students to study Chinese but also sparked the interest of students to visit China (Hui and Wang 2015, 301). Such efforts are expended in the hopes of fostering a future generation of individuals with an improved image of China.

On the other hand, China has also established cultural centres across the world as a way to promote Chinese culture beyond classrooms. Since the first establishment of China Cultural Centres in Benin and Mauritius in 1988, more than 20 cultural centres have been established in Asia, Africa, Europe, Oceania and Central America, with most of the additional locations introduced after 2000. China currently hosts 27 international cultural centres, with a large number of the centres spread out across Asia and Europe. As described in its online introduction, the China Cultural Centre organises cultural activities such as performances, exhibitions and art festivals and provides Chinese language and cultural training courses (China Cultural Centre 2015). In terms of public diplomacy, the China Cultural Centre plays no small role in disseminating knowledge on China through the constant organisation of musical performances and art and calligraphy exhibitions and events among others. Meanwhile, in 2012, China's Ministry of Culture introduced 'Happy Chinese New Year' (HCNY) (欢乐中国 *huanle zhongguo*), a series of cultural festivities centred on the theme of Chinese New Year. Adopting the central tenet of 'happiness, harmony, dialogue and sharing', the HCNY celebrations seek to tell a story of China that is robust and cherishes communal values, which stands in stark contrast with arguments that deem China as a colossal threat (China Cultural Centre 2017).

Prospects of China's Public Diplomacy

This chapter provides a short survey of the development of China's public diplomacy in recent years and some efforts Beijing has expended towards the improvement of its global image. While it is much too early to evaluate the success of China's new charm offensive, previous experiments with soft power by Beijing present several challenges that China may need to address if it hopes to find success with public diplomacy.

First, while China provides a definition of 'public diplomacy' in its official public diplomacy report, to some extent, the definition remains excessively general and difficult to translate into real policies. While an optimistic reading of China's definition suggests the inclusion of 'governments, non-governmental organisations and individuals' is a non-discriminatory act that seeks to exploit the full strength of the nation in realising public diplomacy, an alternative reading raises the question of whether there exists a one size fits all policy guideline for all the actors. After all, diplomacy is traditionally limited to the realm of the state; to move diplomacy outside the state may require policymakers to think outside the box, as private and non-governmental actors may harbour widely different interpretations of the state and its various features. In other words, China is viewed differently across different levels and sectors and narratives may contradict – the success story of one may have nothing to recommend for another. Such challenge warrants attention if

China seeks to claim further success with public diplomacy.

Second, the fact that China remains an authoritative regime generates contradictions with the concept of public diplomacy that are hard to resolve. Even though public diplomacy can be considered an interest driven action regardless of regime type, China's authoritative character exacerbates the issue by hinting at the potential involvement of sophisticated consequences. For example, by enshrining the guideline of 'telling a good story of China and disseminating the voice of China' as propaganda, China proposes a dilemma between the nature of the Chinese regime and public diplomacy. If public diplomacy is guided by the principle of disseminating propaganda, how credible are China's foreign policy communications and actions? Indeed, such tensions have been raised in the past concerning the Confucius Institute. As critics point out, under its disguise to pass on knowledge of Chinese language and culture to the outside world, the Confucius Institute also encourages students to think highly of China and its ruling political authority (Peterson 2017). While such claims remain controversial and rebuffed by China, backlashes have occurred, with institutions such as the University of Chicago and Pennsylvania State University terminating their cooperation with the Confucius Institute and many other institutions around the world becoming more vigilant over China's public diplomacy (Liu 2017). As the case of the Confucius Institute demonstrates, trust remains a crucial ingredient for the success of China's language teaching institutes abroad and ultimately, China's public diplomacy. How Beijing seeks to increase the world's trust in China in the near future remains to be observed.

References

Central Committee of the Communist Party of China Party Literature Research Office. 2013. *Xijinping guanyu shixian zhonghua minzu weida fuxing de zhongguomeng lunshu zhaibian* (Summary of Xi Jinping's Discourse on Realizing the China Dream and the Great Rejuvenation of the Chinese Nation). Beijing: CCCPC Party Literature Research Office.

CCTV. 2016. "Daxing jilupian yidaiyilu zai yangshi kaibo" (Major Documentary "Belt and Road" Aired on CCTV). http://www.cctv.cn/2016/09/05/ARTIpI1WmlmwT3VSoDvU7Rye160905.shtml.

China Cultural Centre. 2015. "About China Cultural Centre," http://en.chinaculture.org/ccc/2015-02/02/content_597924.htm.

China Cultural Centre. 2017. "Huanle zhongguo" (Happy Chinese New Year), http://cn.chinaculture.org/portal/site/wenhua/special_report/springfestival/2017/index.jsp#imglistbox.

"Di shiyi ci zhuwaishijie huiyi zaijin zhaokai" (The 11th Conference of Chinese Diplomatic Envoys Stationed Abroad was held in Beijing). 2009. *People's Daily*, July 21.

"Full text of President Xi's speech at opening of Belt and Road Forum." 2017. *Xinhua News*, May 14. http://news.xinhuanet.com/english/2017-05/14/c_136282982.htm.

Han, F. 2014. "Shibada hou zhongguo gonggong waijiao shiye de fazhan" (The Development of China's Public Diplomacy after the 18th National Congress of the CCP). http://blog.ifeng.com/article/31833706.html&gws_rd=cr&ei=mg4zWe_qEcKz0gTHxorADA.

Hanban. 2017. "Guanyu kongzi xueyuan ketang" (About the Confucius Institute/Classroom). http://www.hanban.org/confuciousinstitutes/node_10961.htm.

Hui, C. and Wang, B. 2015. "Dunzi yiwenhuiyou yiyoufuren – kongzi xueyuan shizhounian fazhan jieshao" (Ten Years Development of the Confucius Institute: An Introduction), in Zhao Qizheng and Lei Weizhen eds., *Bluebook of Public Diplomacy: Annual Report on China's Public Diplomacy Development*. Hong Kong: Peace Book, 293-301.

"Keynote Speech by H.E. Xi Jinping, President of the People's Republic of China, at the Opening Ceremony of the G20 Summit." 2016. http://www.g20chn.org/English/Dynamic/201609/t20160909_3414.html.

Kurlantzick, J. 2007. *Charm Offensive: How China's Soft Power is Transforming the World*. New Haven and London: Yale University Press.

Liu, T. 2017. "Exporting Culture: the Confucius Institute and China's Smart Power Strategy," in David O'Brien, Toby Miller and Victoria Durrer eds., *The Routledge Handbook of Global Culture Policy*. New York: Routledge.

Ma, C. 2009. "Tell a big story well to sell it to the world." *China Daily*, September 8. http://www.chinadaily.com.cn/cndy/2009-09/08/content_8664887.htm.

Nye, J. 2005. "The Rise of China's Soft Power." *Wall Street Journal Asia*, December 29. http://www.belfercenter.org/publication/rise-chinas-soft-power.

Peterson, R. 2017. "American Universities are Welcoming China's Trojan Horse." *Foreign Policy*, May 9. http://foreignpolicy.com/2017/05/09/american-universities-are-welcoming-chinas-trojan-horse-confucius-institutes/.

Tsai, T., Hung, M. and Liu, T. 2011. "China's Foreign Policy in Southeast Asia: Harmonious Worldview and Its Impact on Good Neighbor Diplomacy." *Journal of Contemporary Eastern Asia* 10 (1), 27–30.

Wang, Y. 2016. "Jianghao zhongguo gushi shi shidai shiming" (Telling a Good Story of China is the Mission of an Era). *People's Daily*, September 28. http://theory.people.com.cn/BIG5/n1/2016/0928/c376186-28746111.html.

"Xi jinping: yishi xingtai gongzuo shi dang de yixiang jiduan zhongyao de gongzuo" (Xi Jinping: Propaganda Work is an Extremely Important Task of the CCP). *Xinhua News*, August 20, 2013. http://news.xinhuanet.com/politics/2013-08/20/c_117021464.htm.

Xinhua News. 2012. "Shibada baogao quanwen" (Full Text of the Party Report of the 18th National Congress). November 19. http://www.xj.xinhuanet.com/2012-11/19/c_113722546_11.htm.

Zhao, Q. and Lei, W. eds. 2015. *Bluebook of Public Diplomacy: Annual Report on China's Public Diplomacy Development*. Hong Kong: Peace Book.

Zheng, B. 2005. "China's 'Peaceful Rise' to Great-Power Status." *Foreign Affairs*, 84 (5), 18–24.

6

Can China Link the Belt and Road Initiative by Rail?

SHU LIANG (KARL) YAN

A senior official from the Guangzhou Railway Group enthusiastically introduced the concept of *yilu yidai* to me in an interview. Apparently, he had just learned the concept from an internal study session with his counterparts in the China Railway Corporation (CRC) and was eager to share it (1612I).[1] I was quite confused at the time and thought he must be wrong. Since 2013, the Silk Road Economic Belt has been referred to as the *dai* (belt) whereas the Maritime Silk Road has been referred to as the *lu* (road) – thus, the Belt and Road Initiative (OBOR) (*yidai yilu*). After I had returned to Toronto and started my research on the effects of China's international strategies on the regulation of its railway sectors, I ran into the term Railroad Economic Belt (REB, *yilu yidai*) (Yin-nor 2016, 207). I immediately contacted the cadre whom I had interviewed and confirmed the definition of the concept. In his words, 'you need to have a road before you can connect'. The CRC indeed regards the railway sector as the locomotive that leads China's efforts in constructing the OBOR, as the REB is a strategy that enhances connectivity and deepens OBOR infiltration through the building and exporting of Chinese rails (1722I).

Behind the formulation of the REB stands a ubiquitous Party-state that has the ability to forge a national consensus in pushing through broad-sweeping economic and political reforms. Indeed, the 2013 reform of the Ministry of Railways (MOR) and the creation of the REB show the Chinese central government's commitment to maintaining a steady control on the railway sector in support of its international interests. A state's international ambition has direct effects on its domestic policy making. As a single sector study on the Chinese railways, this chapter builds on the theoretical framework of

---

[1] This is an interview code, similar codes such as 1373I and 1722I are explained in detail in the bibliography section.

economic statecraft and addresses two empirical issues. First, domestically, this chapter addresses the question of control – how the Chinese state has turned its railway sector, one that has been less studied by China scholars, into one that is internationally competitive. To be specific, what kind of relationship has been cultivated by the Chinese state in using its commercial actors to achieve technological and industrial advancement. Second, internationally, this chapter addresses the question of connectivity. Namely, how the export of Chinese rails (transportation and infrastructure) could strengthen regional integration and deepen China's geopolitical interests.

However, it is also important to highlight the complex nature of China's behaviour towards the international order. For example, in the realm of financial governance and developmental foreign aid, socialisation (inclusive of two-way socialisation) of international norms has been one of the key characteristics found in China's international behaviours (Johnston 2007; Chin and Yan 2013). Even in China's new multilateral development bank initiatives, namely, the New Development Bank and the Asian Infrastructure Investment Bank, the goals are to complement the existing multilateral developmental bank system[2] and help make the extant system more efficient. These are evidently found in the rhetoric used by both official documents published by the Chinese state as well as official Chinese media. Much of the reason behind such rhetoric is that China is still in the process of 'learning', through which it needs to localise norms and rules of the said system (Wang 2015). China has been actively pushing for the export of its high speed and regular rails and railway infrastructure in the railway sector. The rhetoric is no longer about 'learning' or 'complementing existing norms'. Instead, 'China's Railway High Speed (CRH) could be considered as the only strategic industry since the Reform and Opening that is developed by China and could change the basic international and domestic political-economic landscape of the 21st century' (Xu 2016, emphasis added). China's high-speed rail (HSR) could thus become an important leverage for China in becoming a new land power, starting with improving connectivity and gaining road rights.

Economic Statecraft

Economic statecraft is a practice through which noneconomic means are achieved through economic means – 'influence attempts relying primarily on resources which have a reasonable resemblance of a market price in terms of money' (Baldwin 1985, 13–14). Norris (2016) narrows economic statecraft by linking it with a state's international grand strategy and does so by operationalising how a state mobilises commercial actors to pursue its international

---

2   E.g. the World Bank, the International Monetary Fund, the Asian Development Bank.

interests. Thus, instead of looking at macroeconomic policies that a state sets (such as tariffs) like Baldwin had done, Norris looks at microeconomic actors and their relationship with the state and examines the helpfulness of such relationship.

Previous studies on China have also focused on how China achieves its strategic goals through economic statecraft. Such goals can either be economic in nature (Alves 2013) (Gallagher and Irwin 2015) or political (Brautigam and Tang 2012) (Reeves 2015). Scholars have also investigated the effects of China's economic statecraft on other countries' domestic structures (Reeves 2015), and the increase of China's geopolitical influence (Urdinez et al. 2016).

This chapter thus takes a state-centric point of view and looks at the state's control of the railway sector in the pursuit of its international interest. The continuous push for greater centralisation in the railway sector lies in the state's active effort in utilising its infrastructural power to support the REB. This chapter makes a theoretical contribution to the economic statecraft literature by unpacking the very type of government-business relationship cultivated by the state and explaining the mechanisms through which a state can successfully control a sector with a concentrated market structure.[3]

The Quest for Standard: Recentralisation of the Railway Sector

On 28 May 2009, US Congresswoman Nancy Pelosi was deeply impressed by the HSR while visiting the Beijing-Tianjin Intercity Railway. Indeed, the railway sector has become a powerhouse for innovation and a platform for internationalisation. Multiple government units' concerted efforts culminated in a great leap forward in technological and industrial advancement. In a conversation with the former head of MOR Liu Zhijun, she asked him how it was all possible. Liu answered succinctly and proudly that this was because of 'the political advantage of the wise leadership of the Chinese Communist Party (CCP), and the institutional advantage of concentrating powers to accomplish big things [*jizhong liliang ban dashi*]' (Li 2010, 7). Indeed, since 2010, the Chinese government has given priority to the development of the HSR as a new strategic industry.

The MOR/CRC is indeed proud of its technological and industrial accomplishments, and the establishment of the 'China Standard'.[4] By the end

---

3   According to Norris (2016, 33), a concentrated market structure is one with 'a few large firms with powerful domestic political equities'.
4   In short, China Standard refers to a set of standards developed by the CRC,

of 2009, the MOR successfully applied 946 patents for the CRH. These patents range from railway engineering, high speed rail technology, and station engineering, all of which would later become parts of a full system of HSR technology with China's own independent intellectual property rights in 2016. The CRC proudly announces that China's world leading HSR industry is the only strategic industry in China that has surpassed its international competitors (The CRC 2016[5]).

A view found in existing scholarship on regulatory regimes in China asserts that controlled competition is the preferred organising principle for champion industries. Indeed, the grand strategy, or 'metavision', shaping China's industrial structure and regulatory regime has been a preference for marketisation and more importantly, controlled competition[6] (Pearson 2005, 313; Pei 2006; Yeo 2012) with the goal of preserving and advancing the role of the state (Eaton 2016). However, from the beginning of state-owned enterprise (SOE) reform, the MOR has been an outlier, as it deviated from the pattern of controlled competition. This was particularly noticeable in the 2013 reform, which resulted in recentralisation (Yin-nor 2016). In 2013, the MOR was broken into an SOE (the CRC) and a regulatory body, the State Railway Bureau (SRB), without introducing controlled competition or any further reforms at the provincial and sub-provincial level (1373I).

The newly created CRC and SRB have overlapping responsibilities in railway regulation – rendering the SRB practically obsolete (Yu 2015). For example, in the drafting of the 2016 edition of the *Med-and Long-term Railway Network Program*, the National Development and Reform Commission (NDRC) requested the CRC to research and propose amendments to the 2008 edition of the Program, *not* the SRB – who is, in principle, responsible for railway development and planning (The State Council Information Office of the PRC 2016). Thus, the CRC remains as a monopoly in the 1) planning and provision of railway and related services, and 2) the coordination of sub-sectors – transportation and rolling stocks (16121I; Zhen et al. 2012).

Whether the 2013 reform was prompted by domestic factors or China's international ambitions remains debatable. One undeniable fact is the highly-concentrated market structure found in the railway sector and its sub-sectors

---

which owns the CEMU's independent intellectual property rights. The goals are to standardise and systematise the production of EMUs using cutting edge Chinese technology.

5   Sources with 'The CRC' as authors are internal documents provided by the China Railway Corporation; please see the bibliography section for details.

6   Controlled competition here refers to the idea of 'restrain[ing] disorder competition' among a limited number of state-owned enterprises in China's strategic sectors (Pearson 2005, 314–315).

after the 2013 reform. The CRC operates under the 'construction-operation model' (*jianyun heyi*), which means the CRC is responsible for railway development, pricing, and infrastructure building, and then coordinates relevant firms in the railway sector in meeting predetermined developmental goals (Zhen et al. 2012, 57). In rolling stocks, the CRC coordinates the China Railway Rolling Stock Corporation (CRRC). The CRRC was created in 2015 after the State Council (SC) had directed the merging of China South Locomotive & Rolling Stock Corporation Limited (CSR) and China North Locomotive and Rolling Stock Industry Corporation (CNR). The purpose is to coordinate domestic market and reduce destructive competition (Zhao 2016). The CRC supervises production and technological innovation by having firms work together with the CRC's engineering and research branches – the China Railway Design Corporation (CRDC) and the China Academy of Railway Sciences (CARS) (161211). Overall, the railway sector could be described as a concentrated market structure under the de facto leadership of the CRC. Such market structure is the direct descendant of 'concentrating power to accomplish big things'. Indeed, in the 2000s, under the leadership of Liu Zhijun, the MOR and the State Council (SC) converged on the idea and pushed for the strategy of Great Leap Forward (*kuayueshi fazhan*) in railway development (Luger 2008; Ma and Zhang 2015; Yin-nor 2016).

The institutional advantage of 'concentrating power to accomplish big things' has helped greatly in pushing through technological advancement in achieving the 'China Standard' and the development of HSR. The Chinese state can effectively control the entire railway sector by sending administrative orders to only one firm – the CRC (Zhen et al. 2012). In 2004, the SC approved the MOR's *Med-and Long-term Railway Network Program*. In the Program, an HSR network that was known as the 'Four Vertical and Four Horizontal Passenger Networks' (*sizong siheng keyun zhuanxian*) was proposed. These passenger networks would allow multiple unit (MU) trains to reach a minimum speed of 200km/h.[7] Such goals in technological advancement and railway industrial upgrade were reiterated in the 2008 edition of the Program. In 2016, the NDRC requested and approved the CRC's amendments to the 2008 Program. In it, the CRC proposed an 'Eight Vertical and Eight Horizontal Highspeed Rail Network' (*bazong baheng gaosu tielu wang*), which would expand China's existing high-speed mileage from 19,000 km to 38,000 km in 2025, and improve existing railway infrastructure to allow MU trains to reach the speed of 350km/h. Within the CRC, the period from 2016 to 2025 is known as the 'Golden Ten Years in Railway Development' (*tielu fazhan de huangjin shinian*) (161211).

---

7   The top speed of passenger trains running on passenger and freight shared networks was 140km/h.

On top of railway infrastructure planning, the MOR/CRC also outlines the general principles of railway technology development through the implementation of the *Policies on Major Railway Technologies* (*tielu zhuyao jishu zhengce*). Both the 2004 and the 2012 versions of the Policies contained specific technological goals for the HSR. For example, in both documents, the minimum headway for MU trains is three minutes.

The MOR/CRC does not, however, simply lay out the foundations and policy goals of HSR development in China. It has been actively leading and coordinating the research, design, innovation, and testing of the CRH (The CRC 2016). For example, the Signal & Communication Research Institute of CARS has been working closely with relevant domestic firms and research centres in the development of the Chinese Train Control Systems (CTCS) (Huawei 2012). Such multi-pronged government-business efforts culminated in the eventual success of the China-standard Electric Multiple Units (CEMU).

In 2004, Liu Zhijun appointed Zhang Shuguang as the Chief Architect of the CRH. By 2010, Zhang made several technological advancements in the CRH, elevating the CRH's operating speed from 200km/h to 380km/h (with a tested top speed of 486.1km/h) and increasing the CRH's safety and comfort levels (Jiao, Liu and Liu 2011, 1 and 3). Liu Zhijun threw his unconditioned support behind the development of CRH by making the MOR the main point of contact for all relevant domestic actors. In 2008, Zhang Shuguang and his team started working with CSR Qingdao Sifang Co., Ltd and CNR Tangshan Railway Vehicle Co., Ltd on a new model of CRH that would adapt to China's different climatic environments and geological conditions. In the process, Zhang was able to bring 25 research universities, 11 research institutes, 51 national engineer and research centres and more than 10,000 academicians, professors and engineers to bear on completing the project (Jiao, Liu and Liu 2011, 1 and 3).

The state had always been behind the MOR in the development of CRH. The SC forcefully coordinated and centralised relevant industries through administrative orders in support of the effort. The SC also established special project teams that are dedicated to pooling different human, material, and monetary resources in support of the MOR (Zhen et al. 2012). One of the special project teams (*jishu cheliang zhuanye weiyuan hui*) specifically defined the role of the MOR as the coordinator and leader in negotiating with foreign ventures who want to enter the Chinese railway sector (Zhen et al. 2012; Caixin 2012). Indeed, all foreign ventures must interface with the MOR before engaging with specific firms in the entire sector. And Zhang was one of the key decision makers in the process. For example, in the purchase of original MU train models and technology transfers from Siemens, Zhang was able to lower nine billion CNY in cost by setting strict market entry barriers (Zhen et al. 2012). The CNR benefited from the MOR's dealing with Siemens as it subsequently used Siemens' parts in assembling the traction system for the CRH380 series (Zhen et al. 2012).

While the CRH380 was still in its research phase, the MOR and the Ministry of Science and Technology signed the *Independent Innovation of Chinese High-speed Train Cooperation Agreement and Joint Action Plan* on 26 February 2008. The MOR and CRC played key roles in coordinating relevant firms and research centres in the pursuit of CEMU (Xinhua 2016). Both CSR Qingdao Sifang and CNR Changchun, under the guidance and leadership of the MOR/CRC, formed an 'industry-education-research-application' network in which relevant firms, universities, and research centres were integrated to research and build the CEMU (Jilin-China 2015; Sohu 2016). Throughout the process, the CARS acted as the key broker and leader. From 2013 to 2014, CARS published a master plan with clear standards in nine MU technological areas including power components, traction system, braking system, and train control system (Lu 2015). With these technological goals, the CNR and CSR then worked with different agencies to complete the manufacturing process. The first CEMU was put into passenger operation on 15 August 2016 when G8041 left Dalian North Station. At the 39th International Organization for Standardization (ISO) General Assembly in Beijing, the CRC Chief Engineer proudly announced that 'the CEMU is gradually surpassing "the European Standard" and "the Japanese Standard"' (Lu 2016).

Enhanced Connectivity: Expanding Geopolitical Interest

China Railway Signal & Communication Corporation Ltd. believes that an internationally competitive industry must be well supported by a complete supply chain, and all parts must also be internationally competitive (NDRC 2016). This is a defining characteristic of the CEMU, which has become a leading feature of the 'going out' strategy of the Chinese railway sector and the Chinese state. In the process of, the CRC has played an instrumental role in leading and directing railway related firms to seek railway cooperation abroad in Belt and Road countries. According to Zhu Pengfei (Chief Engineer of China Railway International Co., Ltd. or CRIC), the CRC 'accelerated railway construction along the Silk Road Economic Belt, comprehensively pushed for the construction of railway construction abroad and fully promoted the export of CEMU' (Zhu 2015, 26). In December 2014, the CRIC was created to facilitate the 'going out' process of the railway sector. The Chairman simultaneously holds the position of Deputy Chief Engineer of the CRC. The signing of the Moscow-Kazan High-speed Railway project in 2014 signals the international debut of CEMU.

However, it is important to highlight that the 'going out' process has been largely treated as an extension of Chinese foreign aid projects, and the Chinese state has always been behind the establishment of these projects. It is noticeable that the state has been controlling the CRC in fulfilling the state's international objectives (Zhao 2016, 415). The CRC has fully utilised its monopolistic market position in the domestic economy to facilitate the 'going out' process for other railway related firms. Its capacity to coordinate and plan railway design, construction, and equipment manufacturing can help mix and match domestic firms with suitable overseas projects. According to the CRC, this method is a new and innovative bank-to-business and business-to-business cooperation models that have effectively raised the competitiveness of the Chinese railway sector (The CRC 2017). For example, in 2015, in the building of an HSR in Indonesia, the CRC formed a consortium with other firms in railway design, construction, equipment, and operation, and led the negotiation with the Indonesians (The CRC 2015). The CRC's role as a leader in the railway sector has been further strengthened by the NDRC in January 2017 as the NDRC and the CRC, along with 12 other ministries, agreed to establish a 'Belt and Road Working Public-Private-Partnership Model'. Such a model will help Chinese firms accelerate the implementation of infrastructure projects in Belt and Road countries (NDRC 2017). In May 2017, the Postal Savings Bank of China announced that it would provide the CRC with more than 200 billion CNY in support of the CRC's efforts in railway and infrastructure building in Belt and Road countries (The Beijing News 2017).

The CRC has also played a leadership role in enhancing connectivity through the REB (The CRC 2017). It has actively engaged in bilateral and multilateral cooperative initiatives with regional and international railway organisations. These initiatives are meant to foster a healthy environment for the export of HSR and to deepen international cooperation between the Chinese railway sector and its counterparts in Belt and Road countries. The Chongqing-Xinjiang-Europe railway line is an example of how the CRC was able to enhance China's connectivity with Europe through freight as goods can be transported from Europe to China, then shipped to various parts of Asia with ease. Chongqing also aims to become the centre of a new 'four-hour aviation economic zone' (*si xiaoshi hangkong jingji quan*), where goods could be transported to Chongqing from large commercial and industrial hubs such as Bangkok, Hong Kong, and Osaka within four hours via air (Zhao 2017). Chongqing could thus become a logistical hub capable of connecting land with air (*tiekong lianyun*) and Asia with Europe. This freight line provides OBOR countries with a variety of options for the transportation of goods and further lowers logistical costs. And the CRC will continue leveraging its advantages in railway freight to promote the transportation of goods along OBOR countries. The Yiwu-London railway line which was put into operation in January 2017 is another example of China's ambition to connect itself with the world, and the CRC was also a key player in its establishment.

Looking at the present moment, China's provision of global public goods indeed rests upon its ability to build large infrastructural projects abroad – the China-Laos Railway, China-Thailand Railway, the Budapest-Belgrade HSR, and the Kuala Lumpur-Singapore HSR (The CRC 2016). This is mainly due to Chinese policymakers' propensity towards promoting infrastructural projects overseas, which is part and parcel of China's developmental model that emphasises state to state loans and infrastructural development (Paltiel 2017). These actions could be considered as a means to 'buy support' for China's global status (Paltiel 2017, 10). China's infrastructural projects in Latin America, including improving and developing railway infrastructure in Argentina and Brazil, have resulted in an expansion of its geopolitical interests by 'fill[ing] the void left by a declining US presence' (Urdinez et al. 2016, 24).

One concrete international implication of the REB, according to the CRC, is the expansion of China's discourse rights in the railway sector (*kuoda le zhongguo tielu huayuquan*) (The CRC 2017). Also, as the REB expands and deepens, road rights could ultimately pave the way for China to become a dominant land power. The strategy of securing economic resources and energy are important strategic goals in geopolitics (Gao 2015), and connectivity has become a method to achieve such a goal – as connectivity aims to bridge different geographical regions together regarding policy, facility, trade, finance, and people-to-people relations. Often, 'institutions of concertation and coordination' are the basis of hegemony and international hierarchy (Cox 1992, 36; Butt 2016). Yet, China has seemingly chosen an alternative path as connectivity directly contrasts with how hegemony and counter-hegemony forces were formed in the past. The concertation, coordination, and even integration of regional powers is not through institution building; instead, infrastructural projects are the locomotive pulling countries together (Butt 2016). In 2017, seven countries, including major powers like China, Russia, and Germany, agreed to jointly build an information-sharing platform for transportation safety and a fast customs clearance system for the China Railway Express (Belt and Road Portal 2017). The signing of such an agreement shows how railway infrastructure projects could deepen the integration of countries in other issue areas – such as technology sharing and standardising custom clearance. Thus, the building of railways could potentially reshape both the ways through which people and goods travel through space and the existing international system. Indeed, as technology and the international system are co-constitutive (Herrera 2006, 2–7), the 'going out' of the Chinese railway sector, compounded with technological breakthroughs in its CRH, could potentially result in international systemic change as China continues to participate in and contribute to the international management and building of HSR (Gao 2012, 16-19).

Discussion and Conclusion

In the railway sector, it seems that institutional inertia played a key role in centralisation. Indeed, China's control of its railway sector had been through the MOR before the 2013 reform and the CRC after. There is a clear chain of command in this sector, with three major layers – the SC and NDRC on top giving general directions, the CRC makes plans and then coordinates, or even herds, other railway related firms towards the general direction given by the SC and NDRC. Thus, by having firm control over the CRC, the SC and NDRC have effective control over the entire railway sector, as the CRC often leverages its monopolistic position in the transportation and service sub-sectors to coordinate market activities in rolling stocks, railway infrastructure, and signalling (1722I). This new type of relationship – directly controlling a monopolistic SOE instead of regulators – is not counterintuitive. And the logic is similar to Gerschenkron's (1962) idea on late industrialisers. Indeed, a complete supply chain is the foundation in building an internationally competitive industry.

This type of relationship is also seen in the 'going out' process, as the CRC serves as both a coordinator and a platform builder. The CRC effectively leads the entire railway sector in the building of railway infrastructure and CRH and CEMU exports along Belt and Road countries. The SC and NDRC then would only need to control the CRC in meeting the state's international objectives. The upside of this type of arrangement is the efficient implementation of state goals, and the state can shield away from domestic and intra-sector competition. The downside of this type of relationship, however, is that the SC and NDRC's international objectives must be highly aligned with the CRC's political and commercial agenda for the CRC to be an effective agent of the state (Norris 2016). The hitherto story of Chinese rails going abroad indicates that state goals and that of the CRC's are indeed well aligned. The fall of Liu Zhijun in 2011 meant the MOR had lost its political leverage in the SC (Ma and Zhang 2015). However, the reform of the MOR did not result in controlled competition. Prima facie, the CRC was satisfied with the reform result as it had pushed back for reform (1373I). Within the CRC, there were also cries for greater centralisation of the entire railway sector – returning to super-ministerial status, a time when rolling stocks and railway infrastructure were integral parts of the MOR (1612II). At least, the CRC's immediate objectives, though remain muddled at the moment, could be met by implementing state directives.

In conclusion, can China link the Belt and Road Initiative by rail? The answer is 'yes', though premature. First, can China build alliances through infrastructural projects? International institutions help continue international regimes after the initial, favourable condition has disappeared (Keohane 1984) – projects based upon mutual interests indeed lack continuation in this respect. To be specific, can the increasingly connected continental Asia and the ensuing change in regional power dynamic forge a counter-hegemonic force against the extant liberal order? Second, the question is whether the Chinese state can effectively and continuously control the railway sector in serving its international ambitions? Beijing's influence over other countries with the provision of international public goods through infrastructural projects is largely dependent upon Beijing's firm control over its commercial actors. The extant relationship shows that the state and the sector are highly aligned with their goals and objectives. The CRC has the capacity to leverage its domestic production capacity against international competitors, and the state can thusly help the CRC in securing contracts abroad with its diplomatic tools and bringing a conglomerate of actors into bear on ensuring implementation success. However, in the implementation phase, can the CRC adapt to different political institutions and business cultures and deal with countries with profoundly different domestic power dynamics? Indeed, many questions are left unanswered and need to be explored in future research.

*The author is grateful to the following for their helpful comments: Gregory Chin, Victor Falkenheim, Asif Farooq, Bernie Frolic, Jeremy Paltiel, and Yin Yang. The author thanks the anonymous interviewees who had spent their precious time with the author, often multiple times.

Abbreviations

CARS   the China Academy of Railway Sciences
CEMU   China-standard Electric Multiple Units or China Standard High Speed Rails
CCP   the Chinese Communist Party
CDRC   the China Railway Design Corporation
CNR   the China North Locomotive and Rolling Stock Industry Corporation
CRC   the China Railway Corporation
CRH   China Railways High Speed, a high-speed rail service operated by the China Railway Corporation
CRRC   China Railway Rolling Stock Corporation
CSR Limited   China South Locomotive & Rolling Stock Corporation
CTCS   Chinese Train Control Systems

HSR	high speed rails or multiple units
ISO	International Organization for Standardization
MOR	the Ministry of Railways
MU	Multiple Units or high speed rails
NDRC	the National Development and Reform Commission
OBOR	the Belt and Road Initiative
REB	the Railroad Economic Belt
SC	the State Council
SRB	the State Railway Bureau

References

Alves, Ana Cristina. (2013). 'Chinese economic statecraft: A comparative study of China's oil-backed loans in Angola and Brazil', *Journal of Current Chinese Affairs*, 1, pp. 99–130.

Baldwin, David. (1985). *Economic statecraft*. Princeton: Princeton University Press.

Belt and Road Portal. (2017). 'Seven Countries to Deepen Cooperation on China-Europe Freight Rail Services', 24 April. Available at: https://eng.yidaiyilu.gov.cn/qwyw/rdxw/11598.htm.

Brautigam, Deborah and Tang, Xiaoyang. (2012). 'Economic statecraft in China's new overseas special economic zones: soft power, business or resource security?', *International Affairs*, 88 (4), pp. 799–816.

Butt, Ahsan. (2016). 'The Construction of a Chinese Hierarchic Order in the Global South', *World Politics in a Time of Populist Nationalism*. 15 December. Available at: http://duckofminerva.com/2016/12/wptpn-the-construction-of-a-chinese-hierarchic-order-in-the-global-south.html.

Caixin – Century Weekly. (2012). 'Tiedaobu haozi 900 yi yinji gaotie jishu', [The Ministry of Railway Spends 90 Billion in Technology Transfer for High Speed Rails], 4 July. Available at: http://www.shigongjishu.cn/Item/11478.aspx.

Chin, Gregory T. and Yan, Shu Liang. (2013). 'Chonggou buleidun senlin tixi: wei zhongguo jueqi chuangzao kongjian', [Creating Space for China's Rise: Reshaping the Bretton Woods System], in Zhang, Jianxin (eds), *Guoji tixi biange yu xinxing daguo guanxi* (*Change in International System and New Great Power Relations*), pp.182–201.

Eaton, Sarah. (2016). *The advance of the state in contemporary China: State-market relations in the reform era*. Cambridge: Cambridge University Press.

Gallagher, Kevin P., and Irwin, Amos. (2015). 'China's economic statecraft in Latin America: Evidence from China's policy banks', *Pacific Affairs*, 88 (1), pp. 99–121.

Gao, Bai. (2015) 'Railway and Road Rights: Historical Lessons on the "the New Silk Road Economic Belt"', *China International Strategy Review*, Beijing: World Affairs Press. Available at: http://www.faobserver.com/Newsinfo.aspx?id=11493.

Gao, Bai. (2012). 'Gaotie yu zhongguo 21 shiji dazhanlue' [The High Speed Rail and China's Grand Strategy in the 21st Century] in Gao, B. (eds.) *The High Speed Rail and China's Grand Strategy in the 21st Century*. Beijing: Social Sciences Academic Press (China), pp. 1–31.

Gerschenkron, Alexander. (1962). *Economic backwardness in historical perspective, a book of essays*. Cambridge, Mass: Belknap Press of Harvard University Press.

Herrera, Geoffrey L. (2006) *Technology and International Transformation: The Railroad, the Atom Bomb, and the Politics of Technological Change*. Albany: State University of New York Press.

Huawei. (2012). 'Huawei's Digital Railway Solution Helps World First Alpine CTCS L3 High-speed Line to go into Passenger Operation', 5 December. Available at: http://pr.huawei.com/en/news/hw-198411-digitalrailway.htm#.WS61J2iGNhF.

Jilin-China, the Official Government Website of JiLin Province. (2015). '" CNR Changchun-made" Chinese-standard EMU Rolled Off the Production Line', 6 July. Available at: http://english.jl.gov.cn/News/GeneralNews/201507/t20150728_2047407.html.

Johnston, Alastair Iain. (2007). *Social states: China in international institutions, 1980–2000*. Princeton, NJ: Princeton University Press.

Li, Kangping. (2010). 'Zhongguo gaotie shidai de xinshenghuo', [A New Life in the New Era of Chinese High Speed Rails], *Guangming Daily* (*Guangming Daily*), 10 April, p. 7.

Lu, Bingyang. (2015). 'Zhongguo 350 gongli biaozhun dongchezu yangche 6 yue xiaxian', [China's 350km/h CEMU off the Assembly Line by June], *Caixin*, 12 May. Available at: http://companies.caixin.com/2015-05-13/100808753.html.

Luger, Katrin. (2008). *Chinese railways: Reform and efficiency improvement opportunities*. Heidelberg: Physica-Verlag.

Ma, Deyong, and Zhang, Zhiyuan. (2015). 'Guannian, quanli yu zhidu bianqian: tiedaobu tizhi de shehui yanhualun fenxi', [Ideas, Rights, and Institutional Evolution: An Analysis on Reform of Ministry of Railway from a Social Evolution Perspective], *Zhengzhixue yanjiu* (*CASS Journal of Political Science*), 5, pp. 96–110.

National Development and Reform Commission. (2016). 'Xianjin anquan, kaifang jianrong, zizhu kekong de zhongguo gaotie liekong xitong', [Advanced and Safe, Open and Compatible, and Self-Controlled Chinese High Speed Rail Control System], 6 July. Available at: http://www.ndrc.gov.cn/fzggz/wzly/jwtz/jwtzgk/201607/t20160706_810628.html.

National Development and Reform Commission. (2017). 'Guojia fagaiwei huitong shisan ge bumen he danwei jianli "yidai yilu" PPP gongzuo jizhi', [NDRC and 13 Ministries and Work Units Established a PPP Work Model for the Belt and Road Initiative], 6 January. Available at: http://www.ndrc.gov.cn/gzdt/201701/t20170106_834564.html. (Accessed 9 May 2017).

Norris, William. (2016). *Chinese economic statecraft: Commercial actors, grand strategy, and state control*. Ithaca and London: Cornell University Press.

Paltiel, Jeremy. (2017). 'Out of the Shadows: Xi Jinping and Peaceful Order in Post-hegemonic Asia', *ISA Annual Convention 2017*, Baltimore, the US, 22–25 February 2017.

Pearson, Margaret M. (2005). 'The business of governing business in China: Institutions and norms of the emerging regulatory state'. *World Politics*, 57 (2), pp. 296–322.

Pei, Minxin. (2006). *China's trapped transition: The limits of developmental autocracy*. Cambridge: Harvard University Press.

Reeves, Jeffrey. (2015). Economic statecraft, structural power, and structural violence in Sino-Kyrgyz relations. *Asian Security*, 11 (2), pp. 116–135.

Jiao, Yang, Liu, Li, and Liu, Chenguang. (2011). 'Ba zhongguo gaotie tuixiang shijie zhi dian', [Pushing Chinese High Speed Rails to the Top of the World], *Keji ribao* (*Science and Technology Daily*), 25 January, pp. 1 and 3.

Sohu Business. (2016). 'Gaotie chuangxin jixu: Zhongguo biaozhun dongchezu jiang chengwei xiayidai zhuli chexing', [High Speed Rails Continues to Innovate: CEMU Will Become the Main Model for the Next Generation of Trains], 15 June. Available at: http://business.sohu.com/20160615/n454531218.shtml.

The Beijing News. (2017). 'Youzheng yinhang 2000 duo yi zhichi tiezong tielu jianshe', [Postal Saving Bank of China will Provide More Than 200 Billion in Support of the CRC's Railway Construction], 12 May, pp. A17.

The State Council Information Office of the People's Republic of China. (2016). 'Fagaiwei juxing "zhongchangqi tieluwang guihua" youguan qingkuang xinwen fabuhui', [NDRC Holds Press Conference on "Med-and Long-term Railway Network Program"], 20 July. Available at: http://www.scio.gov.cn/xwfbh/gbwxwfbh/xwfbh/fzggw/Document/1484562/1484562.htm.

Urdinez, Francisco, et al. (2016). 'Chinese Economic Statecraft and US Hegemony in Latin America: An Empirical Analysis, 2003-2014'. *Latin American Politics and Society*, 58 (4), pp. 3–30.

Wang, Hongru, and Zhu, Jintao. (2015). 'Yatouhang, pingheng de zhidian', [The AIIB: A Point of Balance], *Zhongguo jingji zhoukan* (*China Economic Weekly*) 12, pp. 22–29 and 88.

Xinhua News Agency. (2016). 'Zhongguo biaozhun dongchezu shouce zaike yunxing', [CEMU Operates with Passenger for the First Time], Edited by Huang, Yue, 15 August. Available at: http://news.xinhuanet.com/politics/2016-08/15/c_129230065.htm.

Xu, Fei. (2016). 'Zhongguo gaotie "zouchuqu" de wu da zhangli', [Five Tension Points on the "Going Out" of China's High Speed Rails], a speech made at the *Fourth Summit on Globalization Strategy of China's High Speed Rails*. Leshan, China, 10 December 2016. Available at: http://edu.people.com.cn/n1/2016/1210/c1053-28939535.html.

Yeo, Yukyung. (2012). "Revisiting China's economic regulatory reform." *The Korean Journal of International Studies*, pp. 255–274.

Yin-nor, Linda Tjia. (2016) *Explaining railway reform in China: A train of property rights re-arrangement*. New York: Routledge.

Yu, Hong. (2015). "Railway sector reform in China: Controversy and problems." *Journal of Contemporary China*, 24 (96), pp. 1070–1091.

Zhao, Jian. (2016). *Reform and Restructure of the Chinese Railway Sector and Research on High Speed Rails*. Beijing: China Economic Publishing House.

Zhao, Yufei. (2017). 'Jizhe shouji: jianzheng zhongou banlie "zhangda"', [A Journalist's Diary: Witnessing the 'Maturing' of China-Europe Freight Rail Service], *Xinhua News Agency*, 14 April. Available at: http://news.xinhuanet.com/world/2017-04/14/c_1120811223.htm.

Zhen, Zhihong. et al. (2012). 'Zhongguo tielu tizhi yiwushichu? Cong bijiao de shiye kan gaotie', [Is China's Railway Regime all Wrong? Looking at the High Speed Rail from a Comparative Perspective], in Gao, B. (eds.) *The High Speed Rail and China's Grand Strategy in the 21st Century*. Beijing: Social Sciences Academic Press (China), pp. 50–76.

Zhu, Pengfei. (2015). 'Fahui zhongguo tielu youshi, fuwu "yidai yilu" guojia zhanlue', [Utilize Advantages of the Chinese Railway Sector and Serve the National Strategy of the Belt and Road Initiative], *Zhongguo keji rencai (Science and Technology Talents of China)*, September Edition, pp. 25–27.

Interview Codes

Interview with Shenyang Railway Bureau Cadre, Shenyang-China, 3 July 2013 – coded as 1373I

Interview with Guangzhou Railway Group Cadre, Guangzhou-China, 21 December 2016 – coded as 16121I

Interview with China Railway Corporation Cadre, Beijing-China, 18 February 2017 – coded as 1721I

Documents presented by the CRC

The CRC. (2015) *2015 yinni gaotie zhanlan ji fabuhui cailiao.* [*Materials on Chinese High Speed Rail Exhibit and Press Conference at Jakarta in 2015*].

The CRC. (2016) *Zhongguo gaotie ziliao* [*Materials on Chinese High Speed Rail Development*].

The CRC. (2017) *Tielu zongongsi 2017 nian neibu gongzuo huiyi xinwen sucai.* [*The CRC's 2017 Internal Work Meeting for Publication*].

7

The Transnational in China's Foreign Policy: The Case of Sino-Japanese Relations

CASPER WITS

When observing contemporary relations between the People's Republic of China (PRC) and Japan there seems to be a plethora of unresolved issues that strain the ties between the two countries; most importantly the disagreements regarding memory of the Second Sino-Japanese War (1937–1945) and the territorial dispute regarding the Diaoyu/Senkaku islands. Naturally, a priority when analysing modern China's relations with Japan should therefore be a focus on 'what went wrong'. Fortunately, ample research has been done on the history issue and territorial disputes in post-war Sino-Japanese relations, and how these hamper international relations in East Asia (Rose 1998, Rose 2005, Seraphim 2006, He 2009). At the same time this scholarship, as well as scholarship on the development of post-war Sino-Japanese trade (Soeya 1998; King 2016), has not ignored the remarkable progress made in bilateral relations between the two countries since 1945.

It is the latter angle, tracing 'what went right', that will be explored further in this chapter. We will draw attention to how the Chinese government utilised transnational networks as a basis for developing Sino-Japanese relations in the first decades of the Cold War (before 1972) and highlight how it was this element in bilateral relations that led to many of the breakthroughs and positive developments in the past. The period immediately after the war saw many countries in Asia and elsewhere newly liberated from imperialist control. This led to such initiatives as the non-aligned movement and the search for an alternative basis for international relations, not based on Cold War superpower rivalry, that culminated in the Bandung Conference of April 1955, at which Chinese Premier Zhou Enlai played a major role and where the Japanese were also represented. As Hilton and Mitter have put it, imperialism 'had inspired one set of global interconnections but the opposition to it provoked others' (Hilton and Mitter 2013, 8). While Japan's position in Asia at this moment was ambiguous as a former colonial power and a strong regional ally of the US, there was a lot of sympathy for these efforts among Japanese progressives, and this is where the Chinese saw an opening for conducting its interactions with Japan.

Especially in the first few decades after the founding of the PRC in 1949, the relationship between the two countries faced many difficulties, amplified by the fact that from 1949 to 1972 they did not have official diplomatic relations. The achievement of diplomatic normalisation in 1972 and the *Peace and Friendship Treaty* that was finally concluded in 1978 were the result of an intense process of bridge-building and (nominally) non-governmental contacts spanning decades. At the centre of these efforts was a transnational network involving people from both countries; a network that was in many ways deliberately cultivated by Zhou Enlai and the Chinese Japan hands under his guidance, thereby skilfully utilising the fact that their objectives had considerable support in Japan. Often referred to as People's Diplomacy (*renmin waijiao*) or People-to-People Diplomacy (*minjian waijiao*), the Chinese sought to overcome the fact that there were no official relations by appealing directly to the Japanese people and concentrating their interactions on them. With diplomatic normalisation and the *Peace and Friendship Treaty* a lot of these efforts came to fruition, and they also contributed to a steady improvement in relations, especially concerning trade, through the 1980s.

Many of the Chinese involved in the crafting of these ties had long-standing ties to Japan that were rooted in the pre-1945 era; for example, many were Overseas Chinese who had moved to the PRC from Japan shortly before or after 1949, or Chinese who came from the Northeast and had therefore been exposed to Japanese expansionism from a young age. Many Japanese of course had similar ties to China that could sometimes be traced back decades. Introducing the connections between such actors, and how such people-to-people ties influenced decision making, can provide us with a unique angle for locating modern China's relations with Japan, and the world, in broader 20th century transnational history.

Largely based on memoirs of the Chinese Japan specialists involved in People's Diplomacy, some of the main transnational actors and mechanisms active in Sino-Japanese relations will be introduced with the aim of tracing the deliberate use of such informal ties in China's relations with Japan. This approach gives us an idea of 'what went right' in Sino-Japanese relations and invites us to contemplate whether the past contains any positive lessons for the present. Since a lot of the Chinese tactics connected to People's Diplomacy were honed during the tenure of Japanese Prime Minister Kishi Nobusuke (1957–1960) and were aimed at cultivating ties with those in Japan opposed to Kishi's right-wing politics, this chapter implicitly raises the question of whether such networks can once again be utilised by the Chinese and those Japanese opposed to the policies of Kishi's grandson: current Prime Minister Abe Shinzō.

Japan's Reluctant Choice for Taiwan

With the signing of the Treaty of Taipei on 28 April 1952, Japan officially recognised the Republic of China (ROC) government of Chiang Kai-shek in Taiwan as the sole legitimate government of China. This reflected a new Cold War reality in which the US-Japan alliance was the determining factor for the Japanese government in shaping its foreign policy stance. Nonetheless there was enormous resistance against this among the Japanese public as well as among its leadership. The signing of the treaty was the result of intense US pressure on Japanese Prime Minister Yoshida Shigeru who, though he was a staunch anti-communist, was in fact convinced of the importance of trade with the PRC for Japan's economic growth, and therefore reluctant to forgo relations with Beijing entirely. This sentiment would foreshadow a remarkable engagement with the PRC among many Japanese mainstream and even conservative politicians, as well as the business community, in the following decades. An immediate and more visible reaction to Japan's becoming 'locked' into the US camp in the Cold War and how this robbed the country of many avenues for engagement with the PRC, came from Japanese progressives and the Japanese left. Grassroots organisations such as the *Japan-China Friendship Association* (JCFA), founded in October 1950, spoke for a significant portion of the Japanese people in arguing for the urgency of concluding a peace treaty and diplomatic normalisation with the PRC, without which 'the state of war continued to victimise both peoples – if not with bullets, then by preventing the settlement of humanitarian issues and economic recovery through trade' (Seraphim 2006, 110). Sentiments like these meant that there was great potential for the Chinese to establish people-to-people ties with a variety of Japanese. The initial initiative among Japanese for the improvement of Sino-Japanese relations via such associations as the JCFA was taken by people who had strong connections in China and had often lived there for years prior to 1945 as reluctant participants in Japanese expansionist endeavours. For example, two of the JFCA's prominent members were its first leader Uchiyama Kanzō, who had run a bookshop in Shanghai from 1917 to 1945 which had been a refuge for progressive Chinese intellectuals like Lu Xun; and Itō Takeo, a prominent member of the Research Department of the Southern Manchurian Railway who had spent a part of the war in jail (Seraphim 2006, 111).

China's People's Diplomacy

There were in fact a number of issues that inevitably had to lead to some interaction between the Chinese and Japanese, even with the absence of official relations. A priority for both sides in the 1950s and 1960s was the gradual expansion of Sino-Japanese trade, something that was seen in both countries as essential for reviving their economies after the war (King 2016). To that end several non-governmental trade agreements were signed, and by 1965 Japan had become the PRC's most important trading partner (King 2016, 2). Another issue that called for intense negotiations was the repatriation of the many Japanese still remaining in mainland China after the war. The successful repatriation of a large number of them from 1953 to 1956 was seen as an early success of China's People's Diplomacy and Beijing's cooperation on this issue led to more favourable views of the PRC in Japan (He 2009, 153). With the increase of exchanges in the 1960s came more breakthroughs like the establishment of permanent trade liaison offices and an exchange of foreign correspondents.

To coordinate and manage these interactions with Japanese, Zhou Enlai and his close confidant Liao Chengzhi, who was Director of the Overseas Chinese Affairs Office and a Central Committee member, formed an unofficial group of Japan hands from different branches of the government in the early 1950s, a group that came to be referred to as the *Japan Group*. Liao Chengzhi was in many ways the perfect example of someone whose transnational background made him equally at home in China and Japan. Born in Tokyo in 1908, he was the son of the famous Chinese exiles Liao Zhongkai, a KMT politician and activist, and He Xiangning, a feminist and artist who would later hold many important positions in the PRC, who were close associates of first Chinese President Sun Yat-sen. Liao grew up speaking fluent Japanese. Moving back and forth between the two countries until 1928, after which he would remain in China, he had become an early member of the Chinese Communist Party (CCP) and would become a Central Committee member in 1945. After 1949, Liao would be a central figure in overseas Chinese affairs and the key person responsible for the management of Sino-Japanese relations under Zhou Enlai. This management for a large part consisted of resurrecting and expanding Liao's own impressive transnational network spanning Japan and China, a network that would form the basis of People's Diplomacy. As one of Beijing's key Japan hands Wu Xuewen, a journalist at the *Xinhua* news agency, remembers:

> Liao Chengzhi had many Japanese friends: friends he had

inherited from his father Liao Zhongkai, friends from his studies in Japan when he was young, friends from the anti-Japanese struggle, friends from after the Second World War, and even more from after the founding of the new China; there were new friends that were introduced to him by, or that he got acquainted with via, old friends, as well as new friends introducing [more] new friends. He blended all these friends into Sino-Japanese 'People-to-People Diplomacy' (Wu and Wang 2007, 120).

Around him Liao Chengzhi assembled Japan hands with similar backgrounds who were fluent in Japanese. Three of them are worth mentioning here because it is their recollections on which this chapter is based: Sun Pinghua (from the *Chinese People's Association for Friendship with Foreign Countries*), Xiao Xiangqian (*Chinese People's Institute of Foreign Affairs*), and Wu Xuewen. These three Japan hands were all from the Northeast and had therefore lived in the *Manchukuo* puppet state, and they had studied in Japan before becoming active in the CCP and the 'anti-Japanese struggle'. Together with a small number of other Japan specialists they were encouraged by Liao to undertake a similar effort to befriend a large variety of Japanese. Since this same tight-knit group of people would take care of all Japanese visitors to the PRC, as well as accompany Chinese visiting groups to Japan, they could develop many personal ties with a large variety of people in the country. It was the crafting of these ties that was in many ways their long-term goal, a goal that transcended the topic of any specific negotiation (Wits 2016). As Wu Xuewen puts it:

> Starting with people exchange, [we would] work tirelessly to develop the traditional friendship between the Japanese and Chinese peoples…This was an unprecedented, large "systematic program" that needed an integrated specific long term policy. It required several generations of Chinese and Japanese people's combined efforts and abilities, to deal with the historical issues (Wu 2002, 27).

The ultimate goal of these transnational ties was to make them so strong they would make an eventual diplomatic normalisation inevitable. With the absence of official ties, the Chinese had no choice but to follow a policy of 'using the people as government officials' (*yimincuguan*). Wu Xuewen:

> For changing the relations into official government relations, they had to start from people's interaction, people-to-people diplomacy, and "using the people as government officials".

> This could lead the Japanese government to change its anti-Chinese policy; using an accumulative step-by-step method, working patiently and meticulously to return to official relations and realize the Peace and Friendship Treaty (Wu 2002, 27).

Negotiations on issues like trade and repatriation would be a window for the Chinese to expand their network further, and whenever a (nominally non-governmental) Chinese delegation would visit Japan, Liao and the other Japan hands would go to great lengths to meet as large an amount of people as possible in a more unofficial capacity. For example, when a Chinese Red Cross delegation visited Japan in 1954 to discuss the repatriation issue, Liao Chengzhi was a part of the delegation, his first visit in decades. Many people were eager to meet with Liao, and Xiao Xiangqian as secretary of the delegation was responsible for organising the many meetings that took place after the 'official' negotiations had finished. These additional meetings were with a large variety of people, and the discussions mostly unrelated to the issue that was the official reason for their visit. Lamenting that Japanese evening receptions seemed to be never-ending, Xiao crammed in as many 'unofficial' evening meetings as he could (Xiao 1994, 40).

The first Chinese delegations to Japan took place during the tenure of Japanese Prime Minister Hatoyama Ichirō (1954–1956) who favoured closer relations with the communist powers and realised diplomatic normalisation with the Union of Soviet Socialist Republics (USSR) in 1956. It seemed Sino-Japanese rapprochement was now also a possibility and the goal for the Chinese was to engage with Japanese government officials as much as possible, while ostensibly only engaging in People's Diplomacy. This strategy ran into difficulties when the conservative right-winger Kishi Nobusuke became Prime Minister of Japan in 1957. Sino-Japanese relations would see a steady deterioration during the Kishi years from 1957 to 1960, a period that would also see immense polarisation within Japanese society against Kishi's pro-US (and pro-Taiwan) politics. Interestingly, a reaction to this setback was to double down on the expansion of transnational ties with a wider variety of Japanese, beyond those active in politics and those already invested in the improvement of Sino-Japanese relations. The need to focus on a multitude of sectors in which ties could be cultivated, often with seemingly less political overtones was an aspect of People's Diplomacy that had already come in vogue from the mid-1950s, when

> The idea of the *Japan Group* was for all kinds of organisations to invite Japanese parliamentarians, business people, from culture and the arts, to encourage mutual understanding and friendship between the Chinese and Japanese peoples and a

> good working relationship; this was needed to develop [the relations] in a broader and deeper direction and to increase the substance (Wu 2002, 59).

In meetings evaluating the state of affairs in Sino-Japanese relations in 1955, the *Japan Group* decided that developing cultural exchange had to be a new priority from 1956 onwards (Wu and Wang 2007, 227). To this end former Prime Minister Katayama visited Beijing in 1955, signing an *Agreement on Japanese-Chinese Cultural Exchange* on November 27, which would lead to the establishment in Japan of the *Japan-China Cultural Exchange Association* the following year.

Another notable aspect here is that in addition to casting a wider net among Japanese, the Chinese also started linking their aims of improving Sino-Japanese relations more with the general anti-Kishi sentiment that was gathering steam in Japan in the late 1950s. For example, during the second visit of the Chinese Red Cross in December 1957, despite the unfavourable new situation under the Kishi government, the delegation members strove to continue building on ties already made:

> While the first visit was about making friends widely and entering a new phase, the second visit was about using that base to make a substantial step forward, in order to advance Sino-Japanese friendship in a more broad, more deep, and more dynamic direction. The common view of the Chinese and Japanese peoples was that for the development of Sino-Japanese friendship the two aspects of strengthening Sino-Japanese exchange and firmly opposing Kishi Nobusuke's anti-China policy were both indispensable (Wu and Wang 2007, 179).

The last sentence makes clear that the Chinese now saw a need to invest in ties with a wide net of Japanese progressives, whose goals were potentially aligned with their own. One avenue for interaction was activism concerning nuclear non-proliferation activism, something in which Japan was somewhat of a pioneer. According to Hilton and Mitter, citizens' concerns about nuclear weapons were a global phenomenon and something that generated many transnational interactions, something in which the Chinese were also active (Hilton and Mitter 2013, 8). People-to-people exchanges with all sectors from Japanese society were now encouraged in order to promote Sino-Japanese friendship and most of all to bring about a change in Japan's China policy. In the eyes of the Chinese active in this was a great success:

> Among the Japanese friends that Liao Chengzhi made were well-known people from [the fields of] economics, politics, culture, education, labour, youth and women's [organisations], religion, and so on, many of society's leaders from all sections of Japanese society and who all had influence in their fields (Wu and Wang 2007, 120).

Many of these ties would continue to deepen during the government of Ikeda Hayato (1960–1964) which was again much more favourably disposed towards Beijing. The many people-to-people exchanges taking place in this period led to the creation of the *China-Japan Friendship Association* (CJFA), founded by the Chinese on October 3, 1963. This is much later than its Japanese counterpart (founded in 1950, as mentioned earlier). According to Sun Pinghua the Chinese had resisted the creation of such an association because of the anti-China policies of successive Japanese governments (Sun 1998, 118). While there were and are many Chinese organs for the promotion of People's Diplomacy, this was the first such organ aimed at a particular country. Its goal was mainly to serve as a bridge for people in China; between those working with Japan and groups that might be interested in exchange with Japan. Xiao Xiangqian describes the association's activities within China as 'bringing together those in the frontline of Japan-related work [on the one hand] with academics, cultural figures, and nongovernmental associations in Beijing [on the other]. There were basically no other foreign friendship organisations [in China] where such a colourful collection of people would be assembled' (Xiao 1994, 115).

From Transnational to Diplomatic Interaction

While the numerous nongovernmental exchanges served the purpose of promoting a favourable image of the PRC in Japan and generally increasing China's leverage, these kinds of delegations also served as a convenient cover to send some of the *Japan Group* members to Japan to engage in semi-official negotiations while remaining somewhat under the radar. This was useful so as not to draw the ire of right-wing and pro-Taiwan politicians.

The Japan hand who was employed like this most frequently was Sun Pinghua. On several occasions he was sent to Japan for meetings with political figures, often in preparation for breakthrough visits to China by people like the parliamentarian Matsumura Kenzō, who was the leader of the pro-China faction in the ruling LDP. For example, with the ongoing talks concerning Sino-Japanese trade that would eventually lead to the establishment of trade liaison offices, the Chinese sent Sun to Japan in July 1962 as part of a Chinese delegation of Go players, undeterred by the fact that Sun had not mastered the game (Sun 1998, 105–106). During the same period of intense negotiations concerning both trade and an exchange of journalists, three Japan hands would be sent to Japan again, when Matsumura and Liao decided a delegation of Chinese orchid specialists should visit Japan in April 1963. Matsumura was an orchid lover but the real reason for sending the orchid connoisseurs to Japan was so that they could be escorted by Sun Pinghua and others, to serve as, as Sun put it: 'Orchid Envoys'. In Japan they met many important people from the business world, as well as the government (Sun 1998, 111–115). Probably the most important case was in the summer of 1972 when Sun was added to the delegation of the Shanghai Ballet Troupe to Japan, again notwithstanding his ignorance of the art, in order to discuss a possible Sino-Japanese diplomatic normalisation with the Japanese leadership (Sun 1998, 136–144). Needless to say, this 'Go Diplomacy' and 'Orchid Diplomacy' seems like a prelude to the famous 'Ping-Pong Diplomacy' that contributed to Sino-American rapprochement and in which Japan also played a central role (Itoh 2011). The transnational ties cultivated through people-to-people interaction would prove their use in the heady days before Sino-Japanese rapprochement was finally achieved in September 1972, when the lack of official ties made the network of friendship more important than ever:

> Especially on the eve of diplomatic normalisation, many of Liao Chengzhi's old Japanese friends went back and forth between Tokyo and Beijing, passing on China and Japan's principles and tentative plans regarding the resumption of relations, and even the draft of a joint statement, thereby connecting the paths of Sino-Japanese 'People-to-People Diplomacy' and inter-governmental negotiations, and smoothly realizing the normalisation of diplomatic relations. This was unprecedented in the history of international relations and diplomacy (Wu and Wang 2007, 121).

Conclusion

While in the new era after 1972 the role of People's Diplomacy and transnational networks would be to a large extent superseded by connections on a governmental level, with the current impasse in bilateral relations it is worth looking to the past to learn from the mechanisms that have contributed to the many achievements in post-war Sino-Japanese relations. The idea of stimulating people-to-people interaction is something that has been gaining traction with Chinese scholars such as Zhiqun Zhu calling for People-to-People Diplomacy between China and Japan as a way to counter the current downward spiral (Zhu 2015). The experience in the 1949–1972 era shows that transnational networks, both those that already existed and a variety of newly crafted connections, could be put to use for the achievement of political goals. While conditions, at a time such that international structures connected to the Cold War and the need for trade with Japan made Beijing open to Sino-Japanese interaction in a way that may be less prevalent now, it remains a potent example of how civic action across borders can change seemingly rigid political realities. Opportunities are manifold, with quantitative interaction now much higher than during the period discussed in this chapter, whether its foreign students, cultural figures, or business people doing the interacting.

References

He, Yinan. *The Search for Reconciliation: Sino-Japanese and German-Polish Relations since World War II*. Cambridge UK: Cambridge University Press, 2009.

Hilton, Matthew, and Rana Mitter. "Introduction." *Past and Present*, Supplement 8: 7–28, 2013.

Itoh, Mayumi. "Mr. Gotō Goes to Beijing: The Origin of Ping-Pong Diplomacy." *Sino-Japanese Studies* 18, 2011.

King, Amy. *China-Japan Relations after World War Two: Empire, Industry and War, 1949–1971*. Cambridge: Cambridge University Press, 2016.

"People-to-People Diplomacy in China-Japan Relations"; *The Diplomat*; Zhiqun Zhu; http://thediplomat.com/2015/03/people-to-people-diplomacy-in-china-japan-relations/; March 17, 2015; Accessed: June 29, 2017.

Rose, Caroline. *Interpreting History in Sino-Japanese Relations*. London: Routledge, 1998.

Rose, Caroline. *Sino-Japanese Relations: Facing the past, looking to the future?* NY: Routledge, 2005.

Sun, Pinghua. *Chūgoku to Nihon no hashi wo kaketa otoko* [The man who built a bridge between China and Japan]. Tokyo: Nihon keizai shimbunsha, 1998.

Seraphim, Franziska. *War memory and social politics in Japan, 1945–2005*. Cambridge, MA: Harvard University Press, 2006.

Soeya, Yoshihide. *Japan's economic diplomacy with China, 1945–1978*. Oxford UK: Oxford University Press, 1998.

Wits, Casper. "The Japan Group: Managing China's People's Diplomacy Toward Japan in the 1950s." *East Asia* 33 (2): 91–110, 2016.

Wu, Xuewen. *Fengyu yinqing: Wo suo jinglide Zhongri guanxi* [Good Times, Bad Times: My experience of Sino-Japanese Relations]. Beijing: Shijie zhishi chubanshe, 2002.

Wu, Xuewen, and Wang Junyan. *Liao Chengzhi yu Riben* [Liao Chengzhi and Japan]. Beijing: Zhonggongdangshi chubanshe, 2007.

Xiao, Xiangqian. *Tokoshie no rinkoku to shite* [Good Neighbours Forever]. Tokyo: Saimaru shuppansha, 1994.

8

Soviet Foreign Policy in the Early 1980s: A View from Chinese Sovietology

JIE LI

This chapter will examine the analyses of Chinese Soviet-watchers of Soviet foreign policy against the larger context of China's political setting in the early 1980s, before the rise of Mikhail Gorbachev in 1985, and investigate how those Chinese scholars placed post-Mao Chinese official agendas centrally in their research. It is going to demonstrate that in the early 1980s, Chinese research on Soviet hegemonism (*baquan zhuyi*), Soviet-Yugoslavian conflicts, and Soviet-Third World relations all reflected Beijing's ambitions of challenging the orthodox Soviet model of economic development in the socialist world, competing with the Kremlin for leadership in developing countries, and projecting a fair and benevolent image of Chinese socialism vis-à-vis Moscow. In short, Chinese research of Soviet foreign policy in the early 1980s had primarily been to trace problems of Chinese socialism as experienced by scholars at the time of their research; this was done in order to legitimise state agendas, rather than to seek truth about the Union of the Soviet Socialist Republics (USSR).

With respect to primary sources, it should be mentioned here that this research is based predominantly on the 'national core journals' (*Guojiaji hexin qikan*) published in the People's Republic of China (PRC), such as those dealing with problems of socialism or communism in the world, and the ones concentrating on questions and issues relating to the former Soviet Union. Moreover, the research intends to examine the thinking of Chinese Sovietologists against the backdrop of political changes in early 1980s China. Therefore, China's Party newspapers and journals, and the writings and speeches of contemporary Chinese leaders were also consulted.

The use of the term 'Sovietologists' (or Soviet-watchers) in this paper for those who study and research the state of the USSR is based on Christopher Xenakis' definition. Xenakis defines US Sovietologists broadly, to include 'political scientists, economists, sociologists, historians, diplomats and policy makers'. He uses the terms 'Sovietologists', 'Soviet experts', 'foreign policy analysts', 'Cold War theorists', and 'political scientists' interchangeably, citing the examples of George Kennan, Zbigniew Brzezinski, Richard Pipes, and Strobe Talbott. These individuals are both Soviet-specialists and policy makers, while Hedrick Smith and Robert Kaiser are also Soviet-watchers and journalists simultaneously (Xenakis 2002, 4).

In terms of this elastic definition of the field and the diversity of scholars' backgrounds, the situation in China is generally similar to the situation in the US as described by Xenakis. For example, as we shall see, although some Chinese scholars specialise in either Soviet or world communism, most of those mentioned and quoted in this paper are generalists rather than specialists in Soviet studies. Their articles often express more political zeal than scholarly expertise or analytical insight. Generally speaking, the descriptions by Xenakis of US Sovietologists could also be applied to the Chinese situation. Although the academic training of Chinese Soviet-watchers is in different disciplines and by no means confined to Soviet studies, their research and publications are relevant to Sovietology in one way or another.

Perceptions of Soviet Hegemonism

In the early 1980s, when Sino-Soviet relations were in estrangement and the 1979 Soviet invasion of Afghanistan had exacerbated bilateral relations, the Chinese communist regime called for the state-wide denunciation of so-called Soviet hegemonism. After that, Chinese Soviet-watchers became preoccupied with criticising Soviet hegemonism in their writings. As we will see, both the real Soviet military threat along the PRC border after Moscow's incursion into Afghanistan, and the historical memory of the past Russian invasion of China played key roles in intensifying the hostility of Chinese scholars towards the USSR in the early 1980s.

Deng Xiaoping, who was already the preeminent leader of China after the passing of Mao Zedong, understood the gravity of the Soviet military threat to Chinese security. In a Chinese Communist Party (CCP) Central Committee meeting in 1980, he claimed that 'opposing hegemonism will be on our daily agenda', and 'the struggle against hegemonism is a grave task constantly confronting our country' (Deng 1995, vol 2, 241). Deng once defined 'hegemonism' as denoting the situation when a country 'becomes arrogant' and 'acts like an overlord and gives orders to the world' (Deng 1995, vol 2,

123).

David Shambaugh in his book on Chinese scholarly perceptions of America has devoted several pages to ascertaining the Chinese concept of hegemony. A Chinese scholar at Renmin University defined the term in the following words during an interview he gave to the author:

> When we use this term in China, we mean big countries that try to control or interfere in smaller countries. Many scholars mix up imperialism and hegemony. We do not know if it is a system or a policy. Before the 1980s we thought it was a system, like Soviet social-imperialism. We now define hegemony as a policy. For example, in the past when we called the United States imperialist we meant the system; today we use hegemony to describe its foreign policy (Shambaugh 1991, 79).

Since the Soviet invasion of Afghanistan, accusations of so-called Soviet hegemonism had carried weight within Soviet studies in China. In the first issue of *Xiandai guoji guanxi* (Contemporary International Relations) published by Beijing University in 1981, the editor stated clearly that the journal was committed to 'opposing hegemony, safeguarding world peace, and striving for a favourable international environment' (Editor 1981, 64). In January 1981, in the first issue of *Sulian dongou wenti* (Matters of the Soviet Union and Eastern Europe) published by the Chinese Academy of Social Sciences (CASS), the journal editor Liu Keming criticised the Soviet leadership for causing the first socialist country to degenerate into 'a social imperialist state', and making the USSR become 'the principal source of turmoil in the international society' (Liu 1981, 1). He argued:

> In order to safeguard world peace, it is essential to do research on policies, theories, and origins of Soviet hegemonism, reveal the true face of it, and make people realise its nature and danger. This is an important mission of our studies of Soviet problems (Liu 1981, 1).

The application of the term hegemonism throughout the history of the PRC has been quite evolutionary. In the early days of the regime, the use of the term was in the context of confrontations between the 'two camps' during the Cold War. It was limited to describing the capitalist US and its allies only (Mao 1993, vol 8, 354). During the early days of Sino-Soviet discord in the late 1950s, China started to criticise Moscow's policy of peaceful coexistence with the West and its intention to control Beijing via the construction of long-wave radio stations in Chinese territory (Chen and Yang 1998, 270). In the early 1960s, when Sino-Soviet relations deteriorated, the PRC intensified its attack on the USSR, accusing Moscow of promoting its own values and institutions abroad in a way that resembled 19th century colonialism (Friedman 2015, 40).

According to Shambaugh, the turning point occurred in 1968, when the term 'hegemonism' was employed by the Chinese to denounce Soviet aggression in Czechoslovakia and the 'Brezhnev Doctrine' (Shambaugh 1991, 78). This is because the Brezhnev statement justifying the Soviet invasion had provided a basis for possible future intervention in other socialist states. China immediately felt the danger of such logic and responded vociferously to Moscow (Boyle 1993, 161). The occasion stood as the major component in the escalation of Sino-Soviet tensions and the Kremlin was thereafter equated with hegemonism in China. By the early 1970s, Chinese scholars had begun to fuse 'social-imperialism' together with 'hegemonism' when referring to the Soviet Union, which was being described as 'socialist in word, imperialist in deed'. In their point of view, 'Imperialism refers to capitalist countries while hegemonism refers to countries regardless of system' (Shambaugh 1991, 78–79).

After the passing of Mao, many Chinese scholars were still locked in Maoist rhetoric in the early 1980s. In 1981, CASS Vice-President Qian Junrui demanded that Chinese scholars use 'Mao Zedong Thought' to 'guide our research on the present questions of international relations'. He emphasised that Mao's 'Three Worlds' concept was still 'our theoretical basis and strategic framework', which guided 'the country's cooperation with the Third and Second World, and resistance to the superpowers and Soviet hegemonism in particular' (Qian 1981, 1).[1] To take an example, CASS scholar Xu Kui used the words 'hegemonism', 'global expansionism', and 'socialist imperialism' more than ten times to depict Soviet activities in the world in his 1981 five-page article (Xu 1981, 10–14).

Chinese scholars may define hegemonism by the West as the oppressiveness of capitalism and colonisation. In the case of the Soviet Union, they used the term to refer not only to the Soviet Union's violation of others' sovereignties, but also Moscow's poking its nose into other countries' affairs, as well as its unequal treatment of the socialist member states by subjecting them to the Soviet model. It was a term used by the Chinese to target Moscow's paternalism in the socialist camp of which China was a member. Up to the early 1980s, using the language of hegemonism to portray the Soviets in the PRC reflected China's ambition of competing with the

---

1   On Mao Zedong's 'Three Worlds' theory, see Mao 1993, vol. 8, 441.

Kremlin for leadership in the Third World and the socialist camp. The term, as used by the Chinese, attempted to emphasise that China was a true socialist country while the USSR was not, and to emphasise that the faults of Sino-Soviet conflicts were on the side of the aggressive Moscow.

Chinese criticism of Soviet hegemonism is not only the legacy of the Mao era. The Chinese have long had vivid memories of Tsarist Russia as one of the Western intruders who conspired to take over China over the centuries. In their research on the history of Russian invasions of China and its killing of Chinese inhabitants during the Boxer Uprising and Russo-Japanese War in the early 20th century, Chinese scholars in the early 1980s always equated Tsarist behaviours with contemporary Soviet chauvinism (Liu 1980, 167-168; Zhou 1983, 92–96). In the eyes of the Chinese, Moscow's present search for global supremacy was no more than a Tsarist tradition, 'disguised by the cover of socialism' (Li 1981, 25). Besides, some Chinese scholars in the early 1980s tended to fault the present Soviet regime for being reluctant to abrogate the unequal treaties that the Tsarist government had signed with imperial China. In their writings, they demanded the return of the lost territories that had resulted from those treaties (Zhou and Shi 1980, 104–112; Chen 1981, 45–46). By presenting the history of Soviet hegemonism and aggression in China in this way, these scholars hoped to mobilise support for China's stand in the Sino-Soviet border negotiation taking place then.[2]

Moreover, at the time Sino-Soviet relations were still in a stalemate, aggravated by the long-time shadow of Tsarist intrusions and Sino-Soviet conflicts since the 1960s. It is thus no surprise that the Soviet occupation of Afghanistan, a country neighbouring China, would produce a grave perceived threat to the PRC in the early 1980s. In January 1980, an anonymous commentary with a sinister tone appeared in the CCP mouthpiece *Renmin ribao* (People's Daily):

> Once the Soviet Union has pushed its military force into the Persian Gulf and Indian subcontinent, it sends a dangerous signal. It shows that the USSR will continue its attack on Iran, Pakistan, and other countries. People should not assume that Moscow would target Afghanistan only. There is an urgent question before us: which country will become the next Afghanistan (Remin ribao 1980, 3)?

Chinese scholars not only were critical of the Soviet invasion of Afghanistan, but also felt suspicious of Moscow's desire in advancing on China. CASS scholar Yu Sui warned, 'Both the Soviet invasion of Afghanistan and its

---

2   On the Sino-Soviet border talk in the early 1980s, see Li 1981, 2.

support of Vietnamese occupation of Cambodia would pose a grievous threat to the security of Asia and China' (Yu 1983, 5). Xing Shugang, another CASS specialist in Soviet foreign relations, pointed out that 'Soviet troops stationing in Asia is nothing other than encircling the PRC, sowing discord between China and its neighbouring countries, and obstructing the progress of China's modernisation' (Xing 1981, 4). It seems that Chinese accusations of Soviet hegemony were not merely politically motivated. The Chinese did not want to see Moscow's expansionism becoming rampant in the world, as China would likely suffer from this situation. Chinese denunciation of Soviet hegemonism indicated not only China's long memories of Russian humiliation, but also its feeling of being uncomfortable and insecure when Moscow extended its large military presence on the Chinese border.

Treatment of Soviet Relations with Yugoslavia and the Third World

With regard to Soviet foreign relations with other countries in the early 1980s, the analysis of Chinese scholars corresponded closely with the tone of post-Mao China's state policies. They attempted to respond to and legitimise China's official agendas through their research. There is one particularly significant example of the Chinese treatment of the Soviet-Yugoslavian relations. Although Mao Zedong once branded Yugoslavia as 'revisionist' (Mao 1974, 189), a derogatory term used to stigmatise any socialist countries opting for capitalist reforms, in the 1980s Yugoslavia became the centre of attention in the PRC. Under Deng, China's foreign policy resembled Yugoslavia's stance of being non-aligned and non-confrontational (*Remin ribao* 1984, 2).[3] Chinese leaders greatly admired Belgrade's spirit in defiance of what was seen as Moscow's overlordship, evidenced by Party General Secretary Hu Yaobang's 1983 high appraisal of 'Josip Tito's principles of independence and equality among all communist parties, and of opposing imperialism, colonialism, and hegemonism' (Liu 1983, 3).

Some articles by Chinese scholars in the early 1980s shared the official claims to promote the case of Yugoslavia in their research. Jiang Qi, a professor of international relations at East China Normal University, regarded Moscow's expelling Belgrade from the socialist camp in 1948 as owing to the latter's uncompromising attitude. He remarked, 'It was the origin of anti-hegemony struggle in Eastern Europe' (Jiang 1983, 7). Cai Kang, another scholar at East China Normal University, wrote, 'The non-aligned policy has evolved from a strategy of Yugoslavia to an international movement', and 'it has broken through the shadow of the Soviet-type foreign policy model for the

---

3   The Editorial stated that both 'China and Yugoslavia are pursuing independent and self-reliant foreign policies, and regarding world peace and human progress as major goals of our common international agendas'.

first time in socialist history' (Cai 1984, 43).

Apart from its non-aligned foreign policy, Yugoslavia's economic model (which had shaken the dominant position of Soviet-style socialism) also became an important reason to gather the Chinese support of Belgrade's struggle against the Soviet rivalry. When ailing President Josip Tito's health condition deteriorated, the event became a paramount concern of *Renmin ribao* in the first half of 1980. At the time, the official organ of the CCP carried day-to-day reports from Belgrade, wishing for Tito's recovery and glorifying his contributions. After Tito's death, during the memorial ceremony held in the Yugoslavian Embassy in Beijing, the first CASS President and CCP ideologue Hu Qiaomu paid the following tribute to Tito and Yugoslavian inspiration:

> Comrade Tito's greatest contribution to the contemporary communist movement was that he was the first one to recognise that socialism should not be confined to one model. He initiated a new way of building socialism suited to the concrete conditions of Yugoslavia. Yugoslavia did not follow the over-centralised economic pattern introduced by the Soviet Union. Led by Tito, the Yugoslav people have broken away from the conventional Soviet methods which were formerly considered inviolable, and have blazed a new trail to develop a socialist economy. The Yugoslavian example provided valuable experience for other countries to choose their own road of socialist construction according to their specific conditions (Qi 1980, 1).

In the wake of the Maoist decades, China found that the Soviet model disguised by Maoism had made China poor and backward. China under Deng was eager to find a new way to make China a prosperous and strong socialist country. Yugoslavia's reform experience initiated by Tito, which included the mixing of central planning and market mechanisms and took a distinctive approach to socialism by disregarding the orthodox Soviet methods, struck a chord with the Chinese. Such a distinctive model is exactly the direction of post-Mao China's reforms. Many academic articles in the early 1980s expressed their approval of Yugoslavian socialism in preference to the dogmatic Soviet orthodoxy, and showed a strong desire to learn from Belgrade (Jiang 1982, 58; Wang 1984, 26–32; Zhao 1984, 77).

As such, Chinese scholars' open advocacy of Yugoslavia's position in its conflicts with Moscow was due to not only China's similar stance in non-aligned policy and anti-Soviet hegemony, but also to China's receptivity to Yugoslavia's unique reform experience. After the PRC became economically successful in the early 1980s, Chinese scholars would sometimes speak of Yugoslavia as a sort of maverick, as a countervailing weight to the Soviet brand of socialism. This in turn would validate the exception of the Chinese way of practicing socialism. The treatment of Yugoslavia, in particular, reflects the increasing confidence of Chinese scholars. They were arguing that Moscow should accept a less centralised and more diverse socialist world.[4] Chinese scholars' clear-cut stand on supporting the post-Mao CCP policy of integrating Marxism with China's concrete circumstances and heralding the vision of the rise of Chinese-style socialism, could be reflected in their analysis of Soviet-Yugoslavian troubled relations.

In the early 1980s China did not fail to notice the rise of the Third World, which would play a crucial role in international relations and become a partner with China to contain the superpowers – at least in the CCP's strategic worldview. During his 1982 talk with Javier Perez de Cuellar, Secretary-General of the United Nations, Deng Xiaoping remarked that the international influence of the Third World 'has increased considerably', and 'cannot be overlooked'. He stated that the foundation of China's foreign policy was 'opposing hegemonism and safeguarding world peace', which was also 'the position and immediate interests of the Third World'. Therefore, it would be essential for China and the region to 'strengthen unity and cooperation' (Deng 1995, vol 2, 407–408).

Concomitant with this strategic perspective, Chinese scholars attempted to use post-Mao China's Third World policy as their theoretical framework for analysis. Chinese scholars in the early 1980s seemed to view Soviet relations with the Third World through the prism of Sino-Soviet friction. Their arguments on the subject look more like explaining and demonstrating China's different treatment of the Third World, rather than genuine research of the Soviet policy in the region. In their articles, Chinese scholars strenuously promoted and defended the case of the Third World. Their arguments indirectly symbolised China's stance in challenging the Soviet authority, appealed for the redress of past historical wrongdoings on China done by Tsarist Russia and the Soviet Union, and promoted the moral superiority of Chinese socialism over that of the USSR.

During Mao's later period, China did not receive much goodwill from the Third World, mainly owing to Mao's excessive obsession with bringing Chinese-based socialism to the poor nations. Such a strategy of exporting revolutions had caused resentment in numerous countries, particularly those in Southeast Asia, where it led to a widespread anti-China sentiment (Bolt 2000,

---

4   The Soviet Union in the early 1980s was still unwilling to recognise that China's post-Mao reforms are genuinely socialist in nature. See Marsh 2005, 131-132.

43-47). Before Mao's death in 1976, the PRC was crippled not only by economic stagnation but also international isolation. In the wake of Maoist decades, the new leader Deng Xiaoping expected PRC foreign policy to detach from the radical determinant of Maoism and return to the realities of modern international politics (Deng 1995, vol 2, 248–249). The post-Mao leadership envisioned that China would become a progressive anti-colonial Asian power symbolised by its break with the Kremlin and the Maoist burden, and a true friend of the underdeveloped world (Wang 1985, 42).

In tune with the official view, some Chinese scholars portrayed Moscow as having taken advantage of numerous conflicts to interfere in the Third World, subjecting others to its beck and call (Xing 1981, 8–9; Zhang 1982, 19; Xie 1984, 45). These articles tend to exaggerate the gravity of Soviet hostility and Moscow's ability to dominate the world, although such radical views began to trail off after Gorbachev's accession. Most of the writings presented above seem to conclude that the Soviet Union had achieved complete failure in its relations with underdeveloped countries, become the only troublemaker and common enemy of the world, and ended up in having no friend in the global society.

Meanwhile, Chinese official organs attempted to foster a new image of China. They posited that the country was far from being isolated in the international community after the death of Mao; rather, it had joined the whole world to contain the advance of the superpowers (Mao 1980, 5; Cui 1981, 25). In 1981, Foreign Minister Huang Hua suggested to his Canadian colleague Mark MacGuigan, that China and the West should establish close ties on the basis of containing Soviet aggressive behaviour in the Third World (Li 1981, 1). On another occasion, he remarked that by carrying the banner of anti-hegemony, China would be able to increase its influence in the Third World, which would be conducive to its global status and open-door policy (Ma 1981, 3).

In 1982, CASS scholar Zhang Jinglin claimed that, along with a broad base of the Third World countries, 'An international anti-Soviet camp consisting of China and the West has developed rapidly' (Zhang 1982, 3). Two years later, both Li Jingjie (a CASS researcher) and Zhou Jirong (a professor of political science at Beijing University) agreed that after becoming stabilised and stronger, China would play a larger role in international affairs, namely by halting the war and safeguarding peace (Li 1984, 19; Zhou 1984, 23). These authors seemingly made use of their subject study to argue that China after Mao was far from being separated from the world. Instead, China under Deng was re-engaging the world and earning respect from international society by joining the global campaign against the Soviet advance. As a result of such sharp Chinese denunciations of Moscow's expansionism, the West became eager for Chinese cooperation and sought to aid Chinese reforms, in order to ally with China in resisting the USSR (Lukin 2003, 216).

There are three other reasons for why Chinese scholars had a strong bias towards the Third World and sympathised with those countries involved when it came to Soviet-Third World relations. The first one may be historical. In the eyes of the CCP, both China and other underdeveloped countries shared the common experience of falling prey to imperialist encroachment in the past (Xu 1983, 3), and China, in particular, had been invaded by Tsars since the early modern period and treated unfairly by the Soviet regime after 1949 (Deng 1995, vol 3, 285–287). This historical background of complicated Sino-Soviet Russian relations was deeply rooted in the collective Chinese mind, and inevitably affected the writings of Chinese scholars (Li 2012, 37). Several articles in the early 1980s evidenced a strong grudge against the unequal relations between Moscow and the Third World. They condemned the forced Soviet model of socialism as a kind of neo-colonisation, which did not benefit the Third World, but instead made them backward and isolated (Zhang 1982, 6; Yu 1983, 4; Hong 1983, 49).

Moreover, in the early 1980s some Chinese writings voiced criticism of the Soviet invasion of Afghanistan as being contradictory to the first Soviet leader Vladimir Lenin's principle of internationalism (Lenin 1967, 26–29). On the other hand, they portrayed China as having wholeheartedly supported the Afghan resistance and the emancipation of other Third World nations, while never meddling in their affairs. According to those writings, China was the true disciple of Lenin's teachings, while Moscow's behaviour was incompatible with Leninist internationalism (Fang 1982, 35; Lu 1983, 17; Shen 1983, 9–10). This picture of the PRC as enlightened and committed to fulfilling its internationalist responsibility to the Third World is not a contemporary invention. Mao Zedong once put forth that CCP members should 'build China into a great and powerful socialist country and help the broad masses of the oppressed and exploited throughout the world in fulfilment of our great internationalist duty' (Mao 1993, vol 8, 320). In the 1980s, Chinese Premier Zhao Ziyang said that the aid work to the Third World was China's 'compelling internationalist obligation' (Feng 1983, 2).

Thus, we can see that post-Mao China was aspiring to gain the upper hand over the Soviet Union in the name of the struggle against hegemonism, and more importantly, in the fight for moral leadership over the Third World. By using Lenin's internationalism to accuse Moscow of being chauvinistic, self-serving, and exploitative in its relations with the underdeveloped countries, Chinese scholars instead would project a fair, humble, and benevolent image of Beijing, enabling it to assume the moral high ground vis-à-vis Moscow.

Last, from the early 1980s onwards the post-Mao reforms led to substantial expansion of Chinese national power and a notable growth in its international prestige and influence, while the Soviet Union was in the grip of economic difficulties. Chinese scholars shared a growing pride in what China had accomplished so far vis-à-vis what they saw as the demoralised USSR. Yang Zhangming, a professor at Tongji University in Shanghai, said that many Third World states had been influenced by China and Yugoslavia to develop socialism according to their own conditions, while distancing themselves from 'some socialist states that would offer aid, but with aid, came interference' (Yang 1984, 84). Du Xiaoqiang, a scholar at Qinghua University, suggested that after China's success in reforms, its distinctive style of socialism might 'weaken the impact of the Soviet model on the Third World' (Du 1984, 6).

Chinese scholars at this stage lost no time in seizing the opportunity to portray China as the beacon of the Third World, by professing its respect to other countries' sovereignties and institutions, publicising its divergence with the Kremlin, and promoting the friendship and brotherhood between China and the developing nations. This was done in the hope that Chinese-style socialism would have greater appeal than the Soviet model and take root in not only the poor countries but the wider global society as well.

Conclusion

In the early 1980s, Chinese discussions on Soviet foreign relations with other countries corresponded closely to the PRC's real security concerns on its border, its historical memories of the wrongdoings done by Tsarist Russia and the USSR, and the principle of post-Mao China's Soviet policy. As such, seen from the early 1980s Chinese criticisms of Soviet foreign policy, Chinese Soviet-watchers endeavoured to propagandise and justify PRC's post-Mao domestic and international agendas through their subject study.

As has been demonstrated, Chinese Soviet-watchers did not present many vicissitudes of Soviet international manoeuvres in their writings; instead, through research on the formation and evolution of Soviet foreign policy, they attempted to adjust their analyses to align with China's vision of itself and the world. While not a determinant in China's foreign policy making, Chinese Sovietology is not able to remain outside the confines of Chinese politics. The Party guidepost always transcends the academic norm. Seen from the article, Chinese Sovietology, by providing both principles and tactics, had been making assessments and proposing solutions on economic and political aspects of contemporary China, friendships and struggles in PRC's international relations. Through the interplay of politics and scholarship, scholars attempted to legitimise the CCP rule and the Chinese way of practicing socialism, as well as projected and envisioned the future of China in the reform era.

References

Primary Sources

Cai, Kang 蔡抗. 1984. "Zhanhou nansilafu waijiao zhengcede yanbianhe bujiemeng." 战后南斯拉夫外交政策的演变和不结盟 [The Evolution of Post-war Yugoslavian Foreign Policy and the Non-aligned Movement], *Shijie jingjiyu zhengzhi* 世界经济与政治 (*World Economics and Politics*) 4: 37–43.

Chen, Liankai 陈连开. 1981. "Lunzhongguo lishi shangde jiangyuyu minzu." 论中国历史上的疆域与民族 [On Territories and Nationalities in Chinese History], *Zhongyang minzu daxue xuebao* 中央民族大学学报 (*Journal of the Central University of Nationalities*) 4: 44–51.

Cui, Weibing. 1981. "China Belongs Forever to the Third World." *Beijing Review*, September 28, 25.

Deng, Xiaoping. 1995. "Realize the Four Modernizations and Never Seek Hegemony." May 7, 1978, In *Selected Works of Deng Xiaoping*, edited and translated by the Bureau for the Compilation and Translation of Works of Marx, Engels, Lenin and Stalin under the Central Committee of the Communist Party of China, vol 2, 122–123. Beijing: Foreign Languages Press.

—— "The Present Situation and the Tasks before Us." January 16, 1980, In *Selected Works of Deng Xiaoping*, edited and translated by the Bureau for the Compilation and Translation of Works of Marx, Engels, Lenin and Stalin under the Central Committee of the Communist Party of China, vol 2, 241–272. Beijing: Foreign Languages Press.

—— "China's Foreign Policy," August 21, 1982, In *Selected Works of Deng Xiaoping*, edited and translated by the Bureau for the Compilation and Translation of Works of Marx, Engels, Lenin and Stalin under the Central Committee of the Communist Party of China, vol 2, 407-409. Beijing: Foreign Languages Press.

—— "Let Us Put the Past Behind Us and Open Up a New Era," May 16, 1989, In *Selected Works of Deng Xiaoping*, edited and translated by the Bureau for the Compilation and Translation of Works of Marx, Engels, Lenin and Stalin under the Central Committee of the Communist Party of China, vol 3, 284–287. Beijing: Foreign Languages Press.

Du, Xiaoqiang 杜小强. 1984. "Guoji zhanlue geju duojihua xintan." 国际战略格局多极化新探 [New Analysis on the Multipolar International Strategic Pattern], *Shijie jingjiyu zhengzhi* 世界经济与政治 (*World Economics and Politics*) 4: 1–8.

Fang, Lianqing 方连庆. 1982. "Liening lingdao shiqide suweiai eguodui afuhande waijiao zhengce." 列宁领导时期的苏维埃俄国对阿富汗的外交政策 [Soviet Russia's Policy Towards Afghanistan in the Years of Lenin], *Guoji wenti yanjiu* 国际问题研究 (*Journal of International Studies*) 2: 31–39.

Feng, Meiyan 冯美言. 1983. "Yuanzhu disan shijieshi womende guoji zhuyi yiwu." 援助第三世界是我们的国际主义义务 [Aiding the Third World is Our Internationalist Obligation], *Renmin ribao* 人民日报 (*People's Daily*), September 29, 2.

Hong, Hai 宏海. 1983. "Yishehui zhuyi weifangxiang—sulianzai yafei guojia tuixingde yizhong lilun." 以社会主义为方向—苏联在亚非国家推行的一种理论 [Directing Socialism—A Theory Promoted by the Soviet Union in Asian and African Countries], *Sulian dongou wenti* 苏联东欧问题 (*Matters of the Soviet Union and Eastern Europe*) 3: 44–49.

Jiang, Qi 姜琦. 1982. "Guanyu sunan chongtu." 关于苏南冲突 [On Soviet-Yugoslavian Conflicts], *Dangdai shijieyu shehui zhuyi* 当代世界与社会主义 (*Contemporary World and Socialism*) 2: 36-58.

—— 1983. "Sudong guanxide yanbian." 苏东关系的演变 [The Evolution of Soviet-East European Relations], *Jinri sulian dongou* 今日苏联东欧 (*The Present Day Soviet Union and Eastern Europe*) 5: 1–10.

Lenin, Vladimir. 1967. *Lenin on the National and Colonial Questions: Three Articles*. Translated by Peking Foreign Languages Press. Peking: Foreign Languages Press.

Li, Dasheng 李大圣. 1981. "Huanghua huanyan jianada waizhang." 黄华欢宴加拿大外长 [Huang Hua Offers Banquet to Welcome the Canadian Foreign Minister], *Renmin ribao* 人民日报 (*People's Daily*), August 18, 1.

Li, Huichuan 李会传. 1981. "Zhongsu bianjie tanpande zhengjie hezai? ." 中苏边界谈判的症结何在？ [What Is the Problem of Sino-Soviet Border Negotiation?], *Renmin ribao* 人民日报 (*People's Daily*), June 17, 2.

Li, Jingjie 李静杰. 1984. "Dangqian sulian duiwai zhengce zhongde ruogan wenti." 当前苏联对外政策中的若干问题 [Several Questions regarding the Present Soviet Foreign Policy], *Sulian dongou wenti* 苏联东欧问题 (*Matters of the Soviet Union and Eastern Europe*) 3: 12–19.

Li, Ning 李凝. 1983. "Gengjia jingzhang dongdangde yinian." 更加紧张动荡的一年 [A Year with Greater Tension and Tumult], *Guoji wenti yanjiu* 国际问题研究 (*Journal of International Studies*) 1: 3–10.

Li, Yuanming 李元明. 1981. "Sulian baquan zhuyide lishi yuanyuan." 苏联霸权主义的历史渊源 [The Historical Origin of Soviet Hegemonism], *Hongqi* 红旗 (*Red Flag*) 17: 21–25.

Liu, Jialei 刘家磊. 1980. "Ershi shijichu shaezai haishenwei pohai huaqiaode baoxing." 二十世纪初沙俄在海参崴迫害华侨的暴行 [The Atrocious Crimes Committed by Tsarist Russia on Oversea Chinese in Vladivostok during the Early 20th Century], *Shehui kexue zhanxian* 社会科学战线 (*Social Sciences Front*) 3: 167–168.

Liu, Keming 刘克明. 1981. "Fakanci." 发刊词 [A Few Words on the Initial Issue], *Sulian dongou wenti* 苏联东欧问题 (*Matters of the Soviet Union and Eastern Europe*) 1: 1–2.

Liu, Xing 刘星. 1983. "Huyaobang zainan juxing jizhe zhaodaihui." 胡耀邦在南举行记者招待会 [Hu Yaobang Holds Press Conference in Yugoslavia], *Renmin ribao* 人民日报 (*People's Daily*), May 13, 3.

Lu, Yikun. 1983. "China Will Never Seek Hegemony." *Beijing Review*, February 7, 17.

Ma, Yuchun 马玉纯. 1981. "Weihu shijie heping, fandui baquan zhuyi." 维护世界和平反对霸权主义 [Safeguarding World Peace, Opposing Hegemonism], *Renmin ribao* 人民日报 (*People's Daily*), September 4, 3.

Mao, Jun 毛军. 1980. "Suliande weixie cujinle lianhede qushi." 苏联的威胁促进了联合的趋势 [The Soviet Threat Has Pushed the World to Unite Together], *Renmin ribao* 人民日报 (*People's Daily*), March 15, 5.

Mao, Zedong. 1974. *Mao Tse-tung Unrehearsed: Talks and Letters, 1956–71*. Translated by John Chinnery and Tieyun. Harmondsworth: Penguin.

Mao, Zedong 毛泽东. 1993. "Rende zhengque sixiang shicong nali laide?." 人的正确思想是从哪里来的？ [Where Do Correct Ideas Come From?] May 1963, In *Maozedong wenji* 毛泽东文集 (*Selected Works of Mao Zedong*), edited by Zhonggong zhongyang wenxian yanjiushi 中共中央文献研究室 [The Central Committee of the Chinese Communist Party Literature Research Office], vol 8, 320–322. Beijing: Renmin chubanshe.

——— "Zhongguo renmin jianjue zhichi banama renminde aiguo zhengyi douzheng." 中国人民坚决支持巴拿马人民的爱国正义斗争 [The Chinese People Firmly Support the Patriotic Struggle of the Panamanian People] January 12, 1964, In *Maozedong wenji* 毛泽东文集 (*Selected Works of Mao Zedong*), edited by Zhonggong zhongyang wenxian yanjiushi 中共中央文献研究室 [The Central Committee of the Chinese Communist Party Literature Research Office], vol 8, 354–355. Beijing: Renmin chubanshe.

——— "Guanyu sange shijie huafen wenti." 关于三个世界划分问题 [On the Question of Division of the Three Worlds] February 22, 1974, In *Maozedong wenji* 毛泽东文集 (*Selected Works of Mao Zedong*), edited by Zhonggong zhongyang wenxian yanjiushi 中共中央文献研究室 [The Central Committee of the Chinese Communist Party Literature Research Office], vol 8, 441–442. Beijing: Renmin chubanshe.

Qi, Sheng 齐胜. 1980. "Tietuo zuixian renshi shehui zhuyi buying yige moshi." 铁托最先认识社会主义不应一个模式 [It Was Tito Who Was the First One to Realise that There Should Not Be One Model of Socialism], *Renmin ribao* 人民日报 (*People's Daily*), May 7, 1.

Qian, Junrui 钱君瑞. 1981. "Maozedong sixiang rengranshi yanjiu guoji wentide zhidao sixiang." 毛泽东思想仍然是研究国际问题的指导思想 [Mao Zedong Thought is Still the Guiding Principle of Studying International Issues], *Guangming ribao* 光明日报 (*Guangming Daily*), July 19, 1.

Shen, Yi. 1981. "China Belongs for Ever to the Third World." *Beijing Review*, September 28, 24.

Wang, Ning. 1985. "China's Role in a Multipolar World." *Beijing Review*, January 7, 42.

Wang, Yiying 王益英. 1984. "Zhanhou chuqi sumeizai dongoude duikanghe sudong guanxi." 战后初期苏美在东欧的对抗和苏东关系 [Soviet–US Conflicts in Eastern Europe and Soviet-East European Relations after World War Two], *Sulian dongou wenti* 苏联东欧问题 (*Matters of the Soviet Union and Eastern Europe*) 1: 26–32.

Xie, Xiang 谢翔. 1984. "Bashi niandai sulian yatai zhanluede zhuanbian." 八十年代苏联亚太战略的转变 [The Changes of Soviet Asia-Pacific Policy in the 1980s], *Sulian dongou wenti* 苏联东欧问题 (*Matters of the Soviet Union and Eastern Europe*) 5: 41–45.

Xing, Shugang 邢书纲. 1981. "Guanyu sulian quanqiu kuozhang zhanluede jige wenti." 关于苏联全球扩张战略的几个问题 [Several Questions on Soviet Global Expansionism], *Sulian dongou wenti* 苏联东欧问题 (*Matters of the Soviet Union and Eastern Europe*) 1: 3–9.

Xu, Kui 徐葵. 1981. "Yici jixu jianchi baquan zhuyi zhengcede daibiao dahui." 一次继续坚持霸权主义政策的代表大会 [A Congress for Upholding the Hegemonic Policy], *Sulian dongou wenti* 苏联东欧问题 (*Matters of the Soviet Union and Eastern Europe*) 1: 10–14.

Xu, Ji 许际. 1983. "Disan shijie dejueqi shidangdai toudeng dashi." 第三世界的崛起是当代头等大事 [The Rise of the Third World is the Most Significant Issue in Contemporary Time], *Renmin ribao* 人民日报 (*People's Daily*), April 1, 3.

Yang, Zhangming 杨章明. 1984. "Dangdai guowai shehui zhuyide xianzhuanghe fazhan qushi." 当代国外社会主义的现状和发展趋势 [The Realities and Trends of Contemporary Socialism Abroad], *Dangdai shijie shehui zhuyi wenti* 当代世界社会主义问题 (*Problems of Contemporary World Socialism*) 1: 81–84.

Yu, Sui 俞邃. 1983. "Bolieriniefu dangzheng shibanian huiguhe sugong xinlingdao zhengce dongxiang chutan." 勃列日涅夫当政十八年回顾和苏共新领导政策动向初探 [A Retrospect of Brezhnev's 18-Year Administration and the Policies of the New CPSU Leadership], *Sulian dongou wenti* 苏联东欧问题 (*Matters of the Soviet Union and Eastern Europe*) 3: 1–6.

Zhang, Jinglin 张景林. 1982. "Suliande 'huanhe zhanlue'." 苏联的"缓和政策" [The Soviet 'Détente Policy'], *Sulian dongou wenti* 苏联东欧问题 (*Matters of the Soviet Union and Eastern Europe*) 2: 1–4.

———. 1982. "Shilunyu dangqian fanba douzheng youguande jige renshi wenti." 试论与当前反霸斗争有关的几个认识问题 [Several Questions regarding the Present Anti-Hegemonic Struggle], *Sulian dongou wenti* 苏联东欧问题 (*Matters of the Soviet Union and Eastern Europe*) 6: 1–6.

Zhang, Zhen 张震. 1982. "Luelun suliande 'huanhe zhengce'." 略论苏联的"缓和政策" [On the Soviet 'Détente Policy'], *Guoji wenti yanjiu* 国际问题研究 (*International Studies*) 4: 18–22.

Zhao, Naibin 赵乃斌. 1984. "Shehui zhuyide, zizhide, bujie mengde nansilafu." 社会主义的，自治的，不结盟的南斯拉夫 [The Socialist, Independent, and Non-aligned Yugoslavia], *Dangdai shijie shehui zhuyi wenti* 当代世界社会主义问题 (*Problems of Contemporary World Socialism*) 2: 74–77.

Zhou, Jirong 周纪荣. 1984. "Sumei zhengba taishide bianhuayu qianjing." 苏美争霸态势的变化与前景 [A New Feature in US-Soviet Rivalry], *Xiandai guoji guanxi* 现代国际关系 (*Contemporary International Relations*) 6: 22–29.

Zhou, Shengde 周盛德. 1983. "Lishi qirong diandao." 历史岂容颠倒 [History Cannot Be Distorted], *Sulian dongou wenti* 苏联东欧问题 (*Matters of the Soviet Union and Eastern Europe*) 1: 92–96.

Zhou, Weiyan 周维衍., and Shi Yikui 施一揆. 1980. "Beijiaerhu yidong diqude lishi zhenxiang." 贝加尔湖以东地区的历史真相 [The Historical Truth of the Eastern Territory near the Lake Baikal], *Fudan xuebao* 复旦学报 (*Fudan Journal*) 1: 104–112.

Zhubian 主编 (Editor). 1981. "Bianhou." 编后 [Postscript from the Editorial Board], *Xiandai guoji guanxi* 现代国际关系 (*Contemporary International Relations*) 1: 64.

1980. "Zhide zhuyide dongxiang." 值得注意的动向 [We Need to Pay Attention to the Situation], *Renmin ribao* 人民日报 (*People's Daily*), January 5, 3.

1984. "Jiaqiang youhao hezuo zengjing geming youyi." 加强友好合作增进革命友谊 [Strengthening Close Cooperation and Promoting Revolutionary Friendship], *Renmin ribao* 人民日报 (*People's Daily*), August 19, 2.

Secondary Sources

Bolt, Paul. 2000. *China and Southeast Asia's Ethnic Chinese: State and Diaspora in Contemporary Asia*. Westport: Praeger.

Boyle, Peter. 1993. *American-Soviet Relations: From the Russian Revolution to the Fall of Communism*. London: Routledge.

Chen, Jian and Yang Kuisong. 1998. "Chinese Politics and the Collapse of the Sino-Soviet Alliance." In *Brothers in Arms: The Rise and Fall of the Sino-Soviet Alliance, 1945–1963*, edited by Odd Arne Westad, 246-294. Washington, D. C.: Woodrow Wilson Center Press.

Friedman, Jeremy. 2015. *Shadow Cold War: The Sino-Soviet Split and the Third World*. Chapel Hill: University of North Carolina Press.

Li, Yan. 2012. "In Search of a Socialist Modernity: The Chinese Introduction of Soviet Culture." PhD diss., Northeastern University.

Lukin, Alexander. 2003. *The Bear Watches the Dragon: Russia's Perceptions of China and the Evolution of Russian-Chinese Relations since the Eighteenth Century*. London: M. E. Sharpe.

Marsh, Christopher. 2005. *Unparalleled Reforms: China's Rise, Russia's Fall, and the Interdependence of Transition*. Oxford: Lexington Books.

Shambaugh, David. 1991. *Beautiful Imperialist: China Perceives America, 1972–1990*. Princeton: Princeton University Press.

Xenakis, Christopher. 2002. *What Happened to the Soviet Union: How and Why American Sovietologists were Caught by Surprise*. London: Praeger.

Part Three

International

9

Overcoming the Greatest Distance: China in Latin America

BENJAMIN CREUTZFELDT

On China's map of the world, the space least charted is the region of Latin America and the Caribbean (LAC). It lies the farthest from Beijing and the acquaintance of one with the other was historically limited. Yet, this trans-Pacific relationship has transformed into one of the most dynamic since President Jiang Zemin's visit to seven countries in the region in 2001. His overture was followed by a series of trips by his successor Hu Jintao in 2004 to Brazil, Argentina and Chile, Costa Rica, Cuba and Peru in 2008, bringing in his wake a large entourage of Chinese officials and business people. This awakened the continent to the new possibilities of trans-Pacific contact. Since 2009, top leadership visits from China have become an annual event, and leaders of LAC countries have reciprocated to varying degrees. Bilateral trade has grown in value from $10 billion in 2000 to almost $280 billion in 2015 (cf. ECLAC 2016), and LAC countries represent six percent of China's global imports. Chinese loans and foreign direct investment in the region have also grown exponentially and enabled substantial economic growth even after the financial crisis of 2008.

What makes the relationship particularly interesting for students and scholars of IR is how it fits into Beijing's adaptive but principled foreign policy strategy (see Cui and Pérez García 2016, and also Gallagher 2016). Not only do LAC countries hold the very resources and fertile lands China needs to guarantee its sustainable development, but they are also a grouping of nations with strong potential for market growth and, more interestingly, for social and political advancement within a new global framework. LAC countries have long been within the US's immediate sphere of influence, but since the mid-

20th century the approach of the 'northern hegemon' has tended to be one of benign neglect. Today, most LAC countries are characterised by alarming inequality in terms of income and opportunity, limited government control over outlying areas, and weak regional integration. Powerful elites dominate politics, the economy, education and land ownership, and frequently sacrifice national interests and environmental concerns for their own priorities. China's involvement with this region has the potential to either exacerbate or mitigate these tendencies.

This chapter offers some key points of reference in the trajectory of the Sino-Latin American relationship, outlines the current patterns of engagement, and concludes with a view on future developments. The scholars referenced are the most consistent observers of this relationship over the past ten years and are recommended as sources for further reading.

History and the Shadow of the Monroe Doctrine

Historically traceable contact between China and LACs began with trade during the early Spanish colonial empire in the second half of the 16th century and continued for more than three centuries by means of the Manila Galleons that carried Mexican silver to the Philippines which then paid for goods from China and shipped to Europe (Connelly and Cornejo 1992). Documented contact between China and the countries of Latin America dates to the Qing Empire in the century of its gradual decline, which coincided with a newfound independence of most of Latin America. Foreign influence continued to be strong in economic, political and sometimes even military terms, for the liberators, educated in the European tradition, continued to look to the West, principally to the United States. In 1823, shortly after the Spanish and Portuguese had been driven out, the government in Washington pronounced the Monroe Doctrine, which proclaimed the region as its sphere of influence.

Nonetheless, the nineteenth century saw the first occasion for the China of the Qing dynasty and a number of Latin American countries to look each other in the eye: a confluence of trends led to the emergence of the 'coolie trade' from China to the plantations and early infrastructure projects of Latin America. The first trend was the chaos, poverty and death of tens of millions in rural China, due to social crises exacerbated by foreign intrusion. The second was the need for cheap labour in Latin America as a consequence of the phasing out of black slavery. The land-owning elites were in need of someone to do the hard labour they were unwilling to do themselves, leading to the importation of several hundred thousand 'coolies' from South China (McKeown 2001): forced emigration of almost exclusively male workers for the sugarcane plantations of Cuba and Jamaica, the silver mines, coastal plantations and guano collecting industry of Peru, and a little later, the Panama Canal project. The miserable treatment many suffered during transport and at their destination forced a reluctant and inward-looking Qing government to negotiate its first formal relations with several Latin American countries: the first of these was Peru in August of 1875, followed by Brazil in 1881, and Mexico in 1899. After the foundation of the Republic of China in 1912, the new government inherited the relations established, and these remained firmly in the hands of Nationalist China even after it fled the People's Liberation Army to Taiwan in 1949.

Following the establishment of the PRC, Cuba was a distant first in the region to recognise Communist China. In 1960, President Osvaldo Dorticos Torrado became the first Latin American head of state to pay an official visit to Beijing. The relationship also led to commercial exchanges, with Cuba in the 1960s representing over three-quarters of China's trade with Latin America. On the flipside, Cuba's political position undermined relations with the remaining countries of the region, most of which were decidedly anti-communist. Contact with other countries in the region was limited to cultural diplomacy: acrobats and dancers left a deep impression on generations of the Latin American public, while political groups of all persuasions were invited to Beijing and were enthralled to shake hands with the Communist Party's top leadership. Left-wing insurgents were inspired by Mao Zedong's guerrilla warfare techniques, but there seems to have been no open engagement or training in the 1960s or 70s. China also sponsored the translation and publication of Chinese literature and political texts into Spanish, and of selected Latin American writers to a Chinese reading public. The Institute of Latin American Studies (ILAS) was founded in Beijing in 1961 to advise the government and has established itself as the key institution in China for the analysis of the situation in Latin America. It was closed in 1966 along with all other Chinese academic institutions, and only reopened cautiously in the late 1970s. It publishes the Chinese-language *Journal of Latin American Studies*, in six annual issues.

The thawing of relations between China and the US after 1971 had immediate repercussions in Washington's 'backyard', by implicitly allowing governments to engage more openly with Beijing. Peru, Chile, Argentina and Brazil were among the first in the region to establish formal diplomatic relations with Beijing. China's approach in the 1950s was founded on the principle of non-interference and aimed at building relationships with governments and oppositions regardless of party colour. As a result, not only did left-leaning governments such as Peru and Chile engage with the PRC, but so did right-wing autocrats. Many waited until the 1980s, after the US had recognised Beijing diplomatically. As of 2018, all but nine LAC countries had relations with Beijing.

Opening-up and the One-China Policy

Between the beginning of Deng Xiaoping's market-oriented reforms in the late-1970s and 2016, China's GDP grew from less than one percent of the world economy to over 15%, and its share of global trade increased from less than one percent to almost 12% (Wu 2013). This growth has been taken by many as evidence that rapid and sustained economic development under non-democratic leadership could both dramatically reduce poverty levels and improve living standards for hundreds of millions of people – and do so more effectively than democratic countries. China's experiences with economic development stand in stark contrast to the absence of such sustained and positive growth in Latin America over the same time period (Kay 2002). With growing confidence, China began to actively nurture its relations with Latin America and welcomed the gradual shift in official recognition from Taipei to Beijing from most remaining South American countries, regardless of the ideological leanings of individual governments. At the end of 1985, Premier Zhao Ziyang embarked on what was the first high-level leadership visit from China to Latin America, visiting Colombia, Venezuela, Brazil and Argentina. His discourse was couched in terms of 'Third World' friendship and emphasised the need to strengthen South-South dialogue, while reiterating a commitment to the Five Principles of Peaceful Coexistence. This rhetoric continues to define the political discourse to this day.

Despite these developments, the physical distance and the incipient diplomatic relations, alongside the relative sway that Taiwan has continued to hold over the majority of Central American and Caribbean countries, meant that commercial and political exchange grew only very gradually. Even after the end of the Cold War, the United States has continued to be wary of left-wing governments in Latin America, and China's 'no-strings-attached' policy for loans and investment has been perceived as tacit tolerance of those governments antagonistic to the US. While commercial activities are wide-ranging and move in both directions, the investment has been largely unilateral, from China to the region. China's earliest inroad to large-scale overseas investment was the acquisition of Latin America's largest iron mine, Hierro Peru, in 1992 (Ellis 2014). For almost two decades, the purchase was China's largest outlay of foreign direct investment in Latin America, and Peru's first large-scale privatisation. This endeavour notwithstanding, at the beginning of the millennium Latin America was the least important region of the world in terms of Chinese overseas investment, but this situation has changed dramatically in the following decade. China was soon seen to have a largely positive impact: both directly, through an export boom, and indirectly, through better terms of trade (Creutzfeldt 2012).

Nurturing Diversity with a Single Strategy

Since these cautious beginnings, the relationship between the People's Republic of China and Latin America has grown apace. At the end of 2008, Beijing published its first policy paper on Latin America and the Caribbean, a canvas of intentions that set out broad terms for bilateral cooperation, invariably described as a 'win-win situation' (Roett and Paz 2016). The Chinese leadership has made numerous overtures to the governments of the region in the past few years. One of the most noteworthy was the speech by Premier Wen Jiabao at the UN's Economic Commission for Latin America and the Caribbean on 26 June 2012. Wen's address, under the heading 'Trusted Friends Forever', raised the character of the transpacific relationship to an almost poetic level. He reached back to the Inca and Aztec cultures to draw parallels with China's own millennial history and quoted great literary figures. He then laid out four proposals for furthering cooperation: political links, economic development, food security, and human and scientific exchange. These proposals were backed up with loans, funding, and financial targets.

The government of Xi Jinping has continued the pattern of annual visits to the region, and augmented incentives for cooperation and the targets for trade and investment. In the course of the year 2014, the most emblematic institution of the ever-closer relations between China and Latin America came into being, in the form of the China-CELAC Forum, and in January 2015, Xi hosted the inaugural ministerial summit in Beijing. Political institutional linkages have been growing in parallel, the People's Republic is now a member of the Asia Pacific Economic Council (APEC) which also includes Chile, Mexico, Panama and Peru, and became a shareholder in the Caribbean Development Bank in 1998 and the Inter-American Development Bank (IADB) in 2009. China enjoys observer status in the Latin American Integration Association (ALADI), the Latin American Parliament, the UN's Economic Commission for Latin America and the Caribbean (ECLAC), and the Pacific Alliance. It is also in permanent dialogue with regional economic organisations: Mercosur, the Community of Andean Nations (CAN) and the Caribbean Community (Caricom). The Chinese government has initiated bilateral dialogue forums, such as the China-Latin America business summit (since 2007, under the auspices of the China Council for the Promotion of International Trade, CCPIT), the China-Latin America Think Tank Forum (since 2010, sponsored by the Institute of Foreign Affairs, CPIFA), and perhaps most significantly, the China-CELAC Forum.

Accompanying this thickening of contacts persists a sense of competition, more acutely felt in countries with a significant manufacturing sector such as Mexico, Brazil, and to some extent Colombia. This has led to concerns by analysts and policy-makers over a renewed deindustrialisation of Latin American economies and an over-reliance on low value-added commodity exports (Strauss and Armony 2012). Others point out that natural resources are not a curse, but constitute a significant asset if revenues are reinvested to physically link their economies by investing in infrastructure, and education can be channelled into value-added industries (see Ray et al. 2016). Questions linger over whether Latin American governments are in fact able to take proper advantage of the opportunity (Ferchen 2011). The perceived threat versus potential is complicated by xenophobic fear-mongering; something Enrique Dussel Peters has noted is that a growing racism towards persons of Chinese descent is evident in Latin America and Mexico, especially in entrepreneurial circles (Dussel Peters 2015).

The Road Ahead

Shortly after the US electoral upset in November 2016, Beijing made public its second policy paper for engagement with Latin America and the Caribbean, intending to send the world a reassuring signal in times of turmoil. The new document is a third longer than its predecessor and builds on the strength of many years of growing investment and bilateral trade, new multilateral institutions, strategic frameworks and forums for better cooperation instigated by China (China, 2016).

The text is emphatic about the idea of collaboration and makes explicit the desire to work together in every field of human activity, ranging from industrial and technological development to military, political, cultural, educational and environmental efforts. China's foreign policy is consistently driven by its domestic needs: political stability, sovereign security, and sustainable development. Its Latin America strategy is no exception: it underscores that the development of China is possible only if other developing countries share this goal and are part of a joint process (Myers and Wise, 2016). It conjures up a 'new phase' that reflects Beijing's goal of sharing its development experience with another region of the world, combined with a drive to transfer its excess financial and industrial capacity abroad.

Both of these goals should be welcomed by Latin American governments. Apart from the proven Chinese expertise in the building of roads and railways, ports and energy plants – undeniable necessities for economic and social progress – China is now at the forefront globally in renewable energy sources and industry guidelines for sustainable development. The environmental standards set by the Chinese industry groups are now among the most stringent in the world, and Chinese officials are actively exploring new approaches and standards for corporate social responsibility and political risk analysis.

Latin America, despite the physical distance, has been officially included in the Belt & Road Initiative. The now annual leadership visits include countries from across the political spectrum, with Premier Li Keqiang visiting both Colombia and Cuba in May of 2015, and the November round of countries including both Pacific Alliance and ALBA member nations; in Ecuador, President Xi inaugurated the Coca-Codo hydroelectric dam and signed a new investment agreement with President Rafael Correa; in Peru he met with newly-elected president Pedro Pablo Kuczynski after the two-day APEC summit hosted there; and in Chile, alongside his counterpart Michelle Bachelet, he oversaw the signing of a dozen cooperation agreements.

China trades in many things, but continuity and words backed by a record of strong economic data, are importantly amongst them. At a time of instability in global politics and with the new leadership of the United States questioning fundamental premises of the international system, the continuity of China's declared commitment to the socioeconomic advancement of countries in Latin America, the Caribbean, and elsewhere, offers some cause for optimism.

References

China 2016. *China's Policy Paper on Latin America and the Caribbean.* Beijing: Ministry of Foreign Affairs.

Connelly, Marisela and Romer Cornejo Bustamante. 1992. *China - América Latina: Génesis y desarrollo de sus Relaciones.* Mexico: Colegio de Mexico, Centro de Estudios de Asia y Africa.

Creutzfeldt, Benjamin (ed.). 2012. *China en América Latina: Reflexiones sobre las relaciones transpacíficas.* Bogota: Universidad Externado de Colombia.

Cui Shoujun and Manuel Pérez García (eds.). 2016. *China and Latin America in Transition: Policy Dynamics, Economic Commitments and Social Impacts.* New York: Palgrave Macmillan.

Dussel Peters, Enrique. 2015. *China's Evolving Role in Latin America: Can It Be a Win-Win?* Washington, DC: Atlantic Council, Adrienne Arsht Latin America Center.

ECLAC. 2016. *Relaciones económicas entre América Latina y el Caribe y China: Oportunidades y Desafíos*. Santiago de Chile: United Nations Economic Commission for Latin America and the Caribbean.

Ellis, R. Evan. 2014. *China on the Ground in Latin America: Challenges for the Chinese and Impacts on the Region*. New York: Palgrave Macmillan.

Ferchen, Matt. 2011. 'China-Latin America Relations: Long-term Boon or Short-term Boom?' *Chinese Journal of International Politics* 4: 55–86.

Gallagher, Kevin P. 2016. *The China Triangle: Latin America's China Boom and the Fate of the Washington Consensus*. New York: Oxford University Press.

Kay, Cristobal. 2002. 'Why East Asia overtook Latin America: agrarian reform, industrialisation and development.' *Third World Quarterly* 23: 1073–1102.

McKeown, Andrew. 2001. *Chinese Migrant Networks and Cultural Change: Peru, Chicago, and Hawaii 1900-1936*. University of Chicago Press.

Myers, Margaret and Carol Wise (eds.). 2016. *The Political Economy of China-Latin America Relations in the New Millennium: Brave New World*. New York: Routledge.

Ray, Rebecca, Kevin P. Gallagher, Andres Lopez & Cynthia Sanborn. 2015. *China in Latin America: Lessons for South-South Cooperation and Sustainable Development*. Boston: Global Economic Governance Initiative.

Roett, Riordan and Guadalupe Paz (eds.). 2016. *Latin America and the Asian Giants: Evolving Ties with China and India*. Washington, DC: Brookings Institution.

Strauss, Julia C. and Ariel C. Armony (eds.) 2012. *From the Great Wall to the New World: China and Latin America in the 21st Century*. Cambridge University Press.

Wu Baiyi (ed.). 2013. 转型中的机遇：中拉合作前景的多视角分析 [*Opportunities in Transformation: A Multi-perspective Analysis of China-Latin American Relations*]. Beijing: Jingji Guanli Publishing.

10

China's Multilateral Diplomacy in Africa: Constructing the Security-Development Nexus

ILARIA CARROZZA

This chapter argues for a re-examination of common theoretical approaches to China's socialisation in international relations. I first introduce the debate over China's rise and argue that studies of the country's foreign policy have failed to account for a number of important elements. The literature on socialisation has done a great deal in trying to compensate for such shortcomings. However, whilst I acknowledge the merits of such literature, I also find it problematic for two main reasons: first, the literature on normative change is biased in favour of a Western liberal order. Second, the same literature often neglects that China is both the *object* and *subject* of socialisation dynamics, for instance via the re-articulation of concepts of state sovereignty and intervention. I elaborate on the second problem by looking at Chinas' regional forum diplomacy in Africa, focusing on the construction of security narratives via the Forum on China-Africa Cooperation (FOCAC). I argue that China's FOCAC diplomacy is based on a discourse that frames China and Africa as friends and allies in the common struggle against Western hegemony. Chinese decision makers have been able to successfully socialise African leaders into a narrative of South-South cooperation that calls for increased cooperation and legitimises the security-development nexus which is at the heart of Chinese policies. It is by successfully interpellating African decision makers into this discourse that Beijing officials have justified increased 'interventions' in peace and security.

Socialising China

In a 1999 essay, Segal famously argued that China was overrated as both a power and a market, and that it had repeatedly failed to deliver on what had been promised by its leaders. After analysing to what extent China did or did not matter economically, militarily, and politically, he concluded that it was 'merely a middle power' (Segal 1999, 35). Many scholars after him have either supported or questioned his claim through more detailed empirical studies, and some of these have subsequently translated into debates within the international relations (IR) discipline on whether China is to be classified as a revisionist or a status quo power.[1] China's rise has thus been addressed from a range of perspectives, including realist, liberal, and foreign policy analysis approaches to its position in international politics: Some scholars have argued against a peaceful rise (Mearsheimer 2006; Mearsheimer 2014; Shih 2005); others have been more sceptical as to the country's potential to become a great power (Shambaugh 2013); yet other scholars have taken China's rise as given and explored the ways in which it could unfold (Buzan 2010; Buzan and Foot 2004; Christensen 2011; Xia 2001).

Indeed, the question of whether China matters is an important one. Nonetheless, I believe the approaches above to be limited in their description of the People's Republic of China's (PRC) foreign policy as if it was a monolith. To be sure, understanding the country's foreign policy is no easy task. As Shambaugh maintains, unlike many Western polities that have generally evolved within a singular liberal paradigm, the modern Chinese state has undergone several macro transitions – from the imperial phase, to republican, revolutionary communist, and modernising socialist (Shambaugh 2000). Despite their different scopes, goals, and tools, these different states have had three enduring missions: the modernisation of the economy, the transformation of society, and the defence of the nation against foreign aggression. While some elements of the past have survived, each new system further elaborated them into new institutional frameworks – although marked by sharp departures, none of these states were ever totally new.

Yet, despite foreign and defence policies remaining fairly consistent and in line with the country's domestic priorities in the last three decades, the government has never disclosed any clear document outlining its strategic goals or grand strategy (Wang 2011).[2] Again, foreign policy scholars have tried to provide as accurate descriptions of these processes as possible (Gittings 2008; Wang 1994; Wang 2011). Similar to the studies mentioned above, these also fail to account for the interactions between the Chinese and

---

[1] Much of the debate reflects concerns among policymakers and analysts within the US and tends to be biased. For more on this, see Economy and Oksenberg 1999.

[2] Although, to be sure, China has a reasonably clear and stable set of aims that include increase in the country's power, continued development and increase in prosperity, defence of territorial integrity, and domestic stability under CCP rule (See Buzan 2014 and Hughes 2016).

other actors, decision makers' learning processes, and socialisation dynamics.[3] Approaches to Chinese foreign policy, argues Johnston, provide a limited understanding of the country's involvement in international institutions and normative regimes (Johnston 2008). Instead, he suggests that the PRC has increasingly shown a greater level of integration and cooperation within the international arena (Johnston 2003; Johnston 2013) – which also led him to argue that 'Chinese diplomacy since the 1990s [has been] more status quo-oriented than at any period since 1949 (Johnston 2008, 207). This is because Chinese decision makers have started to acknowledge the positive impact of global economic and information integration on the country's own economic development. Globalisation and multilateralism have thus become part of a 'new identity discourse that describes China as a "responsible major power", a key characteristic of which is to participate in and uphold commitments to status quo international economic and security institutions' (Johnston 2008, 205).

In particular, Johnston argues that Chinese leaders and foreign policy makers have adopted a more cooperative stance on security institutions – defined as 'more or less formal organizations with identifiable names and with more or less obvious criteria for membership or participation' (Johnston 2008, 27) – between 1980 and 2000, through socialisation's micro-processes of mimicking, persuasion, and social influence. He finds that in contrast to a hard realpolitik ideology inherited from the Mao era, contemporary decision makers have shifted their understanding of participation in security regimes as a result of social interaction and as a product of dynamics of identity construction and differentiation (Johnston 2008).

Just after China's entry into the World Trade Organization (WTO) in 2001, scholars started exploring the country's compliance with the norms and rules of international organisations (IOs), as well as the role of the latter in facilitating China's socialisation. Most of this scholarship agrees that while international organisations contribute to the socialisation of participating parties, they also represent a challenge to them, as they simultaneously confirm and constrain sovereignty (Kent 2002). China's newcomer status meant a steep learning curve in the last 30 years, Kent argues, mediated by its many identities, mainly as a great power and developing country, and led China to prefer bilateral arrangements to multilateral mechanisms. However, Chinese leaders soon realised that international institutions could also serve as a platform for constructing the country's international image and legitimacy, as well as a platform to project its power according to the leaders' cultural

---

3   Socialisation is referred to as 'the process that is directed toward a state's internalization of the constitutive beliefs and practices institutionalised in its international environment', as defined by (Schimmelfenning 2000). I follow his definition here.

realist perspective (Johnston 2008; Kent 2002). China is not only motivated by a system-maintaining and system-exploiting approach (norms-taking), but also by a system-reforming attitude (norms-making), and thus has committed to making a shift to a multipolar world (Kent 2002; Kim 1999).

According to this literature, therefore, China has been successfully socialised into IOs – where success is measured as the shift from being a recalcitrant and rogue state to being integrated into an increasingly interdependent Western, though mostly US-infused, system. While I do agree with Johnston that the PRC's increased integration is a more useful criterion to assess the country's behaviour in international politics than the China threat/rise discourse, there are two major problems with such analyses: one that is general, but applicable to the case of China, and one which is topic-specific. First, I follow Acharya in arguing that mainstream IR theories have tended to privilege hegemonic power and socialisation in international order-building (Acharya 2008); the literature on normative change, he contends, is 'biased in favour of a "moral cosmopolitanism"'. It concentrates on moral struggles in which *good* global norms (championed by mainly Western norm entrepreneurs) displace *bad* local beliefs and practices (mainly in the non-Western areas)' (Acharya 2009, 4). Alternative projects, such as non-hegemonic international order theory, go beyond IR's primary concern with great power geopolitics, starting from the premise that while hegemony might produce order, it does so at the expense of weaker actors (Acharya 2008). Non-hegemonic moments can be found throughout history, one example being the Chinese tributary system, which he argues was geared toward benign outcomes, particularly the maintenance of trade, and was very different from European colonialism. In the context of socialisation, hegemony is manifested in the attempt of the (liberal) hegemon to socialise secondary states into liberal norms and rules, reflected in what Park identifies as the focus of socialisation literature not so much on who is being socialised, but rather what they are being socialised into (Park 2014).

Second, scholarship on China's socialisation has ignored that the PRC has also been the agent of socialisation – what scholars have called a two-way socialisation (Pu 2012) – especially via the re-articulation of concepts of state sovereignty and intervention, and this has in turn encountered responses from within regions of the Global South. In the following section I elaborate on the second point, using the example of China's use of regional forum diplomacy in Africa as a tool of security norms-making.

China's Regional Forum Diplomacy: The FOCAC

The FOCAC was established in 2000 as a dialogue platform to foster Sino-

African exchanges on a broad variety of topics and issues, and which follows an exponential increase in cooperation between the two actors from the late-1990s and early-2000s. It can be seen as the institutionalisation of Sino-African relations and the formalisation of long-lasting ties (Taylor 2011). Ministers and heads of states from 53 member countries, as well as the African Union, which was recently included as a full member, gather together with their Chinese counterparts every three years, alternately in China and Africa. The purpose of the meetings is manifold: first, to counter Taiwan's influence; second, to promote an overall Chinese foreign policy strategy towards the continent which emphasises South-South cooperation and economic development; third, to advertise Beijing's leadership position of 'moral relativism' on issues such as human rights, as well as their own vision of the global order (Alden and Alves 2016; Taylor 2011). In practical terms, FOCAC Action Plans discuss future cooperation in the areas of 'trade, investment, poverty reduction, infrastructure building, capacity building, human resources development, food security, hi-tech industries', and, more recently, peace and security (Li and Funeka Yazini 2013).

The FOCAC hence represents a global governance platform for Chinese decision makers to discuss the agenda plans and future development goals with their African counterparts (Benabdallah 2016a). The Forum also provides the Chinese leadership with opportunities to enhance its role in global governance. First, it offers Chinese policy makers a feedback loop from African leaders so that they can continuously adjust and adapt their policies. Second, interaction on such a wide range of subjects enhances the international practice and credibility of Chinese practitioners, soldiers and policy makers alike. Finally, projects implemented via the FOCAC give China a chance to test its development-led model on African contexts and thus gain experience and feedback (Benabdallah 2016a). Indeed, the FOCAC plays an important role in China's regional forum diplomacy, which the PRC has been implementing elsewhere in the world.[4] According to officials in Beijing, regional forums are efficient and time-saving, and they also reflect China's 'new type of major power relations': instead of focusing on major powers, this group cooperation diplomacy is aimed to gather comparatively smaller countries – a move that makes it easier for China to promote its key official priorities and development model (Ekman 2016, 1). Regional forum diplomacy, in turn, is part of a wider attempt to become a global normative power through seeking recognition by other fellow developing countries (Alden and Alves 2017).

---

[4] See for instance the China-Arab States Cooperation Forum (2004), the China-Central and Eastern European Countries Cooperation Forum, or 16+1 (2012), and the China-CELAC (Community of Latin American and Caribbean States) Forum (2015) (Ekman 2016).

This speaks directly to what I have identified as a gap in the socialisation literature on China, namely its ambitions as a norms-maker besides its norm-taking: China's FOCAC diplomacy, I argue, is based on a discourse that frames China and Africa as friends and allies in the common struggle against Western hegemony. In so doing, Chinese decision makers have been able to successfully socialise African leaders into a narrative of South-South cooperation that calls for increased cooperation and is based on the Five Principles of Peaceful Coexistence – namely, mutual respect for each other's territorial integrity and sovereignty; mutual non-aggression; mutual non-interference in each other's internal affairs; equality and cooperation for mutual benefit; and peaceful coexistence. In particular, peace and security have come to be at the forefront of these ties in a way that was almost unimaginable only fifteen years ago.

Through a discourse analysis of FOCAC output documents, as well as speeches given by Chinese Presidents and officials, I show how China has so far been successful at combining and recombining existing linguistic signs (i.e. North/South, developed/developing), thus creating a coherent discourse around security in Africa that has enabled Beijing to span across a relatively wide range of policy options without deviating from such major representations. The analysis of FOCAC-related documents thus highlights continuities in Chinese decision makers' representations of the China-Africa story in the face of increased insecurity and instability on the continent.[5] Since the Forum's inception in 2000, attention to peace and security, and peacekeeping in particular, has gained prominence. This has resulted in a shift in policies from non-involvement to considerable engagement in a variety of security related activities. Simultaneously, the basic discourse that sustains China's Africa policies has essentially remained the same.

First of all, China and Africa are presented as all-round 'friends', with China clearly characterised as a fellow developing country (FOCAC 2009a). Their friendship is a long-lasting one, dating back to the early Ming dynasty – a friendship which had been maintained long enough, and is therefore likely to continue for as long (Sverdrup-Thygeson 2017). Furthermore, in ancient times Chinese and African civilisations used to be 'splendid' and 'distinctive', whilst in modern times they have been threatened by colonialism and have jointly mobilised against 'subjugation' (Hu 2009). In the case of Africa, this refers to the struggles for independence from European colonial powers from the 1950s throughout the 1970s. In the case of China, it refers to British

---

5   I only include a handful of direct quotations from the documents, and I leave it to the interested reader to check on the others. In conducting discourse analysis, I employed a variety of textual mechanisms, including presupposition, predicate analysis, subject positioning, and metaphorical analysis (Dunn and Neumann 2016).

encroachment following the first Opium War (1839–1842) and the 'century of national humiliation', from which China is believed to have recovered only with victory over Japan in 1945 and the founding of the PRC in 1949.

This historical narrative – 'the colony narrative' – is often used as a tool in China's Africa policy (Sverdrup-Thygeson 2017). In short, Sverdrup-Thygeson argues,

> Beijing is [...] challenging the current historicity applied to the African continent by bringing forth a set of historical narratives that serves [...] also to turn the tables with regard to the Western actors that find themselves occupying the unusual role of the "Other" in this new mode of regarding Sino-African history' (Sverdrup-Thygeson 2017, 56).

Hence, China and African countries are depicted as sympathetic members of the same community of developing countries with 'common fundamental interests'. The two then share a temporal identity, which belongs to a glorious past, and an ethical one, which makes them victims of subjugation, colonialism, and imperialism.

Unlike in ancient times, today's international order is not a friendly environment for developing countries: another important representation is 'globalisation' as a 'challenge' and a 'risk'. The first Action Plan states that 'globalisation currently represents more challenges and risks than opportunities to the vast number of developing countries' (FOCAC 2000). The depiction of globalisation as a challenge remained largely stable throughout the first three Forums and was then replaced entirely by concerns about the global financial crisis starting from the fourth Action Plan. In the former case (globalisation as a threat to developing countries), the implication is that developed countries, which have shaped the current world order according to their norms and interests, are benefitting from globalisation, whilst developing countries, including China, are left with a series of arduous tasks. In the latter case (financial crisis as a threat), China, whilst acknowledging the damages it itself had suffered, simultaneously distances itself from those more in need (FOCAC 2009b). Interestingly, both narratives equally justify and legitimise increasing economic contributions to the continent. Either way, it seems Chinese leaders believe that issues of development should not be overlooked even at times of crisis.

Broadly speaking, the unjust current world system is rooted not only in the economic, but also in the scientific and technological gaps between the 'North' and the 'South'. Imbalances between the two are the symptom that '[h] egemonism and power politics still exist. Developing countries are still faced with an arduous task of safeguarding their sovereignty, security and interests' (Jiang 2000). Hegemony is thus represented by the domination of developed countries in the current world order, which are also responsible for practicing power politics, as well as for exploiting natural resources from developing countries. Such hegemony is held responsible for poverty and backwardness which are the 'true' causes of conflicts in the continent (Jiang 2000). The current world order is therefore inequitable, because it was tailored to developed countries' needs.

Finally, adherence to the principles of 'non-interference in other's internal affairs' and respect for state sovereignty is a milestone of China's Africa discourse. China reiterates 'support for [African countries'] efforts in independently resolving regional conflicts and strengthening democracy and good governance and oppose the interference in Africa's internal affairs by external forces in pursuit of their own interests' (FOCAC 2012). Often accused by some of being neo-colonialist,[6] Chinese leaders have rejected such accusations by arguing that:

> The structure of trade between China and Africa that is based on energy and resources should indeed be improved. Meanwhile, the same situation exists between Africa and all its major trading partners. [...] China-Africa cooperation does not match that between Africa and its traditional partners in either scope or depth. [...] One should also recognize that the unfair and unreasonable international political and economic order is still a major obstacle hindering Africa's development. To reverse the situation, it is crucial that those countries leading international relations make an effort (Zhai 2012).

To sum up, the Chinese discourse constructs China-Africa relations within a broader logic of South-South cooperation, whereby the 'South', according to Alden, Morphet, and Vieira, forms a source of identity for both state and non-state actors – an identity that is constantly negotiated at the meetings of the Non-Aligned Movement (NAM), the G77, and other regional and sub-regional organisations and which encapsulates the common experience of colonialism and imperialism.

Ultimately, the 'South' is being used as a mobilising strategy based upon a critique of the asymmetries and inequalities of the contemporary international system (Alden, Morphet and Vieira 2010).

---

6   See for instance: Gaye 2006; Online Debate: Is Chinese Investment Good for Africa? 2007; Cardenal and Araújo 2013; French 2014.

Legitimising the Security-Development Nexus

In the preceding section I identified the main 'master signifiers'[7] that Chinese decision makers have been employing when constructing China-Africa relations within a South-South cooperation framework. Such a discourse portrays policies directed at helping African countries develop economically as a need, a duty, and a priority. Within such a framework, security occupies an important place. However, the extent to which security has been a part of China's Africa policy has changed throughout the years. Arguably, from being relatively marginal in the first two Forums (FOCAC 2000; FOCAC 2003), it started becoming increasingly prominent from 2004-2005. China's engagement in Sudan and in the peace process undoubtedly marks a crucial moment in the PRC's engagement in peace and security in Africa, and the existing IR literature documents well the motives and dynamics of this shift (Barber 2014; Large 2009; Large 2011). From then on, peace and security, and peacekeeping in particular, feature prominently in all FOCAC action plans (FOCAC 2009c; FOCAC 2009b; FOCAC 2015, FOCAC 2018).

The years since the inception of the FOCAC have thus seen a gradual shift to increased Chinese engagement in peace and security on the continent, based on the Five Principles of Peaceful Coexistence, albeit with space for adjustments, and marked by an emphasis on the security-development nexus. It is this security-development nexus that lies at the heart of China's policies.[8] The understanding of peace and security that emerges from FOCAC documents is one very much rooted in China's domestic practices, where security is intimately connected to development: reducing poverty and improving living conditions is considered to be key to achieving peace and, consequently, security (Benabdallah 2016b). China's domestic policies in turn shape its foreign policy towards security in Africa – its own experience in focusing on economic development in order to strengthen stability informs its international approach too. Poverty, backwardness, and lack of development, which China blames on hegemonic powers, are the main causes of insecurity, conflicts, and war. As Xi Jinping argued during the Fourth Summit of the Conference on Interaction and Confidence Building Measures in Asia:

---

7   'Master signifiers' is first used by Derrida; Laclau and Mouffe call them 'nodal points'. They are the result of exposing 'the practices and possibilities engendered by various textual mechanisms within individual texts and discourses in general' (Dunn and Neumann 2016).

8   To be sure, while the link between security and development has its origins in Western thought, from the Enlightenment onwards (see Duffield 2001; Hettne 2010), it does have its equivalent in China, as Benabdallah also notes (2016a), and Chinese policy makers have been especially eager to use the concept in their Africa discourse, making the nexus one of the key elements of their foreign policy towards the 'Global South'.

> Sustainable security means that we need to focus on both development and security so that security would be durable. As a Chinese saying goes, for a tree to grow tall, a strong and solid root is required; for a river to reach far, an unimpeded source is necessary. Development is the foundation of security, and security the precondition for development. The tree of peace does not grow on barren land while the fruit of development is not produced amidst flames of war (Xi 2014).

Such a security-development nexus creates a sort of quasi-causal argument[9]: Since security can only be achieved through development, China is justified in providing substantial economic aid to African countries in order to simultaneously promote security. Such a nexus is considered appropriate by both parties, as Africans seem to have embraced the China model based on development-first policies. Hence, such discourse legitimises developmental, infrastructure, and logistics-related policies in light of the pursuit of peace and security. Arguably, security issues have gained more prominence in China's Africa policy, which reflect a major change in its security policies on the continent. The analysis above has showed that the official discourse has remained constant throughout the years: The centrality of the security-development nexus allows Chinese leaders to modify their policies toward peace and security without changing the narratives behind it. As the largest developing country and leader of the developing world, China has an almost moral obligation to provide economic assistance to African countries. Crucially, economic development is considered an essential tool in achieving security. This is said to be in line with continental priorities, and the African Union itself is premised on the securitisation of development: Security is a prerequisite for development, and the barriers between security, governance, and development are not rigid but rather malleable (Chitiyo 2010).

What can be observed in the discourse as highlighted above, is another often ignored aspect of the relationship between security and development, described as the 'developmentalisation' of security. Both Chinese and Africans seem to agree that 'security forces can, and should on occasion, contribute directly or indirectly to development' (Chitiyo 2010, 26). In the years between 2000 and 2015, China used policies that both emphasised the importance of promoting development in order to achieve peace, and promoted an understanding of peace and security as major factors in achieving sustainable development. Lately, increased contributions to peace and security measures, whilst still accompanied by economic and financial aid, reflect a focus on the securitisation of development. Such shifts in policies were possible to enact even without a change in China's basic

---

9   For more on such quasi-causal arguments, see Weldes 1996.

discourse, because such discourse already contained all the elements necessary to range from a set of policies to the other.

The endurance of China's construction of its own identity as a faithful friend to African countries throughout the years of the FOCAC does not only depend on Chinese leaders' intriguing articulation of such identity and related policies. For the purposes of this chapter, it will suffice to say that China's processes of articulation and interpellation (Weldes 1996) have been successful in constructing China-Africa friendship as opposed to colonialist practices perpetrated by developed countries. Similarly successful has been the construction of the security-development nexus as central to its policies, even when these have shifted from focusing on the importance of economic development as a driver of peace, to focusing on the centrality of security to achieve sustainable development. African leaders have been interpellated into the language of security and development as members of the same group of developing countries with a 'shared destiny'.

Conclusion

In this chapter, I have argued for the need to re-examine common theoretical approaches to China's socialisation in international relations. Whilst acknowledging that the literature on socialisation has done a great deal in compensating for the shortcomings of most mainstream approaches, two main problems remain unaddressed: first, a bias in favour of a Western liberal order and 'good' norms. Second, such literature has neglected that China is both the *object* and *subject* of socialisation dynamics, an example of which can be found in the re-articulation of concepts of state sovereignty and intervention. The most effective way of doing so is through regional forum diplomacy, which in turn forms part of a wider attempt to become a global normative power (Alden and Alves 2017; Benabdallah 2016a).

China has showed ambition to become a norms-maker by trying to move away from ad hoc participation to Africa's peace and security to 'gradualist forms of engagement that include fomenting common Chinese-African values and re-imagining liberal norms on intervention' (Alden and Large 2015, 125). I have taken the example of the FOCAC to show how China has successfully articulated a discourse on Sino-African ties which has gained wide acceptance among African leaders. By constructing its own identity as a fellow developing country which is ready to 'assist' through thick and thin, China has thus established its own interests in peace and security on the continent. Simultaneously, by accepting and embracing such narratives, African leaders have found themselves comfortable in their identity as developing countries in need of assistance from a friend, and have thus established their interests too, in what is being described as a win-win situation.

References

Acharya, Amitav. 2008. "Nonhegemonic International Relations: A Preliminary Conceptualization." *School of Sociology, Politics, and International Studies*. University of Bristol.

Acharya, Amitav. 2009. *Whose Ideas Matter? Agency and Power in Asian Regionalism*. Ithaca: Cornell University Press.

Alden, Chris, and Ana Cristina Alves. 2017. "China's Regional Forum Diplomacy in the Developing World: Socialisation and the "Sinosphere." *Journal of Contemporary China* 26(103): 151–165.

Alden, Chris, and Daniel Large. 2015. "On Becoming a Norms Maker: Chinese Foreign Policy, Norms Evolution and the Challenges of Security in Africa." *The China Quarterly* 221: 123–142.

Alden, Chris, Sally Morphet, and Marco Antonio Vieira. 2010. *The South in World Politics*. New York: Palgrave Macmillan.

Barber, Laura. 2014. *Chinese Foreign Policy in the "Going Out" Era: Confronting Challenges and "Adaptive Learning" in the Case of China-Sudan and South Sudan Relations*. http://etheses.lse.ac.uk/3129/.

Benabdallah, Lina. 2016a. "Towards a Post-Western Global Governance? How China-Africa Relations in(Form) China's Practices." *Rising Powers Quarterly* 1(1): 135–145.

Benabdallah, Lina. 2016b. "China's Peace and Security Strategies in Africa: Building Capacity Is Building Peace?" *African Studies Quarterly* 16(3–4): 17–34.

Buzan, Barry. 2010. "China in International Society: Is "Peaceful Rise" Possible?" *Chinese Journal of International Politics* 3(1): 5–36.

Buzan, Barry. 2014. "The Logic and Contradictions of 'Peaceful Rise/Development' as China's Grand Strategy." *The Chinese Journal of International Politics*, Volume 7(4): 381–420.

Buzan, Barry, and Rosemary Foot. 2004. *Does China Matter? A Reassessment: Essays in Memory of Gerald Segal*. London; New York, NY: Routledge.

Cardenal, Juan Pablo, and Heriberto Araújo. 2013. *China's Silent Army: The Pioneers, Traders, Fixers and Workers Who Are Remaking the World in Beijing's Image*. Allen Lane.

Chitiyo, Knox. 2010. "African Security and the Securitisation of Development." In *Resurgent Continent? Africa and the World*. Nicholas Kitchen, ed. IDEAS Reports - Strategic Updates. London, UK: LSE IDEAS.

Christensen, Thomas. 2011. "The Advantages of an Assertive China: Responding to Beijing's Abrasive Diplomacy." *Foreign Affairs* 90(2): 54–67.

Duffield, Mark. 2001. *Global Governance and the New Wars. The Merging of Development and Security*. London; New York: Zed Books.

Dunn, Kevin C., and Iver B. Neumann. 2016. *Undertaking Discourse Analysis for Social Research*. Ann Arbor, MI: University of Michigan Press.

Economy, Elizabeth, and Michel Oksenberg, eds. 1999. *China Joins the World: Progress and Prospects*. New York: Council on Foreign Relations Press.

Ekman, Alice. 2016. *China's Regional Forum Diplomacy*. European Union Institute for Security Studies (EUISS).

FOCAC. 2000. Programme for China-Africa Cooperation in Economic and Social Development. http://www.focac.org/eng/ltda/dyjbzjhy/DOC12009/t606797.htm.

———2003. FOCAC Addis Ababa Action Plan (2004-2006). http://www.focac.org/eng/ltda/dejbzjhy/DOC22009/t606801.htm.

———2009a. Beijing Declaration of the Forum on China-Africa Cooperation. http://www.focac.org/eng/ltda/dyjbzjhy/DOC12009/t606796.htm.

———2009b. FOCAC Sharm El Sheikh Action Plan (2010-2012). http://www.focac.org/eng/ltda/dsjbzjhy/hywj/t626387.htm.

———2009c. Implementation of the Follow-up Actions of the Beijing Summit of the Forum on China-Africa Cooperation. http://www.focac.org/eng/ltda/dscbzjhy/FA32009/t627504.htm.

———2012. The Fifth Ministerial Conference of the Forum on China-Africa Cooperation Beijing Action Plan (2013-2015). http://www.focac.org/eng/ltda/dwjbzjjhys/hywj/t954620.htm.

———2015. Declaration of the Johannesburg Summit of the Forum on China-Africa Cooperation. http://www.focac.org/eng/ltda/dwjbzjjhys_1/hywj/t1327960.htm.

———2018. Beijing Declaration: Toward an Even Stronger China-Africa Community with a Shared Future. https://focacsummit.mfa.gov.cn/eng/hyqk_1/t1594324.htm.

French, Howard W. 2014. *China's Second Continent: How a Million Migrants Are Building a New Empire in Africa.* New York: Alfred A. Knopf.

Gaye, Adama. 2006. *Chine - Afrique: Le Dragon et l'autruche.* Études Africaines. L'Harmattan.

Gittings, John. 2008. "China's Foreign Policy: Continuity or Change?" *Journal of Contemporary Asia* 2(1): 17–35.

Hettne, Björn. 2010. "Development and Security: Origins and Future." *Security Dialogue* 41(1): 31–52.

Hu, Jintao. 2009. Address by Hu Jintao President of the People's Republic of China at the Opening Ceremony of the Beijing Summit of the Forum on China-Africa Cooperation. http://www.focac.org/eng/ltda/dscbzjhy/SP32009/t606840.htm, accessed April 12, 2017.

Hughes, Christopher. 2016. "China as a leading state in the international system." In: Tsang, Steve and Men, Honghua, (eds.) *China in the Xi Jinping Era.* The Nottingham China Policy Institute Series. Palgrave Macmillan, London, UK.

Jiang, Zemin. 2000. China and Africa-Usher in the New Century Together. http://www.focac.org/eng/ltda/dyjbzjhy/SP12009/t606804.htm.

Johnston, Alastair Iain. 2003. "Is China a Status Quo Power?" *International Security* 27(4): 5–56.

Johnston, Alastair Iain. 2008. *Social States. China in International Institutions, 1980-2000*. Princeton University Press.

Johnston, Alastair Iain. 2013. "How New and Assertive Is China's New Assertiveness." *International Security* 37(4): 7–48.

Kent, Ann. 2002. "China's International Socialization: The Role of International Organizations." *Global Governance* 8(3): 343–364.

Kim, Samuel S. 1999. "China and the United Nations." In *China Joins the World: Progress and Prospects*. Elizabeth Economy and Michel Oksenberg, eds. Council on Foreign Relations Press.

Large, Daniel. 2009. "China's Sudan Engagement: Changing Northern and Southern Political Trajectories in Peace and War." *The China Quarterly* 199: 610–626.

Large, Daniel. 2011. "China and Post-Conflict Reconstruction in Africa: The Case of Sudan." *SAIIA China in Africa Project*. Policy Briefing 36.

Li, Anshan, and April Funeka Yazini, eds. 2013. "Forum on China-Africa Cooperation." *The Politics of Human Resource Development*. South Africa: Africa Institute of South Africa.

Mearsheimer, John J. 2006. "China's Unpeaceful Rise." *Current History* 105(690): 160–162.

Mearsheimer, John J. 2014. *Can China Rise Peacefully? The Tragedy of Great Power Politics*. Updated Edition. New York: W. W. Norton.

Online Debate: Is Chinese Investment Good for Africa? 2007. Council on Foreign Relations. http://www.cfr.org/china/chinese-investment-good-africa/p12622.

Park, Susan. 2014. "Socialisation and the Liberal Order." *International Politics* 51(3): 334–349.

Pu, Xiaoyu. 2012. "Socialisation as a Two-Way Process: Emerging Powers and the Diffusion of International Norms." *The Chinese Journal of International Politics* 5(4): 341–367.

Schimmelfenning, Frank. 2000. "International Socialization in the New Europe: Rational Action in an Institutional Environment." *European Journal of International Relations* 6(1): 109–139.

Segal, Gerald. 1999. "Does China Matter?" *Foreign Affairs* 78(5): 24–36.

Shambaugh, David, ed. 2000. *The Modern Chinese State*. Cambridge University Press.

Shambaugh, David 2013. *China Goes Global: The Partial Power*. New York: Oxford University Press.

Shih, Chih-Yu. 2005. "Breeding a Reluctant Dragon: Can China Rise into Partnership and Away from Antagonism?." *Review of International Studies* 31(4): 755–774.

Sverdrup-Thygeson, Bjornar. 2017. "The Chinese Story: Historical Narratives as a Tool in China's Africa Policy." *International Politics* 54(1): 54–72.

Taylor, Ian. 2011. "The Forum on China-Africa Cooperation (FOCAC)." *Global Institutions*. Oxon/New York: Routledge.

Wang, Jisi. 1994. "International Relations Theory and the Study of Chinese Foreign Policy: A Chinese Perspective." In *Chinese Foreign Policy: Theory and Practice*. Thomas Robinson and David Shambaugh, eds. Oxford: Clarendon Press.

Wang, Jisi. 2011. "China's Search for a Grand Strategy. A Rising Power Finds Its Way." *Foreign Affairs* 90(2): 68–69.

Weldes, J. 1996. "Constructing National Interests." *European Journal of International Relations* 2(3): 275–318.

Xi, Jinping. 2014. New Asian Security Concept For New Progress in Security Cooperation. http://www.fmprc.gov.cn/mfa_eng/zxxx_662805/t1159951.shtml.

Xia, Liping. 2001. "China: A Responsible Great Power." *Journal of Contemporary China* 10(26): 17–25.

Zhai, Jun. 2012. Broad Prospects for the New Type of China-Africa Strategic Partnership. http://www.focac.org/eng/ltda/dwjbzjjhys/zyjh/t951074.htm.

11

Becoming a 'Responsible Power'?: China's New Role during the JCPOA Negotiations

DANIEL JOHANSON

The ancient connections between China and Iran are frequently stressed to underscore the strength and longevity of the relationship. Official statements from both governments take special care to highlight this history. While this is predominantly rhetoric now, centuries ago there was a strong connection through the Silk Road's movement of goods and cultural traditions. China's modern relationship with Iran is anchored in the legacy of the Cold War, but it also includes a strategic element – viewing Iran as a key gateway into the Middle East. China's current relationship with Iran began as China was beginning to move away from its revolutionary history. Even still, ties between reformist China and revolutionary Iran developed, stemming from a number of factors – including economic interests, energy security, and regional stability in the Middle East. This chapter will briefly explore China's role in and importance to Iran, leading to an examination of China's unofficial participation in other nations' sanctions in 2010 – sanctions that arguably led Iran back to negotiations. Next, we will examine China's role in the JCPOA agreement and attempt to identify any new roles or actions that China took in addressing the Iranian nuclear issue. China's participation here is relatively understudied – but shows a key trend towards more active involvement that may impact its future interactions in issues of international security.

The Evolution of China's Role in Iran

Between the 1980s to the late-2000s, China's actions regarding Iran gradually began to change in connection with international consensus and frustration amongst Chinese leadership stemming from a lack of progress and an apparent disregard for international concern. Throughout the 1980s and 1990s, China's overall role in the issue was minimal – save the sale of weapons and weapons technology (Gill 2001, 267; Davis 2012, 4; Calabrese 2006, 10; Lin 2010, 2; Harold and Nader 2012, 4). Even then, much of this ceased in an effort to prioritise relations with the United States in the 1990s (Calabrese 2006, 12; Meshbahi and Homayounvash 2016, 77; Harold and Nader 2012, 8).

As China's role in the international community began to grow throughout the early to mid-2000s, it began to acknowledge the potential repercussions of the Iranian nuclear issue. During this period it viewed this as a bilateral issue between the US and Iran. It is important to note that China did delay referrals for Iran's actions first to the IAEA, and then the UNSC in an attempt to let Iran prove its nuclear intentions were peaceful (Garver 2013, 80–81). These delays were, in effect, 'last chances' for Iran to comply. Yet, once deadlines were passed and unmet by Iran, China allowed for resolutions – and sanctions – to be passed while continuing to stress the need for mediation and cooperation (Katzman 2011, 29–30; Garver 2011, 75).

When circumstances aligned and brought about an environment favourable for negotiations, China's integration with the international community, as well as with Iran's economy were both at a high point. While it was always possible for China to strongly support Iran, China supported an increasing role in ensuring that international security be upheld.

China's Increasing Iranian Interests

It is important, first of all, to understand China's relationship with Iran after the weapons sales of the 1990s ended. Even though Beijing and Tehran's political systems are somewhat at odds, the relationship has had benefits for both parties. As Iran's role in the region became stronger, it also became 'a significant source of vital oil supplies' to fuel China's economy (Swaine 2010, 1; Chen and Yang 2010, 79–81). To ensure continued economic growth, China had increasingly needed to focus on markets abroad and obtaining the necessary raw materials to fuel its economy.

At the same time, the US began pressuring 'Russia, Japan, South Korea, India, and Europe to reduce trade and investment with Iran' (Harold and Nader 2012, 5). So, as China enhanced its role in Iran – in both its domestic and energy markets – other players were leaving. As a result, by 2007 China had become the largest trading partner of Iran – taking the EU's place (Dickey and Ighani 2014). China was viewed by Iran to be a key source of 'investment and technology necessary for ... economic development and modernization'

(Harold and Nader 2012, 5). Sanctions also created an environment in which Iran needed China due to the limiting effect of the sanctions on Iran's access to the external finance and specialists needed to develop its natural gas and oil reserves.

China has predominately filled this gap, not only through funding and expertise – but also through the provision of refined energy supplies (e.g. gasoline) that were banned as exports to Iran. Essentially, Iran became both a market for Chinese goods and a supplier for the Chinese energy industry (Downs and Maloney 2011, 3) This, in part, underscores China's understanding and support for solving the nuclear issue diplomatically. If something were to cause a power shift or exacerbate regional stability, China recognises that it will be the clear loser with higher oil prices and unpredictable supply issues.

To provide a quick overview – Iran's quest for nuclear weapons was viewed as a problem for three key reasons:

> 1) Its relatively open cooperation with North Korea and Pakistan
> 2) A documented support of terrorism in the Middle East and internationally
> 3) A clear hostility towards Sunni Muslim states as well as Israel (Christensen 2015, 121)

In the first half of the 2000s, diplomacy had some success in approaching the issue – first with the Tehran Declaration, and then the Paris Agreement in 2004 (Gaietta 2016, 72). Unfortunately, diplomacy took a backseat after the election of Mahmoud Ahmadinejad in 2005.

Iran then began enriching uranium, resulting in the IAEA referring the issue to the UNSC by early 2006 (Zheng 2007, 19; Sterio 2016, 72). The political climate under Ahmadinejad was full of rhetoric, and while diplomatic approaches continued – Iran also continually failed to assuage the International community's concerns. As a result, from that point until 2010, the UNSC passed six resolutions in an attempt to address the issue.

Early on in its own history, the People's Republic of China saw the development of nuclear weapons to be 'a sovereign right', but now seems to more fully recognise the implications of proliferation on international security and stability (Wuthnow 2011, 174). China believed – or at least was open to the possibility – that Iran's nuclear ambitions had peaceful intentions. As a result, China stressed diplomacy yet allowed for the imposition of sanctions that did not directly target the Iranian people or harm Chinese interests. Throughout this, Iran became increasingly dependent on China – as the sanctions issued after 2010 by the US and EU pushed out most other players (Harvard Belford Center 2015, 9, 18).

China and the 2010 Sanctions

Even though China was not a direct party to the unilateral sanctions – particularly those imposed by the US – after their imposition, Chinese economic activity with Iran began to slow. The same year, it was said that 'the Chinese government [had] informally instructed firms to slow down' (Davis et al. 2012, 18). Additionally, several Chinese companies operating in Iran – including 'CNPC [China National Petroleum Corporation], Sinopec, CNOOC [China National Offshore Oil Corporation], and Zhenrong ... failed to implement their agreements ... or have "gone slow"' in finishing current projects (Harold and Nader 2012, 12). These actions seem to have been the result of some kind of agreement with the United States. One, in particular, that would not sanction Chinese companies' current Iranian investments as long as no new deals were made. So, while China was still active in Iran, new and unfinished projects were either delayed or postponed altogether. Additionally, highlighting this was the fact that from 2010 to 2013 Chinese purchases of Iranian oil fell year on year.

Sanctions, and China's willingness to at least partially comply, clearly had a role in bringing Iran back to the negotiating table. After roughly three years of the sanctions another key roadblock to diplomatic talks was addressed when Hassan Rouhani was elected in 2013. That same year, initial discussions between he and US President Barack Obama created the groundwork that made it possible for further talks in Geneva and Vienna – culminating in the Joint Comprehensive Plan of Action (JCPOA).

China's Role in the JCPOA Talks

After about two years of negotiating, an agreement was reached between Iran and the P5+1 on 15 July 2015. The resultant pact was an attempt to satisfy all involved parties while addressing the key issues surrounding Iran's nuclear quest. After the agreement was approved in the UNSC through UNSCR 2231, the timeline for implementation and removal of sanctions began (UN Security Council 2015).

As a good portion of the negotiations were conducted behind closed doors, portions of the final agreement are still not publicly available (Samore 2015,

1).[1] At this point, much of China's exact role in the negotiation remains unclear – yet it is obvious that China at the very least had a critical role in mediating differences between the US and Iran. It is also clear that a peaceful resolution of the issue and avoidance of all possible military action became a priority (Garver 2016, 1). While, as in prior stages of the issue the main actors involved have been the United States, China was clearly a key component and intermediary. In particular, China appeared to have been useful in persuading Iran about potential economic and political benefits that could be obtained, 'securing international recognition for Iran's 'right' to enrich uranium', as well as mediating any other disputes (Garver 2016, 1; Ford 2015).

Without at least China's approval and minimal participation, negotiations would likely have been more difficult if not impossible. Through its 'active' mediation role and its part in UNSCR 2231, China also has highlighted its more active international role. This is a 'notable precedent in [China's] diplomatic efforts to combat nuclear proliferation and other issues of global governance' (Nejadifar 2016, 59).

The agreement that became the JCPOA was acceptable to all parties involved – even if it did not satisfy all of their initial requirements. The key component that satisfied the P5+1 was that there was a stated limit on 'Iran's ability to produce fissile material for nuclear weapons' – with the allowed amount at a low enough level that Iran would not be able to successfully make a warhead (Samore 2015, 4). Iran's main benefit – understandably – was sanction relief once the agreement was in place. The relief would be phased, first removing UNSC sanctions, and then others that had been unilaterally imposed would follow (Wuthnow 2016, 3; Salehi-Isfahani 2015; Nasralla 2017).[2]

A major component of this relief included the lifting of a US action that sanctioned all international entities that had dealings involving Iran's Central Bank. This action took effect early on, around implementation day – freeing the Chinese companies that had previously restrained their actions in response to the sanctions (Kennedy 2016). Still, while the largest destination for Iranian oil remained China the overall economic situation improved (EIA 2015). Merely a year after the sanctions on Iran were lifted, total foreign investment in Iran had grown by 42% (Financial Tribune 2017).

---

1   This is 'including a side agreement among the P5+1 on future UN action in 10 years and the contents of Iran's "enrichment and enrichment R&D plan," which Iran will eventually submit to the …(IAEA)'.
2   This would happen on 16 January 2016. Though it is important to note the US continues to push the envelope on this through adding more sanctions under Trump.

While China's actions in earlier phases of the Iranian crisis were minimal, they were said to have had a constructive role throughout the JCPOA mediation procedures – potentially 'motivated by a desire to shape [the] diplomatic outcome' (Singh 2015). In general, China seems to have had a key role in mediation and convincing Iran of the value of the deal – while making sure that it was acceptable to all parties.

'Active' Mediation

When involved in the resolution of an international security issue China has long preferred a sort of mediation role, but for the JCPOA negotiations they appeared to take up a much more active approach – at least outwardly. Moving away from past precedents, China acted at various times as a mediator, a bridge between the various actors, as well as an assurer – so as to prove to Iran that the dealmakers were sincere and the agreement would be carried out.

One particular example of this effort was Beijing's numerous attempts to persuade Iran of the value of an agreement via a number of high-level diplomatic visits between June 2013 and July 2015 (Kondapalli 2016, 63). Notably, between June 2013 and October 2016, there were at least five diplomatic visits between the Iranian and Chinese heads of state. It was during these visits that China was said to have emphasised the utility of clearly addressing the concerns of the international community – as if Iran did not, a military conflict was likely. Chinese leaders, including China's Ambassador to Iran emphasised the tangible benefits of avoiding conflict – clearly hinting at the provision of Chinese help to further develop Iran's economy once sanctions were gone (Garver 2016, 2; Pang 2015). China was clearly trying to incentivise Iran to work towards a quick solution with the other engaged parties.

After Xi Jinping became President and General Secretary in late 2012 and early 2013, respectively, China's approach and role in these negotiations were viewed to have become much bolder. In particular, it has been noted that Xi Jinping favours a more active role – which is fitting, as Foreign Minister Wang Yi's has also been seen to favour such an approach (Huang 2015). However, it is worth noting that Hu Jintao's government also 'actively lobbied Washington' in an attempt to have the US resolve the issue directly with Iran (Scott 2015).

One of the most interesting aspects of China's role in the discussion is purely how the Chinese media described China's role. The press, particularly Chinese sources, seems to have stressed China's particular role during the

JCPOA negotiation to have been 'constructive' but also 'objective, fair and responsible' (Hua 2015). In the past, China would have been described as a participant or their work would have been downplayed. Yet, after the announcement of the JCPOA, China's role was actually said to have been 'active'. Most statements highlighted the constructive role China had played – providing little detail though insisting that China's role had been useful or even 'pivotal' and 'irreplaceable' (Mu 2015; Shichor 2016, 3). According to CCTV, China had made 'unremitting efforts', and played 'a significant role' (Huang 2015). The Iranian publication PressTV used a quote attributed to Xi Jinping that described China's actions in the process to have been as 'an active participant, constructor and contributor' with a clear concentration on addressing and solving the issue (PressTV 2016). While most of the actual descriptions of Chinese action were vague and specific examples of this are sparse, most of these media reports show China prioritising the negotiations and describe China's activities in the negotiations to have been focused on proactively mediating and promoting diplomatic resolution wherever possible to ensure that an agreement was reached.

Iran's ambassador to Beijing also offered one of the clearest overviews of China's part in the process, as he said it 'worked as a liaison that has successfully bridged the gaps, neutralised misunderstandings and helped alleviate concerns during the negotiations' (Global Times 2015). China's position in the talks, he believed, raised the confidence levels of Iranian negotiators in the process and in the resultant deal (Joobani and Helmy 2016, 384). He also noted that China had even taken the lead on a few topics – particularly offering to lead cooperative efforts to redesign the Arak heavy water reactor (Fars News Agency, 2016.).

Not all sources, however, agree on China's role. Sources outside of China, Iran, and the Chinese media, however have stated that China's role was not as instrumental as has been claimed. These comments range from an involved party insisting that overall it was a group effort, to others stating Beijing's presence was 'marginal, evasive, and ambiguous' (Almond, 2016; Shichor 2016, 3). Regardless of China's actual role – it is important to note that the mere fact that China presented itself and wanted to be viewed as an active component itself is a remarkable change.

Increasing Involvement

China's actions leading up to, during, and after the JCPOA negotiations show a clear change from their past behaviour. While China has always had an interest in a stable Middle East conducive to Chinese growth, as its investments in the region have grown, stability has become much more of a necessity. China clearly views itself as a stakeholder in the region and in international affairs more broadly and wants to be considered responsible. It increasingly became, or was viewed to have become, more actively involved in the resolution of the Iranian nuclear issue – seeking a resolution to above all avoid a military confrontation.

China's interest in a stable Middle East underscores how its interests and view of the international community have evolved. Rather than continuing to refer to the issue as bilateral as it had in the 1990s, China increasingly views the role of multilateral talks as useful in addressing complex issues. China's implicit support of the unilateral sanctions stem from a similar base as to why it supported the UNSC sanctions – nearly universal support from other powers, Iran's continued defiance and inability to address concerns, as well as the potential danger of an armed conflict to ensure Iran complies (Swaine 2010, 8). Moreover, China is concerned with ensuring that its external environment is stable so that there are no further challenges to its growth (Mesbahi and Homayounvash 2016, 83). Iran put this stability into question, and China counselled mediation and resolution of the situation. When mediation initially failed to address the situation, China allowed for other measures – in particular, sanctions – to help expedite a return to talks.

The way China interacted throughout the JCPOA negotiations shows that China is a key stakeholder that also wants to be viewed as a responsible power. While the term 'responsible power' is frequently dismissed as a US ploy in private, it is undeniable that it is something that has become a part of China's policy dialogue and official vocabulary (Global Times 2010; Global Times 2013). China's actions with regard to Iran show that it views non-proliferation, Middle East stability, and the intersection of the two as issues it is involved in, and ignoring these issues would be, by definition, irresponsible. While many in China may disapprove of the use of 'responsible power', China increasingly wants to be seen as a productive member of the international community.

Altogether, China's actions with regard to the creation and implementation of the JCPOA have shown a China that is aware of and influenced by the values of the international system. Through this, China has worked to address a problem, multilaterally, with other powers within the system.

Analysis of Changes

China's actions with regard to the Iranian nuclear issue has shown a clear evolution, from a 'not-our-issue' sort of view to actively working with the rest of the international community to come to a peaceful resolution. To get here,

China needed to balance its interests – yet even that does not completely explain its shift to a more active role as mediator. If China merely required furthered economic relations and a stable region, it could have simply supported the status quo. Instead, along with the other P5+1 nations, China worked towards a new agreement while encouraging the participation of Iran. This was done with the intent of preventing potential conflict, and hopefully creating long-term regional stability.

China's trajectory has shown a clear progression from inactivity to increased involvement. Many reasons play a part in why and how this developed – China's economic growth, the expansion of its energy requirements, as well as its growing international role. Iran's responses to the international community of ignoring requests, breaching agreements, or the general animosity exhibited by top Iranian leadership also gave China little choice but to side with the international community. Iran was offered numerous chances to comply, but each failure made China's choice easier.

A component of China's behaviour, of course, was conducted in tandem with the rest of the UNSC. As a result of this sort of action, China was likely to have better political and economic relations with the EU and the US. This way China also did not risk alienating itself – as there was essentially an international consensus that the issue needed to be resolved quickly, collaboratively and peacefully. The potential of military action and the resultant regional instability was a key motivating factor for China in ensuring that this issue was resolved quickly. The longer it remained unaddressed, the greater the concerns that the region would fall into deeper trouble, causing regional instability and potentially disrupting oil supplies. Throughout the process, undoubtedly there were points when the US and EU did not agree with China's approach. They were all working towards the same end-goal, however, a stable, non-nuclear Iran.

The Indeterminate Future of the Deal

The future of the deal has numerous components that will determine its success – but the two key factors that could unravel its progress now are Iran's adherence to the agreement and the US's continued acknowledgement that Iran is abiding by the agreed rules. The other signatories of the deal – at least for now – do not appear to question the deal, or want anything but its ultimate success.

For Iran's part, their election in mid-2017 underscored domestic Iranian support of the agreement. By all accounts, Rouhani's win means that a continuation of his existing policies should be expected. In general, the vote was a clear indication of the Iranian people's approval of continued stability and engagement with the world. A win by Rouhani's opponent, Raisi, would have been a return to the rhetoric and sentiment experienced under Ahmadinejad. During his term, Ahmadinejad's rhetoric became trying, and stability was constantly threatened, so a similar administration would be disastrous – especially with the unpredictability of the Trump White House (Weir 2011). Rouhani's re-election with 57% of the vote will give him further support as he continues to further Iran's ties with the rest of the world (Cunningham 2017).

While the Obama administration viewed the JCPOA as a diplomatic success, President Donald J. Trump views things differently. Stretching back to his time on the campaign trail in 2015–2016, Trump continually threatened to leave the agreement. He finally did on May 8, 2018. As a result, the US has imposed two rounds of unilateral sanctions. Firstly, in August 2018, targeting various Iranian industries. Secondly, in November 2018 targeting the Iranian oil sector. While the United States is no longer party to the deal, Europe and China are working together to ensure it is upheld. For the time being, Iran appears to be willing to work with Europe and China on this. Indeed, it is important to note that as recently as 30 August 2018, the IAEA reported that Iran was still in compliance with the agreement. On the whole, it remains unclear what the full impact of the United States' absence and the new sanctions will be – but they certainly complicate the issue.

Conclusion

As we have seen, China's view with regard to its role in addressing international issues has seen a clear evolution over the past 20 years. Between the late 1990s and 2005, China viewed the Iranian nuclear issue to be external to its interests and did not or could not view Iran's development of nuclear technology as a concern – to either itself or the international community. The key caveat here was that if Iran's quest interfered with other relationships, or if there was something to gain from acknowledging the issues, China would recognise and react. Throughout the international attempts to address the issue, China supported Iran and pushed for the international community to give Iran the benefit of a doubt on its intentions – but only to a point. When U.N. requirements were not met or ignored by Iran, China allowed for incrementally stricter sanctions to be passed. Each time, China's goal was to have Iran come back to the negotiating table.

When it came to it – China allowed for a UN Resolution in 2010 that would allow for other nations to unilaterally sanction Iran. While China did not sanction Iran directly, for all intents and purposes it was a key component to its success in bringing Iran back to the table. Without China's assistance these sanctions would not have had as much of an impact as they did. One key thing to note here is that through China's implicit acceptance of other nations' unilateral sanctions, a choice was made to work with international consensus and unofficially participate in the sanctions. This was a clear shift from past precedent and could have implications for future multilateral issues. Additionally, it was also impressive that the Chinese media viewed China's role to be so significant – this in itself is a drastic change. This media coverage may forecast a strong continued presence for China in similar issues in the future. Regardless, with the future of the JCPOA under question as a result of the Trump administration's withdrawal from the agreement and the resulting sanctions, China's actions will likely continue to highlight its support for the necessity of upholding the JCPOA.

References

Almond, Roncevert Ganan. 2016. "China and the Iran Nuclear Deal." *The Diplomat*. March 8. http://thediplomat.com/2016/03/china-and-the-iran-nuclear-deal/.

Calabrese, John. 2006. "China and Iran: Partners Perfectly Mismatched." *Middle East Institute Manuscript*.

Chen Lianqing and Yang Xingli. 2010. "Discussion of the Influence the Iran Nuclear Question on Sino-Iranian Relations" *Journal of Hubei University of Economics* 7 (9): 79–81.

Christensen, Thomas J. 2015. *The China Challenge: Shaping the Choices of a Rising Power*. New York: W.W. Norton and Company.

Cunningham, Eric. 2017. "Iranian President Rouhani wins re-election by a landslide." *Washington Post*, May 20.

Davis, Marybeth et. al. 2012. *China-Iran: A Limited Partnership*, Prepared for the US-China Economic and Security Review Commission.

Dickey, Lauren and Helia Ighani. 2014. "Iran Looks East, China Pivots West." *The Diplomat*, August 25. http://thediplomat.com/2014/08/iran-looks-east-China-pivots-west/.

Downs, Erica and Suzanne Maloney. 2011. "Getting China to Sanction Iran: The Chinese-Iranian Oil Connection." *Foreign Affairs*. March/April 2011.

EIA. 2015. "Iran." *US Energy Information Administration*, June 19. https://www.eia.gov/beta/international/analysis.cfm?iso=IRN.

Fars News Agency. 2016. "AEOI Chief: China Helping Iran Redesign Arak Reactor." *Fars News Agency*, February 10. www.en.farsnews.com/newstext.aspx?nn=13941121000954.

Financial Tribune. 2017. "42% More Foreign Investors in Iran's Capital Market Post Sanctions." *Financial Tribune*, January 18. https://financialtribune.com/articles/economy-business-and-markets/57674/42-more-foreign-investors-in-iran-s-capital-market-post.

Ford, Peter. 2015. "Iran nuclear talks: Can China keep negotiations on track?." *Christian Science Monitor*, March 30. www.csmonitor.com/World/Asia-Pacific/2015/0330/Iran-nuclear-talks-Can-China-keep-negotiations-on-track-video.

Gaietta, Michele. 2015. *The Trajectory of Iran's Nuclear Program*. New York: Palgrave Macmillian.

Garver, John. 2011. "Is China Playing a Dual Game in Iran." *The Washington Quarterly* 34 (1): 75–88.

Garver, John. 2013. "China–Iran Relations: Cautious Friendship with America's Nemesis." *China Report* 49(1): 69–88.

Garver, John W. 2016. "China and Iran: An Emerging Partnership Post-Sanctions." *Middle East Institute Policy Focus Series* 2016 3: 1–8.

Gill, Bates. 2001. "Two Steps Forward, One Step Back: The Dynamics of Chinese Nonproliferation and Arms Control Policy-Making in an Era of Reform." In David M. Lampton. Ed. *The Making of Chinese Foreign and Security Policy in the Era of Reform, 1978-2000*. Stanford: Stanford University Press: 257–288.

Global Times. 2010. "UNSC draws up Iran sanctions." *Global Times*, April 16. www.globaltimes.cn/content/522752.shtml.

Global Times. 2013. "2013:Year of 'Chinese dream' diplomacy." *Global Times*, December 18. www.globaltimes.cn/content/832843.shtml.

Global Times. 2015. "Iran confident in future of nuclear deal." *Global Times*, July 21. www.globaltimes.cn/content/933050.shtml.

Harold, Scott and Alireza Nader. 2012. *China and Iran: Economic, Political, and Military Relations*. Rand Corporation: Santa Monica.

Harvard Belford Center. 2015. *Sanctions Against Iran: A Guide to Targets, Terms, and Timetables*. Cambridge, MA: Belford Center for Science and International Affairs.

Hua Xia. 2015. "China's stance on Iran nuclear issue." *Xinhua*, July 14. www.news.xinhuanet.com/english/2015-07/14/c_134412353.htm.

Huang Jin. 2015. "The inside story on Obama's Call to Zhongnanhai." *DWNews*, July 22. http://global.dwnews.com/news/2015-07-22/59668855.html.

Huang Yufan. 2015. "China Welcomes Iran Nuclear Deal Reached 'Through Dialogue." *New York Times*, July 15. https://www.nytimes.com/live/iran-nuclear-deal-live-updates/China-welcomes-iran-nuclear-deal/.

Joobani, Hossein Aghaie and Nadia Helmy. 2016. "China's Role in the Iran Nuclear Deal: Perspectives From Mainstream Chinese Media." *Asian Politics and Policy* 8(2):382–386.

Katzman, Kenneth. 2011. "Iran: US Concerns and Policy Responses." Congressional Research Service, Report RL32048.

Kennedy, Merrit. 2016. "Implementation Day Arrives: Sanctions On Iran Are Lifted." *NPR*, January 16. www.npr.org/sections/thetwo-way/2016/01/16/463168647/u-n-nuclear-watchdog-confirms-iran-nuclear-deal-set-to-be-implemented.

Kondapalli, Srikanth. 2016. "China and the Iranian Nuclear Issue: Converting Challenges into Opportunities." *Contemporary Review of the Middle East* 3(1): 63–76.

Lin, Christina Y. 2010. "China, Iran, and North Korea: A Triangular Strategic Alliance." *MERIA Journal* 14(1).

Mesbahi, Mohiaddin and Mohammad Homayounvash. 2016. "China and the International Non-Proliferation Regime: The Case of Iran." *Sociology of Islam* 4: 73–92.

Mu Xuequan. 2015. "China continues to play constructive part in resolving Iran's nuclear issue: FM." *Xinhua*, July 2. www.news.xinhuanet.com/english/2015-07/02/c_134377052.htm.

Nasralla, Shadia. 2017. "Iran decides not to upset nuclear deal over US sanctions extension." *Reuters*, January 10. www.reuters.com/article/us-iran-nuclear-idUSKBN14U2CL.

Nejadifar, Fatemeh. 2016. "An Elaboration on the Iran-China Relations in the Path towards and After Joint Comprehensive Plan of Action." *International Journal Series in Multidisciplinary Research* 2(2): 57–63.

Pang Sen. 2015. "The Relationship between China and Iran Prospects Seminar," *Iran-China Friendship Society – Tehran*, March 4. http://China.huan¬qiu.com/News/fmprc/2015-03/5817302.htm.

PressTV. 2016. "Iran nuclear deal proved diplomacy paying off: China president." *PressTV*, April 2. www.presstv.com/Detail/2016/04/02/458677/Iran-nuclear-deal-JCPOA-Chinas-President-Xi-diplomacy-P51.

Salehi-Isfahani, Djavad. 2015. "How Sanctions Relief Can Help and Hurt the Iranian Economy." *Payvand*. June 14, 2015 www.payvand.com/news/15/jun/1092.html.

Samore, Gary. 2015. *The Iran Nuclear Deal: A Definitive Guide*. Cambridge, MA: Report for Belford Center for Science and International Affairs.

Scott, Emma. 2015. "A Nuclear Deal with Chinese Characteristics: China's Role in the P5+1 Talks with Iran." *ChinaBrief* 15(14). https://jamestown.org/program/a-nuclear-deal-with-chinese-characteristics-chinas-role-in-the-p51-talks-with-iran/.

Shichor, Yitzhak. 2016. "Iran after the Sanctions: the Marginalization of China." *Note d'actualité de l'Observatoire de la Chine 2015-2016*. March 2016.

Singh, Michael. 2015. "The Sino-Iranian Tango." *Foreign Affairs*, July 21. https://www.foreignaffairs.com/articles/China/2015-07-21/sino-iranian-tango.

Sterio, Milena. 2016. "President Obama's Legacy: The Iran Nuclear Agreement?" *Case Western Reserve Journal of International Law* 48(1): 69–82.

Swaine, Michael. 2010. "Beijing's Tightrope Walk on Iran." *China Leadership Monitor*. June 28, 2010. http://carnegieendowment.org/2010/06/28/beijing-s-tightrope-walk-on-iran-pub-41080.

UN Security Council. 2015. "Resolution 2231 (2015)." *UNSC*, July 20. http://www.un.org/en/sc/2231/.

Weir, Fred. 2011. "SCO security summit: Are China and Russia losing patience with Ahmadinejad?." *Christian Science Monitor*, June 15. https://www.csmonitor.com/World/Global-News/2011/0615/SCO-security-summit-Are-China-and-Russia-losing-patience-with-Ahmadinejad.

Wuthnow, Joel. 2011. *Beyond the Veto: Chinese Diplomacy in the United Nations Security Council*, Diss. Columbia University. https://academiccommons.columbia.edu/catalog/ac%3A132019.

Wuthnow, Joel. 2016. "Posing Problems without an Alliance: China-Iran Relations after the Nuclear Deal." *INSS Strategic Forum – National Defense University*, 290: 1–12.

Zheng Xuefei. 2007. *The Iranian Nuclear Issue and International Security*. Zhengzhou, Henan People's Press.

12

The Evolution of Sino-Japanese Relations: Implications for Northeast Asia and Beyond

NORI KATAGIRI

China and Japan exert the greatest amount of influence over their neighbours in East Asia. Cooperation between the two economic giants remains robust in trade, foreign direct investment (FDI), tourism, and cultural and educational exchanges while their rivalry has grown with regard to military modernisation, political discourse, and cyber security. The complexity of Sino-Japanese relations stems in part from the fact that they have different political and economic systems as well as historical and cultural differences. They are also bound by the presence of neighbours in Northeast Asia that rival each other one way or another – North Korea, South Korea, and Taiwan – as well as powerful states with regional stakes – Russia and the United States – all of which make the region inherently prone to instability. To further complicate issues, the region was thrust into a period of transition after the election of Donald Trump in November 2016. The US-dominant structure that had held the region together since the end of the Cold War began quickly eroding under Trump's Asia policy, or lack thereof. Mired in one self-inflicted domestic crisis after another, Trump remains generally opposed to a large-scale commitment to East Asia, essentially offering China an incentive to be more revisionist and act with less constraint, while making statements drastically different from past presidents about North Korea and Taiwan. The main question I pursue in this chapter, given the changing circumstances, is how stable Sino-Japanese relations are likely to be for the next few years.

In this chapter, I make two arguments. First, of the many factors that affect the stability of Sino-Japanese relations, one of the most important is the way that national leaders in each respective country interpret the balance of military, cyber, and socio-economic power. Militarily, the two countries compete for dominance in East Asia and control of territory – especially with regard to the Senkaku/Diaoyu islands. Concerning cyber power, China continues to use its first-mover advantage to attack vulnerable systems and steal secrets from its neighbours. In economic and cultural dimensions, China and Japan are tightly interconnected and act on the principle of collaboration over conflict. The age of globalisation, regionalisation, and economic interdependence leaves no immediate losers between the two, while generating no winners, either. Claude Meyer's contention in 2011 that 'for the time being, neither of these two dominant powers can lay claim to overall supremacy in the region' is still valid (Meyer 2011, 7). Although China and Japan continue to distrust each other and blame one another for any problems, they remain interdependent for peace and prosperity, and mutual deterrence is at work against military strikes and embargoes by either side (Katagiri 2017, 1–19). The way the current leaders of both countries, China's Xi Jinping and Japan's Abe Shinzo, interpret the gains and losses of their interactions will have much to do with the way they treat each other throughout their leadership, at least until 2022 for Xi and possibly 2021 for Abe (assuming he wins re-election in 2018).

My second argument is that some changes in the external environment will have unexpected, although not necessarily consistent, impact on the stability of Sino-Japanese relations. Bilateral issues like the East China Sea disputes claimed by China but controlled by Japan, and cyber insecurity are likely to continue. They will become more salient political problems when unexpected things happen, such as when provocative statements are made on Taiwan's future (Taiwan, too, claims the East China Sea islands) and when military actions are threatened against North Korea to dissuade its nuclear and missile programs. These things can easily find their way to drag China and Japan into intense scrutiny of one another's intent. Further, bilateral relations will develop based on the way their national leaders interact with other major powers, especially the United States and Russia. That is, Xi's relations with Trump and Russian President Vladimir Putin will form the foundation of his relations with Abe because Trump's and Putin's behaviours are less predictable. Likewise, Abe's relations with Trump and Putin will be a source of strategic consideration for the Japanese as a junior ally and economic partner in the Far East, respectively, although the nature of both leaders' characters make it difficult for the Japanese to predict what their next actions will be.

Overall, ongoing bilateral interactions show that in the short run, China and Japan are likely to continue economic engagement and military balancing. Over the long run, however, China is poised to have a power advantage over Japan. China is growing faster economically, demographically, and militarily, and retains an advantage in hard power as well as the power to significantly influence events at the United Nations as a permanent member of the Security Council with veto power. Japan has boasted of its soft power to make the country culturally attractive, is making a slow economic recovery of its own, and remains protected by American forces. This means, however, that if Trump were to withdraw the United States from active engagement in East Asia, not necessarily an unreasonable possibility, China would likely become the dominant player, especially in the military sphere.

Military and Cyber Confrontations Shaping Bilateral Competition

Between China and Japan, the balance of military power tilts towards the former, a trend likely to continue over time. The Chinese Communist Party (CCP) keeps social support for People's Liberation Army (PLA) programs artificially high through propaganda and coercion, particularly for those that would be used against Japan (Reilly 2011). China has outspent Japan on defence to acquire advanced military hardware, increased training hours, and conducted military exercises. With regard to the Senkaku/Diaoyu islands, China has invested heavily in upgrading its maritime forces to undermine Japan's control to the extent that Japan's Maritime Self-Defence Forces (JMSDF) and Japan Coast Guard can no longer effectively handle them. Growing aerial intrusions and naval incursions into disputed areas have caused Japan to increase its emergency flight missions. As someone who flew an F-15DJ fighter jet recently at an air base in Japan, I can attest to how seriously Japan Air Self-Defence Force (JASDF) operators run *each* flight in contested areas and how much real coordination it takes them to carry out one mission on the ground and in the air. Yet Japan's response is falling behind. In 2016 alone, JASDF scrambled more than 850 times to Chinese aircraft threatening Japan's airspace, nearly 280 times more than in 2015, separate from those against Russian aircraft (Japan Ministry of Defence 2017). Japan's administrative control of the islands is likely to erode further if the Trump administration decides to reduce its defence commitment to Japan believing that Tokyo should 'pay more' for its own defence. The US role in the territorial dispute would also diminish if the United States attacked North Korea, still a possibility after the April 2017 showdown, because an outright war in Korea would allow Beijing to operate the PLA more freely in East Asia against US Forces in Japan (USFJ). It is unclear if the United States would remain committed to the security order in Northeast Asia as Trump is strongly driven by his purpose to 'make America great again'.

Trust is a rare commodity in the military sphere between the two countries. Few Japanese believe in Beijing's rhetoric about a 'peaceful' rise. Military cooperation between them is limited to multilateral contexts like rare joint exercises. Japan's defence officials unequivocally mention China's military growth as a vital security concern. Japan continues to adjust its defence posture to curtail China's territorial ambitions, by shifting SDF resources from Hokkaido, once a Cold War frontline against Soviet attacks, to its south where Japan has buttressed ground forces with Marine components and deployed a few hundred soldiers on islands near Okinawa, among other things. The adjustment reflects Japanese leaders' intent to counter China's growing power by way of acquiring new equipment and increasing logistical efficiency. The leaders, however, have left post-war social norms and laws largely unchanged, which have severely limited the operability of defence forces (Katagiri, forthcoming). The Peace Constitution's Article 9 remains unchanged – banning the use of force as a means of resolving international disputes. Public support for the SDF remains mild, too, in favour of pacifist resolution of conflict. While it is true that a growing number of Japanese people support the SDF, they do so primarily because the SDF carries out non-military missions, such as humanitarian assistance and disaster relief, rather than defence. For *real* defence operations, the Japanese have turned to USFJ as the legitimate authority, as seen in the 2015 legislation allowing collective self-defence with the United States. Of course, the United States does not take a stand on ownership of the Senkaku/Diaoyu islands, but it acknowledges that the Japanese government has administrative control of the islands and that the islands fall under Article 5 of the mutual security treaty. The question, however, is whether President Trump will honour this when pressed to do so.

In cyberspace China's activism is growing with its first-mover advantage. Cyber operations are relatively inexpensive and effective. When used properly, they can impose heavy costs on targets on the cheap and facilitate the use of military force if necessary. China has capitalised on plausible deniability to target countries like Japan asymmetrically to exploit the offensive-dominant nature of cyber-operations. Even though targets of cyber-attacks in general have learned lessons to make their systems robust, attackers continue to retain the initial advantage of choosing the time and place of attack (Singer and Friedman 2014, 57–60; Segal 2016, 82–90). Accordingly, Chinese military writings have called for a strategy of 'active offense' on enemy command and control, network-centric forces, and first strike capabilities (Pollpeter 2012, 165–189). As a result, cyberattacks have been mostly a one-way street, with agents in China being responsible for a disproportionately large number of malicious attacks on its neighbours. To date, China's cyber agents have been identified as having targeted Japanese government agencies, including the Ministry of Defence and Self-Defence Forces, as well as large private organisations like JTB. China's attacks have put Japan on the defensive without *real* defence, however, as Prime Minister Abe's Liberal Democratic Party remains unable to cross the constitutional hurdle to adopt a retaliatory cyber doctrine and robust counter-offensive measures to deter attacks. Most Japanese officials I speak with say that the government knows the severity of the damage it incurs and that it has to do more to curtail further attacks, but then they privately acknowledge that it has done little to fix the problem. Of course, there are questions about whether China can actually use the stolen information in ways that significantly increase its ability to absorb stolen data and reinforce its aggressive aspirations (Lindsay 2014/15, 44). For now, however, China continues to steal a massive amount of industrial and government secrets from Japan to the extent that the asymmetry of cyberattacks is steep in Beijing's favour.

These issues across the security and cyber dimensions have shaped the tension between the two, while still providing reasons for cooperation. To add to this already complex picture, Sheila Smith argues that several critical political issues have separated the two in the past few years – including historical disagreements, food safety, as well as political rhetoric on both sides. She points out a few contentious issues including Japanese politicians' visits to the Yasukuni Shrine, China's export of poisoned dumplings, and the territorial disputes in the East China Sea. None of these offer a clear-cut path to compromise, yet they shape the way they interact with each other (Smith 2016).

Keeping the Balance through Socioeconomic Cooperation

Intense rivalry in the military and cyber domains aside, the two countries have experienced a boost in trade, FDI, tourism, and cultural and academic exchanges. This perhaps represents the only beacon of hope for better relations. It is important to note, however, that economic interdependence is based less on mutual trust than the unilateral drive to economically gain – so as to eventually outdo the other. Still, China has been Japan's largest trading partner, while Japan is China's second largest following only the United States. In 2015 Japan granted 3.8 million visas to Chinese nationals, an increase of 85% over 2014, which represented 80% of all visas Japan issued to all nationalities that year (The Japan Times 2016).

There are two problems that may hamper economic cooperation in the short run. First, the growing trade deficit with Beijing remains a concern for Tokyo, as it negatively affects Japan's relative power in the long run. In 2015, for instance, Japan's trade deficit was $17.9 billion (Japan External Trade Organization 2016). Anticipation of continued trade deficit may decrease incentives for cooperation in Japan, making it easier for lawmakers to be nationalistic towards China and call for less peaceful means to solve bilateral problems like the territorial dispute (Copeland 2014). Tokyo has complained about Chinese involvement in stealing intellectual property, which the CCP has unsurprisingly refused to acknowledge. Cyber-attacks targeting Japanese industrial secrets may strain Japan to such an extent that Japan would seek to retaliate economically, although to do so would bring back even more painful counteractions.

Second, while bilateral trade remains robust, there are different types of political dynamics at play in *multilateral* economic projects where the relations are more complex and competitive. Certainly, China and Japan are among the leading nations that participate actively in a number of regional organisations, such as APEC, ASEAN+3, and ASEAN Regional Forum (ARF). Yet there are critical new groups where the two nations compete against each other for influence. Beijing seeks to find ways to maximise the use of the many regional economic projects it leads, including the Regional Comprehensive Economic Partnership (RCEP) and the Asia Infrastructure Investment Bank (AIIB) – of which Japan is not a member. Japan is a partner of China's with regard to the promotion of the RCEP, but it is unclear how long this cooperation will last. These regional economic projects are heavily affected by external events including, most notably, Trump's policy. The presumable end of the Trans-Pacific Partnership (TPP) brought about by Trump's reluctance has now put the Japanese on track to lead a multilateral negotiation to pursue a TPP-minus-America. Until the deal is made, the TPP's disappearance is likely to strengthen China's regional influence relative to Japan.

Managing Political Flashpoints

In addition, the external strategic environment remains critical in shaping Sino-Japanese relations, especially the way China and Japan have diplomatically aligned with other countries in the region. On one hand China has 'friends' (but not formal allies) that it *could* rely on – primarily Russia and Pakistan. However, both of these states pursue different sets of political ambitions from China. Certainly, Russia confronts US global interests in a manner that occasionally aligns with China's. Since the 2016 US presidential election, modest expectations of the possibility of rapprochement between Trump and Putin have been raised. The possibility, however, is a wildcard; it can turn out well enough to positively shape Beijing's relations with Trump, or go so bad that it may spill over to Sino-US relations to deteriorate them. In the meantime, Prime Minister Abe's recent overture towards Putin through unilateral economic investments is also important, as it made Japan's Russia policy less confrontational than previous administrations. The move, however, has not necessarily been successful for hammering out a resolution of the Northern Territories/Kurile Islands dispute. China is also close to Pakistan, which offers the use of a strategic naval port at Gwadar to the Chinese navy.

This allows for China to check India's naval power and exert influence beyond the Indian Ocean. This concerns Japan because its cargo ships pass through the Indian Ocean and 80% of its oil imports come from the Middle East. Accordingly, Japan has closely worked with India to prevent this. Finally, China shares with North Korea a common interest in checking Japan's power, but the chance of collaboration between China and North Korea has weakened in recent years as Pyongyang continues to ignore Beijing's calls for restraint. China's weakening control of North Korea means that it will be less likely and able to use North Korea as an instrument of policy at negotiation tables with the United States and Japan. In sum, Chinese strategic alignment does not strongly constrain Japan's national interests, but it does not boost them either.

Japan's growing military ties with some of the Southeast Asian and South Asian states – especially the Philippines, India, and Australia – allow it to have an encirclement strategy against China. The ties with the Philippines allow SDF ships to operate near the contested areas of the South China Sea, both with the US Navy and independently. Japan's reasoning for this is not to aggressively act against the Chinese Navy but rather to secure sea lanes and freedom of navigation as much of Japan's energy import comes through the Strait of Malacca. Common strategic sense pulls Japan and India together to tighten commerce, weapons sales, and officer exchange. India and Japan also view Chinese advances into the Indian Ocean as harmful to their interests. India has historically abhorred making foreign commitments and is geographically distant from Japan, but both nations meet periodically to discuss methods of cooperation. Finally, Australia remains wary about China's advance and is a regular participant in multilateral military exercises that include the SDF.

In this context, it is important that China and Japan find ways to manage political flashpoints that may arise as a result of unexpected changes in their external environment. Specifically, if Trump does something without thinking hard enough about consequences that end up upsetting regional stability, China and Japan may clash. Two scenarios are especially possible. One potential situation is if Trump moves away from traditional policy to publicly encourage Taiwan to declare independence. Trump's early missteps towards temporarily rejecting the One-China Policy emboldened Taiwan President Tsai Ing-wen. This served as a fresh reminder that a statement short of actions can quickly escalate putting cross-strait relations into confusion. Even though Trump changed his mind after China's protest, the incident left behind a sense of opportunity for Taipei which it could exploit in the future. This also brought a sense of fear and uncertainty in Beijing about what Trump would do next. Japan's informal diplomatic relations with Taiwan could change if Abe decides to align with Trump's Taiwan policy. If, hypothetically speaking, Japan decides to follow Trump in supporting Taiwan's call for independence, this would in turn put China and Japan in direct confrontation.

The other scenario is North Korea, where Kim Jong-Un's regime has become even less predictable since the April 2017 showdown with Trump. China's declining 'control' over North Korea and inability to discourage missile and nuclear development has increasingly allowed North Korea to do things that annoy many including the Japanese. Kim appears to know his limits, but he acts almost recklessly in the eyes of foreign countries because he has no choice but to keep face outside to ensure internal stability. Andrei Lankov predicted that North Korea's end would come suddenly and violently (Lankov 2012, 187–228). It would be in China and Japan's interests to work together to minimise any impact a collapse in North Korea would have on regional stability particularly the danger of a nuclear explosion, proliferation or mass outflows of Korean refugees.

Conclusion

China and Japan regularly hold high-level bilateral talks and routinely participate in multilateral discussions about regional cooperation, but trust deficits keep the two nations apart. In China, the CCP has managed to contain nationalist sentiment and public demand for greater autonomy to the extent that allows the Party to continue to pursue aggressive economic development projects. The CCP has done so by making efforts to restrain its citizens by cooling public anger towards Japan (Reilly 2011). In Japan, however, incidents like the high-profile, uncivil demonstrations against Japanese businesses in 2012 remain vivid in the minds of the Japanese, and CCP's effort to rectify its image seems too political to be true. Furthermore, to most Japanese eyes, the CCP's effort is hardly sufficient. China's supposed restraint has failed to convince ordinary Japanese that China has become friendlier by any measure. Public surveys constantly put both nations' public opinions of each other at low points, and without mutual efforts, that reality is unlikely to improve anytime soon. The cyber hacks and rivalry over the islands make it quite hard for both nations to improve relations quickly. The international community can, for now at least, rest easy, as socioeconomic interdependence and deterrence against military strikes prevents further deterioration of relations.

References

Copeland, Dale. 2014. *Economic Interdependence and War*. Princeton: Princeton University Press.

Japan External Trade Organization. 2016. *JETRO Survey: Analysis of Japan-China Trade in 2015 (Based on imports of both countries)*, February 17.

Japan Ministry of Defense.2017. *Joint Staff Press Release*, April 13. http://www.mod.go.jp/js/Press/press2017/press_pdf/p20170413_01.pdf.

Katagiri, Nori. "Between Structural Realism and Liberalism: Japan's Threat Perception and Response." Forthcoming in *International Studies Perspectives*.

Katagiri, Nori. 2017. "What Democratization, Trade Expectations, and Military Power All Mean for the Future of Sino-American Relations." *Asian Security* 13(1): 1–19.

Lankov, Andrei.2013. *The Real North Korea: Life and Politics in the Failed Stalinist Utopia*. New York: Oxford University Press.

Lindsay, Jon.2015 "The Impact of China on Cybersecurity: Fiction and Friction." *International Security* 39(3): 7–47.

Meyer, Claude. 2011. *China or Japan: Which Will Lead Asia?* New York: Columbia University Press.

Pollpeter, Kevin. 2012. "Controlling the Information Domain: Space, Cyber, and Electronic Warfare." In Ashley Tellis and Travis Tanner (Eds.). *Strategic Asia 2012-2013: China's Military Challenges*. Seattle: National Bureau of Asian Research.

Reilly, James. 2011. *Strong Society, Smart State: The Rise of Public Opinion in China's Japan Policy*. New York: Columbia University Press.

Segal, Adam. 2016. *The Hacked World Order: How Nations Fight, Trade, Manoeuver, and Manipulate in the Digital Age*. New York: Public Affairs.

Smith, Sheila. 2016. *Intimate Rivals: Japanese Domestic Politics and a Rising China*. New York: Columbia University Press.

Singer, P.W. and Friedman, Allan. 2014. *Cybersecurity and Cyberwar: What Everyone Needs to Know*. Oxford: Oxford University Press.

The Japan Times. 2016. "Japan issued record number of visas to Chinese in 2015, up 85%." *The Japan Times*. June 6.

Note on Indexing

E-IR's publications do not feature indexes. If you are reading this book in paperback and want to find a particular word or phrase you can do so by downloading a free PDF version of this book from the E-International Relations website.

View the e-book in any standard PDF reader such as Adobe Acrobat Reader (pc) or Preview (mac) and enter your search terms in the search box. You can then navigate through the search results and find what you are looking for. In practice, this method can prove much more effective than consulting an index.

If you are using apps (or devices) to read our e-books, you should also find word search functionality in those.

You can find all of our e-books at: http://www.e-ir.info/publications

www.ingramcontent.com/pod-product-compliance
Lightning Source LLC
Chambersburg PA
CBHW021103080526
44587CB00010B/353